The Selling and Self-Regulation of Contemporary Poetry

The Selling and Self-Regulation of Contemporary Poetry

J. T. Welsch

ANTHEM PRESS

Anthem Press
An imprint of Wimbledon Publishing Company
www.anthempress.com

This edition first published in UK and USA 2021
by ANTHEM PRESS
75–76 Blackfriars Road, London SE1 8HA, UK
or PO Box 9779, London SW19 7ZG, UK
and
244 Madison Ave #116, New York, NY 10016, USA

First published in the UK and USA by Anthem Press in 2020

Copyright © J. T. Welsch 2021

The author asserts the moral right to be identified as the author of this work.

All rights reserved. Without limiting the rights under copyright reserved above,
no part of this publication may be reproduced, stored or introduced into
a retrieval system, or transmitted, in any form or by any means
(electronic, mechanical, photocopying, recording or otherwise),
without the prior written permission of both the copyright
owner and the above publisher of this book.

British Library Cataloguing-in-Publication Data
A catalogue record for this book is available from the British Library.

Library of Congress Control Number: 2021938499

ISBN-13: 978-1-83998-180-7 (Pbk)
ISBN-10: 1-83998-180-6 (Pbk)

Cover photo by Ed Centeno, used with permission.

This title is also available as an e-book.

CONTENTS

Acknowledgements   vii

Introduction: Poetry and the New Creative Industries   1

Part I New Markets

1. The Generation Game: Anthologising the New Consensus   21
2. Shortlisted Against My Ruins: The Economy of Scandal in the New Prize Culture   43
3. Poetry as Content: The Network Value of Lyrical Thought   59

Part II New Products

4. Full-Length: The Invention of the Modern Poetry Collection   75
5. Poetic Devices: Technologies of a Retro-Future   91
6. Debut Fever   105

Part III New Policy

7. Creative Capitals: The Place of Cities in Global Poetry Networks   121
8. Fake Muse: Plagiarism, Conceptual Writing, and Other Sins of Authenticity   137
9. All Our Exploring: Poetry's Critical Turn   153

Part IV New Producers

10. Poetry and Work: Some Thoughts on *Paterson*   169
11. The Poet as Entrepreneur   183
12. The Promise of Professionalism   201

Afterword: The Poetry Game   215

Index   227

ACKNOWLEDGEMENTS

This book wouldn't have existed without the support of Katherine Ebury. Aside from the model of fastidiousness and social bearing in her own research, she has brought a sense of perspective to more breakdowns and middle-of-the-night deliberation than anyone deserves. John McAuliffe has been another guiding spirit, going well beyond the duties of a PhD supervisor since I finished 10 years ago. Colleagues at the University of York have provided invaluable advice and mentorship, both on the writing process and specific drafts, especially Matthew Campbell, Helen Smith, Hugh Haughton, Alexandra Kingston-Reese, Emilie Morin, David Atwell, Adam Kelly, Bryan Radley, Michael McCluskey, Erica Sheen, Cathy Moore, Nick Gill, Sam Buchan-Watts, Emily Roach, and all of the students on my 'industry' modules over the years. Beyond personal support, this manuscript would not have been finished without research leave from the York's Department of English and Related Literature in 2018–19. I'm also endlessly grateful to everyone at Anthem Press and the reviewers of this manuscript for their emboldening feedback.

Other friends have been similarly indulgent of my bringing so many conversations back to creative industries themes, including James Fraser, Sam Reese, Iain Bailey, Rebecca Pohl, and Andrew Frayn. Every chapter here is profoundly indebted to exchanges with poets and publishers over the past decade. Whether or not they are conscious of specific contributions, it is impossible to imagine this book without the input and encouragement of Rachael Allen, Paul Batchelor, Stephanie Burt, Anthony Caleshu, Kimberly Campanello, Matthew Cheeseman, Tom Chivers, John Clegg, Joey Connolly, Stephen Connolly, Abi Curtis, Nia Davies, Kit Fan, Michael Farrell, Steven Fowler, Nathan Hamilton, Jeff Hilson, Nasser Hussain, Kirsten Irving, Evan Jones, Luke Kennard, Caleb Klaces, Ágnes Lehóczky, Melissa Lee-Houghton, Frances Leviston, Kathryn Maris, Will May, Adam Piette, Deryn Rees-Jones, Ruby Robinson, Andy Spragg, Jon Stone, Claire Trévien, David Wheatley, Jane Yeh, and many others.

Gratitude is also due to editors and publications where material for this book previously appeared. A version of the first part of the first chapter was published in *B O D Y* as 'Generationalism in British Poetry' in 2014. A version of Chapter 3 will be included in a forthcoming volume on poetry and the essay from the University of Victoria Wellington, following a conference there on the topic in 2017. Chapter 10 was commissioned by Gregory McCartney at *The Honest Ulsterman*, where a version of it was published in 2017. The final chapter was commissioned by Emily Berry for *Poetry Review*, where a version of it was published in Autumn 2018. Other chapters began life as conference papers at the universities of Bolton, Dundee, East Anglia, Goldsmiths, Manchester, Plymouth, and the Institute for English Studies, London.

In keeping with the arguments that follow, I have no doubt of the role these support networks, structures, and privileges have played in the production of this book. Among them, Katherine and my parents, siblings, and other family have had an influence beyond measure. Lovely Sasha, in particular, has been the most steadfast writing companion anyone could ask for.

Introduction

POETRY AND THE NEW CREATIVE INDUSTRIES

Beyond the Golden Age

2007 seems a simpler time in hindsight. The Global Financial Crisis seems to mark a clear turn, whether it began that summer or at any number of earlier signs ignored. In the long tail of the Great Recession and political fallout that continues more than a decade later, the effects are still being tallied and felt. In popular dramatisations and documentaries, there is a predictable focus on the big-shorting wolves of Wall Street, with less scope for wider, more complicated cultural shifts. In these retellings, the dot-com bubble around the millennium's turn was followed by a sunny period of growth, ostensibly regaining the stability of the 1990s, while actually feeding a new frenzy of speculation around sub-prime mortgages. In August 2007, a run on the UK bank Northern Rock and the lowering of the US Federal Reserve interest rate, which had been rising since 2003, were the first harbingers for those of us outside trading circles of the worldwide economic crisis to come.

In the story of the Great Recession, the fate of arts funding is often overshadowed by more urgent crises in social services, healthcare, and other support structures. When it is discussed, there is often a sense of cultural production at the mercy of global finances. In March 2007, UK prime minister Tony Blair delivered a speech in the Turbine Hall of London's Tate Modern, suggesting that 'the last ten years' might be seen as a 'golden age' for the arts, thanks to his government's cultural investments. With prophetic irony, he addressed concerns by those who might be 'nervous that the golden era may be about to end', amid worries about an upcoming spending review or the cost of civic projects like the 2012 London Olympics. 'All of us in government take great pride in what has been achieved this past decade', he assured the artists, patrons, and journalists present. 'We have avoided boom and bust in the economy. We don't intend to resume it in arts and culture.'[1]

Two months later, Blair announced his resignation, precipitating a period of national turmoil that continues in the Brexit crisis. By comparison, the effect on arts investment was swift and profound. In December that year, before the depths of the global situation were clear, nearly two hundred arts organisations in the United Kingdom were told they would lose their funding, in what the *Guardian* reported as the 'most bloody cull since the Arts Council was set up more than 50 years ago'.[2] After further spending reviews when the Conservative-led coalition took power in 2010, Art Council England's budget was slashed by another 30 per cent, with additional reductions throughout the next decade. Similar cuts followed a bailout of banks in Ireland, where the Irish Writers' Centre lost its funding as part of a €9 million reduction to Arts Council Ireland's budget. In the United States, where private contributions are the primary source of arts funding and where public funding had been on decline since 2001, the end result was the same. As a 2018 report produced by Grantmakers in the Arts explains, 'Private contributions for the arts appear to be more sensitive to the effects of economic downturns than is true for private contributions overall.'[3] Its figures show an overall decline of 20 per cent in US arts funding for 2008, including a disproportionate decrease in philanthropic support. Foundations and sponsors also made significant reductions, with funding for the arts decreasing disproportionately within overall grant budgets. The impact on writers was fairly direct, with the UK Authors' Licencing and Collection Society (ALCS) reporting that the percentage of authors who earn a full-time living from writing had fallen from 40 per cent in 2005 to 11.5 per cent by 2013. Wherever arts funding had come from before, despite Blair's assurances, the golden age was over.

This book considers the repercussions for poetry in the decade after 2008. From the start, however, I want to highlight the broader forces behind the shifts it examines. In the first instance, it is essential that the story be expanded beyond any simple notion of 'the crash' as the primary cause for these changes, while also looking beyond the state of arts funding as the primary effect. For individuals and institutions involved with poetry, the most significant changes of the past decade are manifest more generally in 'poetry culture' – by which I mean the values, behaviours, and activities which characterise that loosely defined community. Although those who make and read poetry have undoubtedly been affected by funding cuts and shrinking regional economies, this book is my attempt to understand specific effects in their poetic contexts, investigating the practices and debates around poetry, as poets, publishers, and organisations have responded, however indirectly, to wider economic, political, and cultural shifts. Therefore, this is not a book about poetry as a literary form, but rather, the manner and means by which poetry conducts its business. And in that regard, it is still very much a book about language. While it is hardly unique in its focus on the structures and institutions that sustain poetry as a field of production, it places a new emphasis on the language *around* poetry as a factor in its making. This language around poetry, I argue, displays the most visible symptoms of these changes, while it also plays a more visible role in poetry's business since 2008, for reasons outlined below.

The Creative Turn

As Blair's Tate speech made clear in its anxiously self-satisfied look back at the previous decade, the language around creative work had been changing well before the 2007–8 crash. Ten years before, New Labour announced its intentions in a 1997 election pamphlet entitled *Create the Future: A Strategy for Cultural Policy, Arts, and the Creative Economy*. While the focus on 'cultural policy' extended rhetoric reframing the 'cultural industries' as an economic sector since the 1980s, a greater emphasis on the '*creative* economy' and the '*creative* industries' reflects an important shift in thinking near the end of the century, which Sarah Brouillette describes as 'the creative-economy turn'.[4] Within months of the landslide May 1997 election, Blair's government established the Department of Culture, Media and Sport (DCMS), which soon began publishing policy documents that refined their vision of the new creative industries.[5] Even before Blair's 2007 speech, the success of this long-term intervention was marked by reports like the *Cox Review of Creativity in Business* (2005) and *Creative Growth: How the UK Can Develop World Class Creative Businesses* (2006), the latter produced by the National Endowment for Science, Technology and the Arts (NESTA) as part of the DCMS's Creative Economy Programme. Through its influence on funding strategy, infrastructure investment, and public conceptions of creativity, this policy language plays a crucial role in the way that poetry now sees and structures itself as an industry.

The dual intentions of this new creative discourse are also clear in the remit of these documents. In their respective forewords, NESTA's chief executive Jonathan Kestenbaum introduces 'a commercial analysis of the UK's creative industries', while George Cox, the chairman of the Design Council appointed to conduct his independent review, sets out to examine 'how to exploit the nation's creative skills more fully'.[6] Therefore, from NESTA's perspective, re-conceiving the 'cultural industries' as the 'creative industries' was a means for reassessing an existing sector, developing its economic potential by encouraging a more commercial or professionalised approach. As the NESTA report explains:

> Many creative owner-managers take an 'organic' approach to the growth of their businesses, by adding slowly to their customers and clients through the distinctiveness of their creative work. However, the purpose of creative business is to harness and exploit creativity in a commercial context and for commercial ends.[7]

By imposing a less organic, less slow, and less distinctive sense of 'purpose' through a more expansive definition of creative business, such policy accentuates the need for 'a greater awareness of business strategy skills and related core skills such as financial planning' among businesses, organisations, and practitioners identified as part of the existing creative sector.[8] The *Cox Review*, on the other hand, begins by literally redefining 'creativity', extending the word's connotations to areas of business that might not typically see themselves as creative. The definitions, on the first page after the foreword, start with the c-word:

> *'Creativity'* is the generation of new ideas – either new ways of looking at existing problems, or of seeing new opportunities, perhaps by exploiting emerging technologies or changes in markets.[9]

In this understanding of *creativity*, severed from cultural or artistic associations, the word signifies a broad principle for growth. 'Greater creativity is a key to greater production,' Cox writes, 'whether by way of higher-value products and services, better processes, more effective marketing, simpler structures or better use of people's skills.' Like the NESTA report, Cox proposes 'a greater clarity of purpose that focuses on commercial growth'.[10] The difference is that a position like NESTA's concerns commercial growth within the creative industries, while Cox and others are focused on the application of creative models and language to other industries. In either direction, such language is used to integrate activities and ways of thinking that might be associated separately with either art or commerce. Creative workers supposedly have much to learn about business, and vice versa.

While these two reports foreground the British context – with NESTA suggesting that 'in the past ten years, UK policymakers have led the world in recognising and supporting the creative industries'[11] – their language reflects a creative-economy turn on both sides of the Atlantic and in other English-speaking countries. As NESTA sees it, 'Policymakers from across national governments, and not just the traditional advocates for these sectors, need to concentrate on the opportunities and challenges facing these industries from an economic point of view.'[12] New Labour's turn-of-the-century cultural drive was just one large-scale expression of a political-economic philosophy codified by writers like Charles Leadbeater (later an advisor to Blair) and the American urban theorist, Richard Florida. Florida's *Rise of the Creative Class* (2002) in particular, according to Brouillette, 'has become a handbook for government officials and done more than any other work to crystalize and disseminate globally the ostensible virtues of the conception of culture that New Labour campaigned on and then fostered as it governed'.[13] The collective upshot of these texts, reports, policies, and coordinated media coverage, as Oli Mould puts it in *Against Creativity* (2018), is that 'capitalism of the twenty-first century, turbocharged by neoliberalism, has *redefined* creativity to feed its own growth'.[14]

The impact of creative industries rhetoric and thinking on poetry, despite its marginality as an industry within the larger creative sector, is one of this book's central concerns. Again though, it is worth connecting this particular agenda with economic, cultural, and technological developments, whose effects on poetry are bound up with its relation to the creative industries. At the highest level, the unavoidable term for these entangled developments is *neoliberalism*. For all the word's uses and abuses in public discourse, neoliberalism is perhaps best summarised as an ideology imposing economic principles onto everyday life. In policy terms, it is the cumulative result of deregulation and privatisation pursued in earnest throughout the 1980s and 1990s, following various economic crises in the 1970s. In practice, it leads to every area of activity being construed as a competition for resources and market share. As in the examples above, language is a primary tool for this ideology's normalisation, through which creative activity is reoriented towards new economic purpose in the 'creative industries', in which individual 'creative entrepreneurs' are encouraged to see themselves as innovators or disruptors within the 'creative economy'. Even for those resistant to the language of new creative-speak, neoliberalism's commonsensical posture makes it difficult to guard activities against co-option into measures of productivity and competition. From romantic notions of the individual imagination to the most punk aesthetics or claims to independence from the market, all are eagerly absorbed by neoliberalism's exploitation of creative labour. But before saying a bit more about the strange continuity between art's claims to autonomy and new entrepreneurial ideology, it's worth noting a few other ways in which the financial crisis sits within a wider cultural turn.

Again, it's hard to look back at 2007 without some sense of lost innocence. Until the 'crash' and the coming US election took over news reports the following winter and spring, popular media was still dominated by entertainment news, with top Google searches for the year focused on American Idol, Britney Spears, or Paris Hilton. Television viewing was still mostly a scheduled event, with HBO's *The Sopranos* finishing in June 2007, but followed in July by the premiere of *Mad Men*. Any industry dejection over the final *Harry Potter* book's publication in July was offset by the many films to come. Judd Apatow productions cornered the summer box office with *Knocked Up* and *Superbad*, with the launch of the Marvel Cinematic Universe safely a year away. Even in December, global stock markets remained steady enough to suggest, in the *Telegraph*'s review of world events, that '2007 may be remembered as the year in which Iraq turned the corner.'[15] Barack Obama had announced his presidential run in February. Things were looking up.

Other events would have far-reaching effects on people's work and lives. On 9 January 2007, Steve Jobs announced a new Apple product intended to revolutionise daily interactions. 'iPhone is like having your life in your pocket,' he told the world. 'It's the ultimate digital device.'[16] The following week, Netflix, which had built up its DVD rental service over the previous decade, announced it would start streaming video online. The smartphone boom created by the iPhone proved essential to the spread of social media. Twitter, launched in 2006, had been slow to catch on before mobile use catapulted the platform from 5,000 tweets per day in 2007 to 50 million per day by 2010.[17] Facebook, which had also been publicly available since 2006, saw enormous growth around the 2008 US election, when it finally overtook Myspace with 145 million registered users. Whatever corporate scandals, election meddling, or mental health crises these services have incited in the decade since, they have profoundly and permanently changed the way people communicate and interact with 'content'. This includes the means by which poetry is made, read, and sold, from always-connected networks between individual poets and publishers, to online spaces for promotion and dissemination.

If poetry after 2008 is distinguished by increased political engagement, efforts around accessibility and inclusivity, and the visibility of performance-based or internet-oriented poetry, there is a practical sense in which all of these developments were made possible by technologies that support a more connected and outward-looking conception of poetry culture. In Cox's terms, these are the 'emerging technologies' waiting to be 'exploited'. They have helped contemporary poetry fulfil, in its own way, his report's demand for 'higher-value products and services, better processes, more effective marketing, simpler structures or better use of people's skills'.[18] The chapters that follow are balanced between those benefits and their costs. Again, rather than frame this book as a study of poetry in the wake of the financial crisis or specific economic changes, it considers the cumulative effects of these inseparable developments.

Anxieties of Autonomy

The image of poetry as a relatively small area of activity under the influence of these major economic, political, cultural, and technological shifts returns us to a question broached above, regarding poetry's independence as an art form. One paradoxical implication for the integration of creative and economic activities within this new conception of the creative industries is that these appear to be naturally separate spheres, thus in need of such interventions to mutually 'exploit' the economic potential of creative work and creative potential of other industries. There are also moments where the presumed separation of art and commerce becomes more explicit. The NESTA report concludes, for instance: 'Now, a growing market is out there to be won by creative businesses that are willing and able to innovate, and that do not see any inherent conflict between creative and commercial excellence.'[19] Here, the gamified sense of a market 'out there to be won' (a prevalent way of thinking I'll return to in my Afterword), comes with the implication that creative excellence needs to recognise the game in order to play it. Thus, the 'inherent conflict' is fairly one-sided. Whether the aim is to make creative work more profitable or to apply creative models to business more generally, creative industries policy is inevitably focused on extracting either labour or ideas from creative workers, with far less sense of the creative or cultural benefits in return. Therefore, it's not surprising that many writers and artists regard such rhetoric and initiatives as an encroachment on their creative autonomy.

The problem of autonomy – its reality or its historical and material conditions as an ideal, partly defined by its vulnerability to exploitation – has been expressed in various terms, not only by those with a direct stake in poetry's prospects, but also by thinkers considering the broader relationship between art and commerce. It's worth mentioning some of these available positions, before explaining my own. Karl Marx, for instance, in material drafted for *Capital* in the 1860s (and in a passage I'll return to in Chapter 11), makes a clear distinction between what we might call creative work and creative business. He actually uses poetry as an example:

> Milton, who did *Paradise Lost*, was an unproductive worker. In contrast to this, the writer who delivers hackwork for his publisher is a productive worker. Milton produced *Paradise Lost* in the way that a silkworm produces silk, as the expression of his own nature. Later on he sold the product for £5 and to that extent became a dealer in a commodity.[20]

The description of Milton's labour as 'unproductive' simply refers to the fact that it was unwaged, so that the writing itself did not directly produce any surplus value for the market. In Marx's poetic image of the silkworm, the poet's work is further distinguished from the 'hackwork' of writing done under contract as an organic 'expression of his own nature'. It's only later that the product – and, crucially, not the labour itself – becomes a commodity for sale. In his influential 2012 essay, 'The Work of Art in the Age of Real Subsumption', Nicholas Brown points to this passage to explain the difference between 'formal' and 'real subsumption' in Marx's terminology. The separation of cultural labour from the market is what marks a distinction between the two historical phases, in what Brown interprets as a developmental process. In Milton's day – and still in Marx's, from Brown's perspective – artistic production remained in a state of formal subsumption, in which the work of an artist like Milton could be conducted independent of the market. Despite the fact that the results of that work might 'later on' be sold, under formal subsumption, in Marx's terms 'there is no change as yet in the mode of production itself'.[21] This contrasts with 'real subsumption', in which production has been reconfigured towards the market at every stage, closing the gap between autonomous artistic practice and the commodification of its products. By describing the poet's work as fundamentally different from the hack writer's contracted labour, Marx implies art's natural resistance to subsumption. Brown, as his essay's title suggests, believes the process of real subsumption is now complete, echoing Frederic Jameson's suggestion (now nearly thirty years ago) 'that aesthetic production today has become integrated into commodity production generally.'[22]

This contemporary sense of subsumption reaching its inevitable conclusion, with aesthetic production fully integrated into commodity production, follows various twentieth-century interpretations of the 'inherent conflict' between art and its markets, which build on Marx's analysis with different emphases. Broadly speaking, Marx's two degrees of subsumption suggest that artistic pursuits are either idealised as autonomous activity, regardless of the potential for later commodification, or else art becomes like any other industry, with its labour fully integrated and products designed with commercial potential at stake at every stage. From the 1940s, however, Theodor Adorno expanded on this dualistic view, arguing that *some* creative work, forms, or genres (mostly modernist art and literature in his examples) was still capable of successfully resisting commodification, while other work had now been absorbed into what he and Max Horkheimer dubbed 'the culture industry'.[23] In the latter case, Adorno explains, 'Cultural entities typical of the cultural industry are no longer *also* commodities, they are commodities through and through.'[24] Thus, while a broader application of Marx's terms might question the autonomy of art in general, Adorno offers a position between full autonomy and full (or real) subsumption, which applies to some but not all creative work. This selective notion of artistic autonomy has been especially useful for poetry, with the obvious gap between its resources or modes of production and those of big-budget films, for example, or other creative sub-sectors that contribute more obviously to economic appraisals of the creative industries. Even within poetry, an Adornian distinction between autonomous art proper and culture industry commodities has contributed to divisions and debates that I consider in chapters here.

Later in the twentieth-century, the sociologist Pierre Bourdieu offered another view on what he describes as 'fields of production' – shifting the focus from a strict distinction between production and markets, and towards a more comprehensive and dynamic set of social relationships between individuals and institutions, within which art is made, valued, and consumed. While these relationships and interactions might have an economic context, Bourdieu suggests that so-called restricted fields, such as poetry or literature, are shaped in greater part by the circulation of 'symbolic' capital. In this case, the perception of autonomy serves an important function in the 'legitimation' of these art forms, and in its cultural value, as expressed in the form of symbolic capital. In practice, for example, poetry's 'restricted audience (often only a few hundred readers)' and 'consequent low profits' make it 'the disinterested activity *par excellence*'.[25] In other words, its relatively low economic value becomes part of its heightened cultural value. Thus, rather than see autonomy as art's natural state prior to marketisation, Bourdieu understands the value of autonomy as a historical response to the emergence of art markets in the nineteenth century. In this 'apparent paradox', he explains, art's growing industrialisation 'to some extent prepared the ground for a pure theory of art'.[26] In turn, poetry's perception as 'the most perfectly autonomous sector of the field of cultural production' results in an 'economy of practices [...] based, as in a generalized game of "loser wins," on a systematic inversion of the fundamental principles of all ordinary economies'.[27] Its claim to autonomy is precisely what makes it valuable in this 'inverted' economy, and the relationship between symbolic capital and real capital becomes far more complex. Rather than treating art and commerce as separate spheres, creative works take on a 'two-faced reality' as both 'a commodity and a symbolic object'.[28]

Self-Regulation

This book follows Bourdieu's sense that the field of poetry is a special case, but does so with a greater attention to the collective energy put into maintaining its exceptional status. I also follow Bourdieu's emphasis on the importance of perceptions, when it comes to questions of poetry's market relations. Claims for autonomy or market complicity are rarely verifiable in any empirical sense. They persist among poets and other artists, I argue, due to their experiential force. A *sense* of autonomy takes on personal and socially recognised values within the work and its bodily production. For some, this implies a delusion to be overcome. 'Why should lyric production be any less touched by the process of technicization and capitalization than another?' Jennifer Bajorek asks. 'Poetry has always been plugged into the more general fields of production and reproduction, the material, the mediatic, and the technical. It has always been wired.'[29] Yet, this commonsense insistence that poetry has *always* been wired into capitalist production overlooks the historical specificity of different claims to autonomy. It also neglects the specific pressures facing poets and publishers, for whom the experience and perception of independence has a direct impact on the material resources that sustain their practice. As in Bourdieu's paradox, Jesse Zuba has recently shown the extent to which 'the creation of poetic authority itself crucially depends on pursuing a condition of relative autonomy'.[30] At times, these perceptions of relative autonomy might be demonstrably at odds with a poet's actual working conditions. Nor is it confined to specific types or schools of poetry. Indeed, the ideology around creative independence is so pervasive, Zuba argues, that even work that positions itself as 'countercultural poetry is energetically responsive to the same crisis of autonomy that animates the work of the university-based mainstream.'[31]

Interpreting claims to autonomy in the context of art's industrialisation doesn't mean ignoring their obvious roots in notions of selfhood propagated by earlier Enlightenment Philosophy and Romantic Literature, inspiring what Nancy Yousef calls 'the anxious imagination of autonomy'. Although its later iterations focus on freedom from market relations, the legacy of Romantic individualism is also legible in that period and since, Yousef suggests, as attempts to suppress feelings of dependence and vulnerability more generally.[32] My attempt to understand the 'anxieties' or 'crisis' of autonomy experienced by poetry in recent years begins by acknowledging autonomy's experiential and economic values, which are themselves interrelated. But it also requires a historically specific sense of those anxieties, in relation to the political and cultural shifts described above. The state of contemporary poetry culture is not helpfully analysed by trying to determine once and for all its state of commodification or subsumption. If nothing else, the continuing efforts of governmental economic policy suggest the process is incomplete – as in NESTA's frustration with slow, 'organic' creative workers stuck in a Milton-silkworm mode. At the same time, creative industries policy and rhetoric has had clear, but complex effects. Within the wider field, Jasper Bernes and Daniel Spaulding describe publishing as a 'borderline case', 'in which enterprises may be organised along either capitalist or non-capitalist lines'.[33] And at times, they might be both. As they write: 'No sane person doubts that artworks go to market, and only hopeless romantics would deny that they are often produced with that market in mind.'[34] Without drifting into the philosophical or psychoanalytic contexts in which Yousef approaches the autonomous imagination, I want to keep in mind that sense of what different poets, publishers, or others who work with poetry might have 'in mind'. On any given day, the work of poetry might feel more or less autonomous. On any given day, these perceptions might be differently affected by material conditions.

Therefore, the central argument of this book, which surfaces in different guises in different chapters, is less about autonomy versus market integration, and more about a fluid process of self-regulation. As with many art forms, the relationship between poetry and its market remains indeterminate. But its distinction among the arts, I argue, lies in the specific means by which individuals, organisations, and the field of poetry as a whole work to maintain a careful balance between autonomy and dependence on material or financial resources. Among the arts, poetry is uniquely bound by its autonomous image, foregrounding relatively cheap, flexible, and solitary labour – even compared with fiction, with its typically greater involvement of agents, editorial teams, marketing teams, sales strategy, reviews, and reader feedback. On the other hand, poetry's niche or 'restricted' audience, despite whatever legitimacy it might confer in Bourdieu's terms, also heightens the feeling of precariousness throughout the field. These layers of anxiety, for survival of the form and individual survival within a field of limited resources and opportunities, all feed into poetry's heightened self-regulatory functions.

At the organisational level, poetry's self-regulation occasionally takes the form of actual rules, in the fine print of eligibility guidelines for prizes, funding, or submission to publishers, for example. In other cases, it is manifest in the 'gatekeeping' decisions of editors, judges, funding bodies, or those in charge of appointing these figures. At other times, and as importantly, poetry's self-regulation takes more tangible forms, through the physical spaces it requires for production, performance, teaching, or collaboration, and issues of access around these, either in relation to disabilities or geographical distance. Perhaps more consistently than any of these, however, poetry's self-regulation takes discursive forms, either in specific instances – the values expressed by reviews, promotional blurbs, articles, think pieces, or blog posts – or in the daily hum of discourse and debate, via online or offline social networks where positions are continually being re-negotiated and communal values policed. While quietly (or not so quietly) regulating the exchange of poetic capital, these mechanisms of self-management and self-assessment more generally ensure poetry never becomes so autonomous that it surrenders what remains of its cultural relevance, but also that it isn't seen to be straying so far towards market concerns that it loses its cultural legitimacy.

While many of these regulatory mechanisms have had their place in poetry for centuries, a key concern for this book is the extent to which poetry's natural proclivity for self-regulation has responded to the valorisation of more entrepreneurial modes of self-exploitation under neoliberalism, especially in creative fields. Again, these practices have also adapted to the historical conditions outlined above. The economic necessities and technological possibilities for self-assessment are perhaps greater than ever. And at any ideological level, self-regulation is the most essential component of neoliberal models – justifying, at the state level, the steady process of industrial and financial deregulation since the 1970s, and for individuals, normalising entrepreneurial thinking and behaviours in all areas of life. Beyond the perceived value of self-regulation, an absolute belief in the self-sufficiency of individuals and entire industries has emerged as the necessary corollary of extreme laissez-faire free-market policy in recent decades. In practice, the principle of self-regulation helps rationalise the shift of responsibility to individuals, encouraging them to internalise processes of self-evaluation, self-management, and, ideally, self-improvement. Michel Foucault calls this 'governmentality' – understood as a mentality of self-government, but also as the point of continuity between self-government and the government of any larger community or field of activity.[35]

This is the context in which economic policymakers fetishise creativity, celebrating the self-exploiting potential of workers with an inherited or otherwise rationalisable stake in their autonomy. The historian Robert Hewison (in another passage I'll return to near the end of the book) shows how New Labour policy capitalised on this dynamic in the United Kingdom, adapting Florida's conception of the 'creative class':

> Creative Britain needed a creative economy in order to ensure the continuous innovation on which growth depended. This would be served by a 'creative class' whose occupation was the production of signs and symbols that could be consumed in commodified form. Creative Britain would be populated by young and eager people, who, in spite of their techno-savvy, clung to the romantic image of the struggling artist, whose individualism would make the breakthrough that justified their insecurities and self-exploration.[36]

While this description highlights the manner by which art's romantic notions of autonomy become a screen for precariousness and self-exploitation, it is worth reiterating the point above about the variety of conscious and unconscious experience under these self-regulatory forces. Even where an editor or prize judge might be making a deliberative decision, knowingly contributing to the regulation of values within the field, there is still a deeper sense in which the invisible force of self-regulation links their decision with the expression of values inherent in the work they are judging, as well as larger values inherent to poetry as an art form *and* commercial product. The poet, publisher, critic, judge, and reader are joined by their transmission of evaluative forces. Foucault describes this in biological terms, in which a generalised process of self-regulation, in place of top-down disciplinary models, becomes a 'technology which aims to establish a sort of homeostasis, not by training individuals but by achieving an overall equilibrium that protects the security of the whole from internal dangers'.[37] It is this metabolic balance within poetry's many-limbed organism that I have in mind in arguing for poetry's exceptional methods of self-regulation. For that reason, it should be clear that nothing in this book is intended as a critique of individual poets, publishers, or organisations. Recognising as best as I am able the regulatory function of academic criticism, my aim is to offer a useful sense of the 'body-poetic' as it struggles for survival in this contemporary moment.

Overview

As might be clear from the above, this book combines approaches broadly associated with literary criticism and sociology. In some reductive sense, these two disciplines, respectively, might be said to have complementary conceptions of art's autonomy or its integration into other human activity, with literary studies giving a primacy to the text that the social sciences give to larger structures. That said, these approaches have been productively bridged in recent decades. From the literature side, the expansion of book history, bibliography, and publishing studies has been matched by the more focused study of material culture or economic humanities, for example. The social sciences, on other hand, have played a leading role in the development of what is now sometimes referred to as 'creative industries studies'. This emerging field, shaped by key texts like David Hesmondhalgh's *The Cultural Industries* (first published in 2002, now in its fourth edition), has been further defined in recent years by other UK-based scholars, such as Angela McRobbie and Mark Banks. Attention to the nature of creative labour and ethical issues germane to the creative industries in McRobbie's *Be Creative: Making a Living in the New Culture Industries* (2015) and Banks's *Creative Justice: Cultural Industries, Work and Inequality* (2017), for example, has been invaluable to my thinking. I've already mentioned Oli Mould's focused critique of creative rhetoric in *Against Creativity* (2018) and essential historical work like Robert Hewison's *Cultural Capital: The Rise and Fall of Creative Britain* (2014). Within this area, studies like Alison Gerber's *The Work of Art: Value in Creative Careers* (2017) consider artistic work beyond the United Kingdom; and the field as a whole has been recently 'legitimised' by publication of *The Oxford Handbook of Creative Industries* (2017).

It's unavoidable, perhaps, that more general analysis of the creative industries – which tends to focus on examples from the visual arts, fashion, music, or film and TV – might seem to have limited scope for less obviously market-driven fields such as literary publishing. In that regard, Sarah Brouillette's

Literature and the Creative Economy (2014) has proven a groundbreaking and indispensable model for situating literary production within this century's 'creative-economy turn'. Work like Jasper Bernes's *The Work of Art in the Age of Deindustrialisation* (2017) and edited collections like Mitchum Huehls and Rachel Greenwald Smith's *Neoliberalism and Contemporary Literary Culture* (2017) extend these neo-Marxist approaches, while the focus on theories of labour and consumption also supplements work on the publishing industry itself, like Claire Squires's *Marketing Literature: The Making of Contemporary Writing in Britain* (2009), and the growth of 'creative writing studies' in the wake of Mark McGurl's *The Program Era* (2011). Nevertheless, with few exceptions, the study of literature as an industry has been overwhelmingly focused on the production and consumption of fiction. Books that do look at poetry, such as Bernes's or Jesse Zuba's *The First Book: Twentieth-Century Poetic Careers in America* (2018), provide useful historical foundations for poetry's economic contingencies, though often foregrounding the situation of individual poets or poems.

The Selling and Self-Regulation of Contemporary Poetry is my attempt to apply the insights of this thriving critical field to contemporary poetry. In four sections on New Markets, New Products, New Policy, and New Producers, its twelve chapters are intended to be readable as self-contained discussions of issues or trends in poetry since 2008, while together building on the broader notion of self-regulation defined above. In that regard, these chapters progress from higher levels of regulation for the field as a whole, into their manifestation at the level of organisations, institutions, and finally individuals – with much natural overlap between.

The opening section on New Markets establishes the parameters of my material-historical approach. The first chapter, on 'generationalism' in contemporary poetry, considers recent anthologies and list campaigns which capture the impulse towards generational frames, a key mechanism for regulating a consensus of values among new poets. Chapter 2 turns to the function of prizes in the public reception of poetry, with an emphasis on the growing role of social media and participatory journalism in regulating the cultural value associated with these awards. Chapter 3 extends this focus on online networks, concluding the first section with a consideration of poetry's circulation as digital 'content', and shifts in online reading culture epitomised by the sharing of viral poems.

The second part on New Products balances these digital contexts with a re-examination of poetry's physical products. Chapter 4 considers the so-called full-length collection as a material form, the historical development of which has responded to broader industry changes. Chapter 5 connects recent developments in publishing technology – including ebooks, print-on-demand, and their varied use by bigger or smaller publishers – with the 'ambivalent ontologies' of online poetry. This section concludes in Chapter 6 with a study of 'debut culture', manifest in the prominence of first collections on prize lists and publishers' lists in recent years.

The third part considers New Policy, broadly defined as the unofficial infrastructure and language governing the flow of poetic capital. Chapter 7 opens this section with a critique of poetry's city-centric biases, in which historical investments in the artistic or radical potential of urban spaces increasingly dovetail with economic models of networked, 'creative' cities. This is followed in Chapter 8 by a set of case studies involving various forms of fakery and the shared regulatory impulses exposed in the policing of plagiarism, conceptualism, and hoaxes. Chapter 9 completes this section by examining poetry's place in contemporary writing's 'critical turn', in which changes in reading culture and creative writing as an academic discipline have encouraged new possibilities for research-driven and project-oriented poetry.

The final section on New Producers turns more pointedly to individual poets' stake in these wider developments, beginning with a meditation on the status of poetic labour, centred around its depiction in Jim Jarmusch's 2016 film, *Paterson*. This is followed in Chapter 11 with a critique of creative entrepreneurialism, returning to the debates around autonomy raised in this introduction and a growing 'entrepreneurial imperative' in contemporary poetry. This is balanced in the final chapter by a re-evaluation of poetry's more general professionalisation, reconciling the pressures of individualistic entrepreneurialism with a more inclusive and communal model of poetry as a 'profession'. A short afterword offers a few thoughts, going forward, on the impact of 'gamification' as a self-regulatory mechanism.

In all of this, I have done my best to consider the specific contexts of different regions and poetry communities. While I admit there is, given my circumstances, an inevitable emphasis on examples from the United Kingdom and the United States, comparisons across English-speaking countries and beyond are an important part of the analysis of online spaces especially. In my focus on public discourse and poetry's most visible effects – in prize culture, media coverage, and so on – there is also an admitted tendency towards 'mainstream' print poetry, though again with an awareness and occasional examples of more marginalised writing within the field as a whole, including performance-based work, experimental modes, and the work of smaller presses. I have also done my best to make these discussions as useful as possible to those with different experiences or knowledge of either poetry culture or its academic contexts.

Notes

1. Tony Blair, 'Blair's speech on the arts in full', *Guardian* (6 March 2007).
2. Mark Brown, 'England's arts face bloodiest cull in half a century as funds are cut for 200 groups', *Guardian* (17 December 2007).
3. Steven Lawrence, 'Arts Funding at Twenty-Five: What Data and Analysis Continue to Tell Funders about the Field', *Grantmakers in the Arts*, Special Report vol. 29, no. 1 (2018), 9.
4. Sarah Brouillette, *Literature and the Creative Economy* (Stanford, CA: Stanford University Press, 2014), 13.
5. In addition to George Cox's *Cox Review* (2005) and NESTA's *Creating Growth* (2006) discussed earlier, significant New Labour policy documents in this area includes the DCMS's *New Cultural Framework* (also known as the *Creative Industries Mapping Document*, 1998), *Culture and Creativity: The Next Ten Years* (DCMS, 2001), 'Government and the Value of Culture' (Tessa Jowell, Secretary of State for Culture, Media and Sport, 2003), *Staying Ahead: The Economic Performance of the UK's Creative Industries* (Will Hutton for The Word Foundation, 2007), *Creative Britain: New Talents for the New Economy* (DCMS, 2008), *Beyond the Creative Industries: Mapping the Creative Economy* (NESTA, 2008), and the 2010 party manifesto, *Creative Britain*.
6. NESTA, *Creating Growth*, 1; Cox, *Cox Review*, 1.
7. NESTA, *Creating Growth*, 3.
8. Ibid.
9. Cox, *Cox Review*, 2.
10. Ibid., 2–3.
11. NESTA, *Creating Growth*, 2.
12. Ibid.
13. Brouillette, *Literature and the Creative Economy*, 5.
14. Oli Mould, *Against Creativity* (London, Verso, 2018), 3. Emphasis in original.
15. David Blair, 'Review of 2007: World Events', *Telegraph* (20 December 2007).
16. Transcript available on various sites.
17. Claudine Beaumont, 'Twitter users send 50 million tweets per day', *Telegraph* (23 February 2010).
18. Cox, *Cox Review*, 2.
19. NESTA, *Creating Growth*, 49, after several earlier repetitions.
20. Karl Marx and Frederick Engels, *Collected Works: 1861–1864*, vol. 34, trans. Ben Fowkes (New York: International Publishers, 1994), 448.
21. Karl Marx, *Capital: A Critique of Political Economy, Volume One*, trans. Ben Fowkes (London: New Left Review, 1976), 1026. One obvious objection to Marx's example is that Milton's writing process was hardly autonomous to begin with, given the unpaid and uncredited involvement of his daughters in the work.
22. Fredric Jameson, *Postmodernism: Or, the Cultural Logic of Late Capitalism* (Durham, NC: Duke, 1991), 4.
23. Adorno and Horkheimer's theorisation of the culture industry was first articulated in the chapter 'The Culture Industry: Enlightenment as Mass Deception', in *Dialectic of Enlightenment* (1944, first translated into English by John Cumming in 1972).
24. Adorno, 'Culture Industry Reconsidered', in *The Culture Industry: Selected Essays on Mass Culture*, ed. J. M. Bernstein (London: Routledge, 2001), 99–100.
25. Pierre Bourdieu, 'The Field of Cultural Production, or: The Economic World Reversed', trans. Richard Nice, in *The Field of Cultural Production: Essays on Art and Literature* (Cambridge: Polity, 1993), 51.

26 Bourdieu, 'The Market of Symbolic Goods', in *The Field of Cultural Production*, 113–14.
27 Bourdieu, 'Field of Cultural Production', 39.
28 Bourdieu, 'The Market of Symbolic Goods', 113.
29 Jennifer Bajorek, *Counterfeit Capital: Poetic Labour and Revolutionary Irony* (Stanford, CA: Stanford University Press, 2009), 14.
30 Jesse Zuba, *The First Book: Twentieth-Century Poetic Careers in America* (Princeton, NJ: Princeton University Press, 2018), 4.
31 Ibid., 93.
32 Nancy Yousef, *Isolated Cases: The Anxieties of Autonomy in Enlightenment Philosophy and Romantic Literature* (Ithaca, NY: Cornell University Press, 2004), 18.
33 Jasper Bernes and Daniel Spaulding, ' "Truly Extraordinary", Review of Dave Beech, *Art and Value: Art's Economic Exceptionalism in Classical, Neoclassical and Marxist Economics*', *Radical Philosophy*, no. 195 (Jan./Feb. 2016), 54.
34 Ibid., 52.
35 Foucault discusses the concept in various places. See, for example, *Security, Territory, Population: Lectures at the Collège de France 1977–1978*, ed. M Senellart, trans. G Burchell (Basingstoke: Palgrave Macmillan, 2007).
36 Hewison, *Cultural Capital: The Rise and Fall of Creative Britain* (London: Verso, 2014), 5–6.
37 Foucault, *Society Must Be Defended* (London: Picador, 2003), 249. Foucault also emphasises the unconscious nature of self-regulation with his conception of its *dispositif* (sometimes translated as 'apparatus' or 'mechanism'). Bourdieu's notion of *habitus* places a similar emphasis on 'a set of *dispositions* which incline agents to act and react in certain ways.' (As defined in John B. Thompson's introduction to Bourdieu's *Language and Symbolic Power* (Cambridge, MA: Harvard University Press, 1991), 12).

PART I

NEW MARKETS

Chapter 1

THE GENERATION GAME: ANTHOLOGISING THE NEW CONSENSUS

This chapter examines the function of anthologies and anthologising lists as devices of self-regulation. As selective surveys of whatever range of poetry they aim to represent, anthologies play an obvious role in canon formation; and as commercial products, anthologies of living poets are poised especially between the promotion of individual writers, the promotion of poetry as an art form, and the promotion of more specific agendas and perspectives within the poetry industry. Whatever their publishers', editors', and contributors' intentions, it goes without saying that the introductions, marketing blurbs, and selection processes for anthologies of contemporary work are bound by the double-imperative of selling that work and deciding what work is worth selling. This chapter focuses on a particular strategy employed by recent anthologies to these ends: the generational frame. In recent years, generational anthologies have been a means for asserting poetry's bright future, but also for projecting an image of consensus into that future, beyond historical divisions that appear antithetical to a shared vision and sense of community. The first half of the chapter focuses on a wave of generation-defining volumes published in the United Kingdom between 2009 and 2014, followed by a discussion of the 'New Generation' and 'Next Generation Poets' lists published in 1994, 2004, and 2014. Together, these UK anthologies and lists offer striking examples of the wider attempts by contemporary print poetry to recognise, on one hand, new voices emerging from a complex historical moment and to consolidate, on the other hand, the regulatory power of print publishing for a rapidly changing audience.

Section I: The Anthology Generation(s)

It's hard to argue with the generational anthology's promise: Go on, it says, pick me up. If it's verse you're after, here's a handy sampler – a safe way to begin exploring the strangely well-hidden world of contemporary poetry, learning the names and trends that will let you feel you're part of that conversation. Like a mixtape from a wise older sibling, an editor or team of editors has done the hard work for you. These are the ones worth reading, the title and preface assure you. It was a difficult choice, they confess (for the sake of those not chosen), but in the end, they feel this dozen or two dozen or twelve dozen poets give us an authoritative snapshot of poetry as it stands today. Everyone wants to know what's happening and who's who, and everyone loves a group photo.

These generational snapshots aren't new to poetry. Somewhere between Palgrave's *Golden Treasury* (1861), which included only dead poets, and Alvarez's *The New Poetry* (1962), which proved a template for generations to come, the 'Living-Poet' anthology, as Laura Riding and Robert Graves call it, had become established enough to warrant their 200-page *A Pamphlet against Anthologies* in 1928. Graves and Riding are particularly scathing about publishers' cynical uses of the form. Although 'intended to give the reader a picture of the poetic world', they perpetuate an 'anthology system' against which poets themselves would find it 'almost impossible to hold out'.[1] T. S. Eliot, having discussed 'the general question of anthologies' with a fellow poet (very likely Graves), found they agreed that 'the work of any poet who has already published a book of verse is likely to be more damaged than aided by anthologies.'[2] As Riding and Graves put it: 'All these collections are mere wanton re-arrangement of poetry that has its proper place elsewhere, or nowhere at all.'[3]

Whatever one's opinion of the format, it seems right to acknowledge its history, as Roddy Lumsden's does, placing *Identity Parade: New British and Irish Poets*, which he edited in 2010, 'in a tradition of generational anthologies which stretches back for decades'.[4] Over the past 25 years, readerly interest in generational surveys has sustained the publication of more than 20 anthologies offering their versions of the best new British (or British and Irish) poetry. Again, it's hard to argue with the value of having as many perspectives as possible, especially when any claim to represent the true flavour of a generation also involves a degree of taste-making. But bursts of popularity for this sort of anthology – from those around Bloodaxe's *The New Poetry* and the Poetry Society's 'New Generation' list in 1993–94, to five major generational anthologies in each year between 2009 and 2014 – suggest the influence of wider trends. Rereading this recent history, a story begins to emerge, less a coincidence of individual volumes than an ongoing conversation between them about how (and why) to frame a generation. A clearer historical perspective will also allow us to better assess the generational frame's social and political implications.

1982–91: Pre-History

In 1982, Blake Morrison and Andrew Motion's *Penguin Book of Contemporary British Poetry* followed the every 'decade or so' pattern Lumsden identifies, after Alvarez's 1962 volume and Edward Lucie-Smith's *British Poetry Since 1945* in 1970. One contentious feature of Morrison and Motion's volume was its inclusion of a number of Irish poets, among whom Seamus Heaney's annoyance is perhaps best known. In 'An Open Letter', he famously responded: 'Be advised / My passport's green. / No glass of ours was ever raised / To toast the Queen.'[5] This political slippage is significant within the history of the generational anthology thereafter, partly because it points us to Gerald Dawe's *Younger Irish Poets*, published in the same year as Motion and Morrison's 'British' selection. In turn, Dawe's book inspired the developing trend, partly by way of its 1991 follow-up, *New Younger Irish Poets*. As controversial as the Penguin anthology had been, the publication of Dawe's two volumes of 'younger Irish poets' set in motion a publishing dialogue that has had a surprising impact on two waves of generational anthologies since.

Peter Forbes's editorial in the summer 1991 issue of *Poetry Review* invokes Dawe's second Irish anthology to criticise the lack of British counterpart this time around. Forbes admits such a new 'canon-making' anthology appears 'unthinkable', due to the 'hectic pluralism and special interest serving' factions then at work in British poetry. From this comparison, he pens what, in retrospect, appears to have been an extremely effective clarion call:

> This loss of the sense of the canon has weakened British poetry. There is an audience beyond the insiders, who would like to know what is happening in poetry – it is no use saying there's any amount of it scattered around: a few key anthologies are essential. […] Despite the chorus of criticism that greeted Morrison and Motion's *Penguin Book of Contemporary British Poetry* in 1982, the dissent has not spawned a serious rival.[6]

1993–94: A 'New' Wave

Forbes' was also pre-empting his own intervention, in the form of the 'New Generation Poets' special issue of *Poetry Review*, published under his editorship in the spring of 1994. According to Forbes, the initial spark for the 'New Generation' was a conversation between Bill Swainson, Christopher Reid, and Robin Robertson, over drinks at the National Poetry Competition awards ceremony in January 1993. If the 'New Gen' list and marketing campaign around it was designed to be the most high-profile response to Forbes' own call, his introduction to the special issue also frames it as a competitive response to David Kennedy, Michael Hulse, and David Morley's *The New Poetry*, with which Bloodaxe had beaten him to the punch in the autumn of 1993. Any 'group portrait' of this kind is a 'risky venture', Forbes explains, adding: 'It totally defeated the editors of *The New Poetry*, for example.'[7] But like Forbes, the slightly earlier Bloodaxe volume, taking its name from Alvarez's 1962 anthology, also cites Dawe's *New Younger Irish Poets* as a seemingly 'inconceivable' model 'if transposed to other parts of the British Isles'.[8]

Kennedy, Hulse, and Morley's implicit response to Forbes's lament for the 'loss of the canon' comes in their contrary emphasis on a 'new pluralism', and their description of their book as more 'defining' than 'definitive'.[9] Bloodaxe itself boldly underlined this paradoxical approach to indefinitive definition and pluralistic canon-making by publishing Linda France's *Sixty Women Poets*, which criticises *The New Poetry*'s 'all-male editorial team' and asserts itself as 'a necessary sister volume', on the same day in September 1993.[10] In the New Generation issue of *Poetry Review* the following spring, Forbes responds to both Bloodaxe volumes – which had, after all, taken up his initial challenge – by dismissing their claims to 'new pluralism' as 'journalistic clichés'. 'At first sight,' he admits, 'the list of twenty New Generation poets is perhaps narrower than it might have been', but redefines their 'wilful individuality' as the 'true plurality'.[11]

Without rehashing further details of these squabbles (though I return to this question around pluralism in my conclusion), it is worth acknowledging that the two Bloodaxe volumes and the New Generation Poets issue are only three among a burst of generational anthologies in this early 1990s wave, responding explicitly or not to Dawe's second Irish volume and Forbes' subsequent call. The first of Carcanet's *New Poetries* series (with the pointed plurality of its title) and Ian Hamilton's *Oxford Companion to Twentieth-Century Poetry in English* were both published in 1994 as well. Neither takes the typical shape, since the Carcanet volume introduces only eight poets – working against what editor Michael Schmidt calls 'the reductive tendency of recent "generational" anthologies'[12] – and Hamilton's a critical introduction, rather than verse samplers. Yet they both insert themselves into the vibrant anthology conversation of that moment, echoed further in the revival of Penguin's *Modern Poets* series the following year and Anthony Thwaite's *Poetry Today* anthology in 1996.

Relative to that burst, however, the later-1990s show a marked lull in the generation-defining volumes. This might be explained as a simple matter of market saturation or a return to the pattern with 'a gap of a decade of so', as Lumsden suggests in *Identity Parade*.[13] In that case, the lack of a print anthology for the Poetry Book Society's 'Next Generation' list in 2004 is an obvious lapse. 1998's *Penguin Book of Poetry from Britain and Ireland since 1945*, co-edited by Robert Crawford and New Generation alum, Simon Armitage, and Picador's *The Firebox: Poetry from Britain and Ireland after 1945*, edited by Sean O'Brien, had both expanded to something wider than the single-generation span of Edward Lucie-Smith's *British Poetry Since 1945* from 1970. On the other hand, Graywolf's *New British Poetry*, co-edited by Don Paterson (another New Gen poet), was published in 2004 only in the United States for its intended audience. In the meantime, other types of publication filled the 10- or 15-year gap into the new century, including Carcanet and Penguin's aforementioned series, the University of East Anglia's *Reactions* volumes (2001–5), and Faber's one-off attempt at an annual magazine with *First Pressings* in 1998.

2009–14: Another Wave

By contrast, a resurgent interest in generational anthologies over the five-year period between 2009 and 2014 included more or less annual volumes. With this new wave came renewed self-questioning about the usefulness and definition of a 'generation', if that's what these group portraits were still aiming for. If nothing else, the rules for eligibility were increasingly arcane. Where Bloodaxe's *The New Poetry* (1993) was open to anyone who hadn't been included in the 1982 Penguin anthology, the New Generation Steering Group (made up of various editors, publishers, and as many marketing experts) devised strict guidelines: under 40, first published after 1989, with a full collection of 32 or more pages in print. Clare Pollard and James Byrne's *Voice Recognition: 21 Poets for the 21st Century* (Bloodaxe, 2009), on the other hand, only included those who had not published a full collection. The following year, Lumsden's much longer *Identity Parade: New British & Irish Poets* (Bloodaxe, 2010) included poets who had 'either published first collections within the past 15 years or will make their debut within the next year'.[14] And within that, no one over 50, unless they first published in the last 10, rather than 15 years.

The scope of *Identity Parade* also allowed Lumsden to cordon off a separate generation, age 26 and under, for the following year's *Salt Book of Younger Poets* (2011, co-edited with Eloise Stonborough). Todd Swift's *Lung Jazz: Young British Poets for Oxfam* (2012) expanded its definition of what it calls 'YBPs' to those 'born in or after 1970'. The following year, in *Dear World & Everyone in It* (Bloodaxe, 2013), Nathan Hamilton admits to breaking most of his own rules, by admitting any UK poet under 'more or less 35 when *The Rialto* feature [from which the anthology developed] started'.[15] These varying criteria and the titles of some of these volumes highlight the importance of age markers, as well as emerging opportunities for 'young' poets they celebrate. The introductions all note a sea change in poetry culture, citing new prizes for young poets, new magazines, a revival of the pamphlet form, new reading venues and corresponding popularity of live readings, social networking, new funding opportunities, and not least the boom in Creative Writing courses, within universities and beyond. As Byrne and Pollard write in *Voice Recognition*: 'For many years the poetry world has belonged to older writers. [...] Being a poet was uncool.' But as of 2009, 'there are more avenues to gain attention as a young writer than any time before.'[16] In retrospect, Tom Chivers, whose Penned in the Margins press's first foray into publishing was the 2006 anthology *Generation Txt*, also deserves credit for anticipating this wave and for his prescient criticism of 'a general unwillingness amongst some in the "industry" to engage seriously with young writers'.[17]

Generationalism

At the very least, this history shows these books appeared neither in isolation nor of their own accord. Rather, the exchanges between volumes and the obsession with defining each new generation suggest a deeper social phenomenon, which we might call 'generationalism'. This was the term coined by historian Robert Wohl in his 1979 study of *The Generation of 1914*, where he defines it as 'the phenomenon of generational thinking'.[18] Generationalism, in other words, describes a heightened awareness or preoccupation with generational categories. As the sociologist Jonathan White glosses the term, it refers to 'the systematic appeal to the concept of generation in narrating the social and political'.[19] The anthologies above all attest to this systematic appeal, with each of them using the g-word at some point – sometimes in their title, sometimes in contention, but most often in support of their varied criteria and explicit premises.

Generationalism seems innocent enough, and historically well grounded, given how readily we divide, say, the Romantic poets into first and second generations of that movement. In their case, it seems obvious that Byron and Shelley would have a different social and political outlook to the Lake Poets, given their very different relationship to the French Revolution and other events. Wohl argues that 'generational consciousness had its deepest roots and its first stimulus in the new concept of time and attitude toward change that developed in the late eighteenth century'.[20] From the nineteenth century onwards, he writes, the rise of generationalism is further entangled with a fixation on young people as 'the standard-bearers of the future in the present'.[21] From the angry young iconoclasts of Late Romanticism, inspired by the Young Werthers of the Sturm und Drang, through an Oedipal chain binding Kant to Nietzsche and all the fathers and sons of Turgenev or Dostoyevsky, we see the High Modernists of the First World War's 'Lost Generation' defining itself against forebears. As Wohl notes, the ubiquity of generational thinking, after 1900 especially, can be traced in dictionaries and manifestos. By now, we're well accustomed to sorting the twentieth century into the Greatest generation, the Beat generation, the 1968 generation, the Baby Boomers, the MTV generation, Generations X and Y, and any other brand names a clever journalist cares to coin.

Into the late twentieth and early twenty-first centuries, generationalism's brand potential is also blatant in the Pepsi and Star Trek references of which New and Next Generation poets must have quickly tired. The 2012 London Olympics aimed similarly to 'inspire a generation'. As White puts it, 'Generationalism may be one of the many ways politics increasingly resembles a marketing exercise.'[22] In that case, however, the market value of generationalism has also been reinforced by more insidious political appropriations. In the late 1980s, for instance, a right-wing special interest group, Americans for Generational Equity (or AGE), drew on generous funding from corporate interests, defence contractors, banks, and insurance companies to propagate feelings of generational conflict, in which the younger generation was pitted against the selfish Baby Boomers' debts. Although this rift has since become a truism of mainstream media and politicians from all sides, AGE's underlying agenda was an attack on national healthcare and the welfare state, with attempts to raise the retirement age, and privatise pensions. Articles and bestsellers with similar motives soon spawned a crowded subgenre, spurred by provocations like *On Borrowed Time: How the Growth in Entitlement Spending Threatens America's Future* (1988), co-authored by political analyst Neil Howe and Peter G. Peterson – a former Lehman Bros CEO and secretary of commerce under Nixon. In the United Kingdom, the influence of Howe and William Strauss's many follow-ups, including *Generations* (1991) and the *Millennials* series (*Millennials Rising, Millennials Go To College, Millennials in the Workplace*) persists in former government minister David Willetts's bestseller, *The Pinch: How the Baby Boomers Stole Their Children's Future – and Why They Should Give It Back* (2010) and an 'Intergenerational Commission', conducted by the Resolution Foundation think tank, where Willetts serves as executive chair.

These texts, along with many imitators and counterarguments, have promoted generational thinking in public debate, inevitably felt in the rise of generational anthologies in this same period; and those complied by younger editors seem particularly disposed to applying notions of wider generational conflict to poetry hierarchies. *Generation Txt*'s complaint about the 'general unwillingness [...] to engage seriously with young writers' or *Voice Recognition*'s about 'the poetry world [belonging] to older writers' resurface in *Dear World*'s call for 'avoiding older, oppositional attitudes', just as they all echo Forbes' earlier critique of 'the old Establishment' and 'older alternative powerbases'.[23]

In this sense, the drama of generational conflict adopted by politicians and economic commentators in recent decades is itself an appropriation of a much older narrative of cultural turnover, typified by the repeated usurpation of nineteenth-century literary movements. As Peter Riley begins his unflinching review of *Dear World & Everyone in It*:

> Dear Nathan Hamilton, You do know don't you, that the tactic of announcing a new, fresh, lively, optimistic, young poetry which will replace a stale, gloomy, heavy, old poetry, is as old as poetry itself? Of course you do.[24]

The Problem with Generations

As seductive as these narratives of generational conflict might be, younger commentators have become increasingly sceptical of pandering rhetoric or inadequate responses to structural inequality. In 2018, for example, the Intergenerational Commission's 'New Generational Contract', proposing a £10k grant to all 25-year-olds, was laughingly dismissed as inadequate reparations. Laurie Penny's rebuttals of Willetts in the *New Statesman* in 2010–11 – 'It's not baby boomers who have stolen our future, Mr Willetts. It's you.' – have been followed by online outlets like *Spiked* repeatedly imploring fellow 'twentysomethings' to 'call off the generational jihad', while books like Jennie Bristow's *Baby Boomers and Generational Conflict* (2015) argue that 'the primary impact of "generationalism" is to mystify the causes of social problems', instilling 'a simplistic narrative that relies on blaming older people for the myriad problems of the present day'.[25] These critiques also show the extent to which the red herring of generational conflict is founded on the presumption of the generation as a meaningful and cohesive social group.

Such pushback also joins a tradition of sociological analysis at least as old as Karl Mannheim's essay, 'The Problem of Generations', first published in 1928. Like Wohl, Mannheim is particularly concerned with the fetishised link between 'youth' and 'progress' in much generational thinking. The rise of evolutionary theory in the late nineteenth century may have added a biological sheen to narratives of generational advance, but the manipulative mobilisation of youth movements had also become a standard political manoeuvre by the early twentieth century. Where the previous groupings of Young Germany, Young Ireland, or Young Vienna brought together artists and writers under shared social and political concerns, early twentieth-century political movements had learned to convert such youthful energy towards showy or dangerous nationalisms. As a counter-strategy perhaps, this left many content in the later twentieth and early twenty-first century to neutralise the potential for political commitment by selling Gen-Xers, grunge kids, hipsters, or millennials images of their own supposed apathy through their preferred media channels.

Poetry anthologies are clearly not above such ploys for youth support, although many of the examples above add to it the neoliberal trick of defining a collective by its 'wilful individuality' (New Generation Poets) or the 'essential individualism which I see in this generation' (*Identity Parade*). *Dear World* aims for a 'plurality' not dissimilar to the 'new pluralism' announced in *The New Poetry, New Poetries I, First Pressings*, and other volumes 20 years prior. In this way, the vagueness of the generational frame becomes the means for reconciling these pluralities of wilful individuals. The blankness of generational identity also encourages presumptions of shared experience. As Bourdieu suggests, the 'very marked tendency to think of the whole social order in terms of a scheme of divisions into generations' also 'follow[s] the logic which often makes intellectuals extend to the whole world characteristics of their own microcosm'.[26] Generational thinking, in other words, is also a habit of bubbles.

The consequences of imposing generational categories are obvious when comparing them to identity groupings such as class, gender, or race. As White writes, 'All such categories risk projecting undue uniformity onto the social world, and political claims thus denominated are potentially repressive of certain individuals even while empowering for others.'[27] Unlike gender or sexual identities, for instance, but perhaps more like that of race, White describes the category of generations as 'impermeable'. In other words, no one is allowed to choose their generation or remove themselves from it. 'For this reason,' White explains, 'those assigned to [a generation] are especially powerless before whatever public connotations that category may acquire, and limited in their ability to take distance from claims made on their behalf.'[28] As so-called millennials know too well, after trolling complaints over their avocado obsessions and snowflake sensitivity in recent years, generationalism is a tool for putting others in their place, and its associations are hard to shake.

Despite or perhaps because of their redundancies, the 2009–14 glut of generational anthologies marked a new phase of British poetry, exerting a regulatory and structuring force on the post-crash decade, not least by providing an important set of credentials at a time of expanding professionalisation. Another benefit of the loosely 'pluralist' generational frame is the implication of meritocracy: poets are included because of the quality of their poems, rather than affinities with certain schools or movements. While the generationalism of these books undoubtedly reflects wide social-political agendas, the second half of this chapter looks more closely at the New/Next Generation campaigns, in order to consider the specific aversions to poetic factionalism driving these projections of a 'broad church' consensus.

Section II: The Fear of Factions

With her 2012 book, *Beyond the Lyric*, Fiona Sampson draws what her subtitle calls 'a map of contemporary British poetry'. The book's method is made more scientific in its introduction, where Sampson proposes 'a quasi-Linnaean classification of poets'. 'By observing poems and grouping them according to type,' the book 'identifies thirteen tendencies (or species) in contemporary British poetry'.[29] In a promotional piece for the *New Statesman*, entitled 'One land, many voices', Sampson explains her motivations. As editor of *Poetry Review*, she felt frustrated by the 'strangely little attention' poetry receives from arts journalists, at a time when British poetry was 'flowering'. She writes:

> Slowly, I came to realise that the tremendous variety of the current poetry boom could actually be putting readers off. Rather than being seductive, it might be overwhelming.[30]

When first published, *Beyond the Lyric* took a fair drubbing in reviews, with many critics questioning the logic of Sampson's taxonomy and her suitability for the task. In the *Times Literary Supplement* (*TLS*), William Wooten quipped: 'It's not just that Sampson's categories don't work for me, they don't work for her either.'[31] Part of the problem, it seems, lay in Sampson's attempt to reconcile these 'thirteen species' with her insistence upon their co-existence in 'a mutually respectful community', in which the 'multiplicity of influences' and 'multiple allegiances' is cause for celebration, not rivalry.[32] For David Wheatley, Sampson's word 'community' retains 'an entirely unsullied and utopian charge', as part of her enthusiasm for poetry in general. With cutting charity, he offers 'that Sampson has loved contemporary poetry perhaps not wisely but too well to take up this challenge in quite the critical spirit the task requires.'[33]

Following the spate of generational anthologies discussed above, this chapter turns now to contemporary poetry's general unease with factions, such as those described by Sampson. In many ways, I suggest, Sampson's self-defeating attempt at categorisation is typical of a more general and well-meaning enthusiasm for poetry that views any acknowledgement of divisions as a threat to the community's whole. In some cases, this fear of factions might seem entirely justified by past conflicts, while the discussion below shows the extent to which this consensus has been enforced in ways that cover over meaningful difference.

Again, the blank generational frame has offered a useful tool for asserting these 'utopian' or otherwise presumptuous notions of 'community'. Although British poetry's fear of factions might be as old as the 'post-war consensus' in UK politics, reflected in the non-descript or ironic names for 'The Movement' or 'The Group' assumed by mid-century writers, the first New Generation list in 1994 offered a chance to stake out a new kind of consensus, perhaps more inflected by the 'Third Way' political consensus of that decade. Many of the poets filling in questionnaires for the 'New Gen' promotion agreed that 'talk of movements should be discouraged'. Michael Donaghy added to his response: 'Yes, "Movements" are dreamt up by publicists to help us sell poetry or by journalists and academic bores to help us understand it.'[34] As ironic as Donaghy's critique of superficial groupings dreamt up 'to help us sell poetry' might be, his comment also substantiates the image of the New Generation as an anti-movement. In line with Peter Forbes's dismissal of 'journalistic clichés' above, the legacy of the New Gen list is its celebration of isolated individual achievement (or 'wilful individuality', in Forbes's words), in a consensus superseding the distinctiveness of would-be factions.

A History of Violence

Like Donaghy, I'm an American import. Arriving in the United Kingdom in 2002, I was struck by the apparent solidarity of the British poetry community. Unlike the formidably diffuse US poetry landscape, it seemed everyone not only knew everyone, but was relatively tolerant of differences in practice. Even when, at that time, I read or heard someone like Keston Sutherland denouncing Don Paterson (or vice versa), these ill-mannered exceptions only proved the rule of etiquette. Later, I did wonder if Sampson's map was doomed by a general sense of any categorisation as vulgar. However, the second thing I noticed was that the rhetoric of consensus was often accompanied by vague references to a less congenial time, now safely passed. In *The New Poetry* (1993), Michael Hulse, David Kennedy, and David Morley contrast their anthology's generation with that past:

> The new poetry highlights the beginning of the end of British poetry's tribal divisions and isolation, and a new cohesiveness – its constituent parts 'talk' to one another readily, eloquently, and freely while preserving their unique identities.[35]

Ten years on, David Herd and Robert Potts, who edited *Poetry Review* together just before Sampson, are similarly defiant. 'When we were interviewed for the position we were asked how we would handle the factionalism of contemporary poetry,' they write in one of their final editorials:

> We said, boldly (foolhardily), that we would ignore it. Our strong sense, as readers of British poetry of the past decade [i.e. 1994–2004], was that the categories according to which the territory was divided, the shorthand by which British poetry was routinely assessed had come to be damaging.[36]

The sentiment persists in 2010, when Roddy Lumsden, introducing *Identity Parade*, describes the cohort included in the book as 'a more harmonious one'. He writes: 'This might well be the generation of poets least driven by movements, fashions, conceptual and stylistic sharing.'[37] Reading this narrative of the path towards unity, beyond of the darker days of 'tribal divisions', it's hard not to wonder how such progress was achieved. Partly, it's an historical question: What was the peace process that delivered such harmony? And partly for now: How, we might ask, is the hard-won consensus implied by such statements enforced? I want to argue for the crucial role played by the New Generation and Next Generation campaigns, along with the broader mood of generationalism they helped inspire, in maintaining that accord.

It's clear that any search for the terms of reconciliation would benefit from a better sense of the dark history than the comments above allow. Yet, the vagueness with which that past is invoked is typical of post-conflict psychology – for those who remember, it doesn't bear repeating. The rest of us should be grateful of the 'wilful naivety' adopted by Herd and Potts, and not reopen old wounds. As Alan Brownjohn put it in 2007: 'Nowadays, unless you speak to a few scarred survivors, you might not realise that the Poetry Society "wars" of the 1970s ever happened.'[38] Brownjohn's occasion for breaking the silence was a review of Peter Barry's *Poetry Wars*, a book which describes the 'Battle of Earls Court', 30 years before, with the sort of archival meticulousness and implicit nostalgia for which another sort of reader might turn to the latest account of Stalingrad. Rather than recount a sordid history better told by Barry, a flippant summary might go: Once upon a time, the 'radicals' of the so-called Poetry Revival movement found themselves in charge of the Poetry Society, did what they could to change it, then lost it back to the conservative 'establishment'. According to Barry, both sides really lost in the end. The 'two tribes', as he calls them, 'had *both* been superseded' by the end of the 1980s, by which time a hybrid approach had become the new 'hegemony'.[39] 'In that sense,' Barry concludes, upbeat in 2006, 'we are now in a "post-dualist" poetry world.'[40]

A Free-Market Future

It's worth contrasting this 'Third Way', 'post-dualist' position with Barry's earlier suspicion, in *Contemporary British Poetry and the City* (2000), to the 'new consensus' still emerging. 'It would be naïve,' he writes,

> to imagine that the old divide between mainstream and margin has simply been 'Berlined' – that the wall between them has been toppled, giving us an 'end-of-history' world of recent poetry. What has happened is that, yes, there has been a change. [...] But the new situation is that there are now *more*, not fewer, zones and divisions than before; yet they are now *more fluid*.[41]

Linda France, on the other hand, introducing 1993s *Sixty Women Poets*, adopts a more dialectical position:

> What is new here is that these opposing forces are seen as co-existing, part of the same whole; as if duality has been exposed as yet another inherited out-worn tradition, used too frequently to divide rather than to unite.[42]

But whether the post-Poetry Wars consensus is envisioned as an 'active, constructive dialectic' (in France's view) or something 'more fluid' (in Barry's), the sense of working beyond factional divides is consistent in these accounts and as a premise for generational anthologies from the mid-1990s onwards. It is in this reconciliatory context, reminiscent of the 'Third Way' politics also consolidated in the period, that the first New Generation list was conceived and announced. That said, very little of the official language around the project is explicitly reparative. Having rejected the 'journalistic clichés' of 'the new pluralism' in his editorial to the spring 1994 special issue of *Poetry Review*, Peter Forbes not only emphasises the 20 New Gen poets' 'wilful individuality', but characterises the group by its 'isolation and intensity', responding to the wider 'social atomization' of the 1980s.[43] Forbes' main concession to the 'fluidity' described by Barry is in labelling the New Gen poets 'the true fruit of postmodernism': 'All cultures are now available to add to one's own inheritance.'[44] In this view, the world is their post-tribal oyster. It is interesting, then, to see where, in a mini-essay in that same special issue, New Gen poet Sarah Maguire already raises concerns regarding this particular brand of 'postmodern' pick-n-mix, connecting it explicitly with political-economic ideology:

> The unbridled relativism of certain aspects of postmodernism strikes me as being deeply reactionary, the free-play of signifiers having more

in common with the so-called 'free' trade and the free-play of money markets than its promulgators would perhaps like us to believe.⁴⁵

In an important sense, the 'unbridled relativism' suggested by Forbes's sense of 'all cultures' being open to appropriation by a new post-faction poetry goes beyond the post-dualist hybridity suggested by Barry's new hegemony or France's constructive dialectic. Instead, the British poetry industry's adoption of neoliberal triumphalist positions in the 1990s is perhaps best and most bluntly signified by Sean O'Brien's 'deregulated muse', in the title of his 1998 book of essays. Through such rhetoric, the advancement of free-market poetics toes a fairly consistent line from the 'wilful individuality' celebrated in New Gen 1994 to 2010s *Identity Parade*, both in its titular metaphor and in Lumsden's praise for 'the essential individualism which I see in this generation'.⁴⁶

'Generation' (Again)

Alongside the waves of generational anthologies discussed in the first part of this chapter, the New/Next Generation Poets, not least in their name-brand, have made an essential contribution to the wider trend of generationalism. Given the number of these class portraits produced over the past 25 years, and in the five years from 2009 especially, those involved in the 2014 Next Generation promotion may have felt they were competing with the project's own influence. My reading of the 2009–2014 wave of gen-anthos emphasised the dubiousness of the 'generation' as a social category, partly due to its manipulation by vested political and economic interests, and the 'undue uniformity' or 'public connotations' its members were 'powerless' to resist, in White's terms. Yet, the New/Next Gen lists further complicate this regulatory dynamic in their own resistance to claims or connotations made on behalf of poets included in the three lists thus far. New Gen 94 poet (and future British laureate) Simon Armitage acknowledges this rhetorical ambiguity around the project in his introduction to the 2004 Next Generation list, which he judged:

> We'd had the Movement, we'd had the Group. We'd even had the Martians. Now, a new clutch was ready to hatch [...] The New Generation was underpinned by literary and philosophical ideas. Allegedly. [...] We were a School. We had things to say, we were good at saying them, and we wanted to be heard. That, if I remember rightly, was how the argument ran.⁴⁷

It's difficult to say whether Armitage is remembering rightly or not, since the notion of the New Generation as a cohesive 'School' runs so contrary to the Poetry Society's own language, and to the 'deregulated' individualism championed throughout the 1990s. But whether or not it is a straw man, Armitage is plainly dubious, and in this way, supports the company line. Whatever 'literary and philosophical ideas' were 'allegedly' shared by his cohort is impossible to say. Like its compatibility with Donaghy's anti-movement sentiments, the power of the generational frame lies as much in its rejection of coherent qualities. As Stan Smith describes the New Gen project, 'Poetic movements have been manufactured before, but perhaps this is the first one to be constructed by a committee.'[48] By 2014, through their committee-manufactured nature, the lists, much like the hollow 'pluralisms' of 'individuals' in the anthologies above, had come to signify whatever was required of the new consensus, or nothing at all.

Unlike the weekly polemics against millennials in certain corners of the media, the appeal of British poetry's post-dualist agreement lay in its reluctance to typecast the new generation, tending instead towards nebulous platitudes. In the 2014 list, which officially recognises the 'most exciting' poets, judges' chair Ian McMillan finds 'an exhilarating mix of style and subject, reflecting a truly diverse range of voices'. Fellow judge Clare Pollard adds only that the latest Next Generation poets seem to write a lot of sequences.[49] With the nearly 40-year age gap between the oldest and youngest poets on the 2014 list, the nominal 'generation' finally proves the ultimate non-category category, acting in that regard as the ultimate buffer against any tribalism that might otherwise resurface.

An End of Consensus?

There are two ways of viewing the presumed consensus which generationalism facilitates. Alan Brownjohn reads Barry's *Poetry Wars* as a 'warning'. 'Few on either side could be proud of their part in the ferocious struggles,' he writes, as a veteran of what Barry calls the 'conservative' side: 'Altogether it was a sorry period. It can only be hoped that Peter Barry is right in believing that modernist poetry now has its fair chance; and presumably doesn't need to storm frail citadels like the Poetry Society.'[50] Thank goodness, in other words, that we've achieved such peace, where everyone can have their 'fair chance'. Robert Sheppard offers a different assessment of this post-war togetherness in his review of Barry's book in *Jacket*. From his perspective, as a veteran of the other side in Barry's account: 'The chorus of democratic poeticality that seems to dominate several *fin de siècle* British anthologies promotes a broad church that includes everybody but the "radicals" and their heirs.' Yet, even Sheppard ends his review with a strange echo and agreement with Brownjohn's hopeful sentiments, saying he hopes Andrew Motion's words in the foreword to Barry's book 'prove true': 'One can only hope that, with the Laureate leading the chorus this time, a true plurality will emerge.'[51]

Sheppard is right to call attention to the 'radicals' overlooked by the Post-Gen consensus. As Keith Tuma puts it, 'New Gen presented an acceptable "literary" collection for the 90s.' It was, in that sense, 'a cynical but certainly in the short term successful exercise in the imposition of a cultural hegemony for the times'.[52] The question remains whether that time is up, and whether Barry and Tuma's 'hegemony' is still in force. By various measures, the status of a generational project that saw 'short term success' in the 1990s and in another burst between 2009 and 2014 appears to be in doubt. The tone of the New Generation project had already shifted by its 2004 sequel, when the name had been changed to Next Generation and organisational responsibility passed from the Poetry Society to Poetry Book Society, which meant, somewhat ironically, that the 2004 and 2014 lists were never commemorated in a physical volume. Anthologies of the latter wave also showed signs of diminishing returns, with the success of Bloodaxe's *Voice Recognition* (2009), *Identity Parade* (2010), and *Dear World* (2013) rendering Salt's *Book of Younger Poets* (2011), Oxfam's *Lung Jazz* (2012), or *The Poetry Business Book of New Contemporary Poets* (2014) fairly redundant, as group portraits go. It won't have helped that 2015 saw the low point of poetry sales for the decade, nor would Salt's contentious announcement in 2014 that they would cease publication of single-author collections in favour of anthologies.

On the surface, *Beyond the Lyric*'s and the New/Next Generation's strategies for defending the consensus might appear contradictory, with Sampson's taxonomy cutting across generationalist discourse. Nevertheless, in their commitment to a 'community' of individual achievement, over collective action or factions, they share what David Wheatley sees in Sampson's book as a resistance to 'the possibility of conflict between rival groups and generations as a driver of poetic history'.[53] They also share a curiously specific tactic for establishing their pluralistic authority at their outset. Sampson lays out her credentials as objective and disinterested map-maker by contrasting herself with Ian Hamilton, which might seem petty, more than a decade after his death, if it weren't for the specific language with which she condemns Hamilton to a bygone 'monopoly on literary patronage'.[54] In this, she might as well have quoted directly from her *Poetry Review* predecessor, Peter Forbes, whose New Generation editorial describes Hamilton's 'chain-letter' method for compiling the *Oxford Companion to Twentieth Century Poetry* as the 'last gasp' of an outdated 'system of patronage'.[55]

If this is the sort of 'partisan development of particular schools' (Sampson's words) which the new consensus cannot abide, what daring or foolishness it must have taken for Nathan Hamilton to admit adapting his uncle's method in editing 2013s *Dear World & Everyone in It*, asking selected poets to recommend further contributors. And Nathan Hamilton is nothing if not upfront about his own biases, as he skewers some of the new consensus's sacred truths:

> It is impossible, and silly to pretend, to be comprehensive or impartial [...] It is impossible to be comprehensive in representing the amount and the variety of activity in the poetry scene. Conversely, it is impossible to be impartial in a world this small, where many of the individual poets will be known to you and a number of them may be friends you don't want to make sad.[56]

Although Hamilton teasingly echoes the dominant discourse at one point, wondering whether 'categorising poetry is just a bad idea', it doesn't stop him from playfully comparing different poets to different Star Trek species, wondering if poetry could be described in terms of colour groupings, and finally, and perhaps more earnestly, advancing a distinction between poets more concerned with either 'product' or 'process'. But perhaps a better indicator that the enforced consensus may have outlived its usefulness is in the sense that the 2014 Next Generation's 'pluralistic' reach may have exceeded its grasp. Of course, it's hardly a failure of that list's promotion that the biggest hook for media outlets was its inclusion of 'performance poet' Kate Tempest. ('Kate Tempest storms next generation poets list,' ran the BBC headline.) But perhaps this demonstrates a promising failure to absorb a meaningful and practical difference into a notional consensus. It's just one example, but these and other noises of productive difference continue to grow in discussions around British poetry, without fear of what it might mean for the 'frail citadel'.

Postscript: Five Years On

When I presented early versions of the analysis above at conferences in August 2013 and March 2015, it was hard to imagine an end to the flood of anthologies and generation-defining lists. Five years on, it seems obvious that it couldn't go on forever. Either readers had enough of the competing group portraits or they did their job in marking an era, giving way to the 'gap of a decade or so' before another generation needs defining. But in that same period, other more fundamental shifts in the way poetry is produced and consumed suggest that the *next* next generation will require a different approach. On the one hand, there have been clear material changes for poetry production in the latter part of what increasingly seems a decade of two halves. The power balance between poetry's print and digital cultures has shifted most dramatically (in all the ways discussed in Chapters 3 and 5). Not only does the visibility of digital and alternative formats trouble the traditional framing of generations according to publication of first print collections (see Chapters 4 and 6), but the expansion and 'fluidity' of global online poetry networks also calls national groupings into question.

More than this, related shifts in poetry culture have made the generational frame appear inadequate to its diversity. Repeated insistence on 'pluralism' and a 'true plurality' now sounds like language belonging to the late-1990s (though it's still used in 2010s *Identity Parade*), from a time when unqualified 'multiculturalism' was central to New Labour's consensus politics. Discussions around diversity now recognise the importance of acknowledging meaningful difference, as well as the importance of resisting slippery rhetoric in which, say, an emphasis on aesthetic or formal diversity obscures writers and readers very different lived experiences. While Forbes's shrugging off of 'journalistic clichés of the new pluralism, regionalism, and the rise of the working class voice' might still appeal to certain editors, it's hard to imagine such tone deafness around a major publication going unquestioned. With greater sensitivity to the privilege involved in self-styled 'post-identity' poetics or cultural appropriation, we can also see how prescient Sarah Maguire was in her wariness of any 'postmodern' notion that 'all cultures are now available to add to one's own inheritance'.

Without suggesting we have collectively progressed beyond generational thinking, poets and readers in the age of social media bubbles are undoubtedly more attuned to risks and privileges of 'extend[ing] to the whole world characteristics of their own microcosm', in Bourdieu's words. Less positively, the culture of credentialism encouraged by generational anthologies is hard to disentangle from the entrepreneurialism and professionalisation of poetry discussed in Part IV of this book. You wouldn't have to look far for a journalist or publisher or listed poet paraphrasing *Voice Recognition*'s 2009 blurb, 'Who are the best young poets today?' In that sense, the 'individualism' of newer poets might prove too 'wilful' for collecting. It seems more likely, however, that the growing complexity of poetry networks and communities, along with the new channels for poetic exchange noted above, will make the generational frame too arbitrary for purpose. If, as White notes, 'an important question becomes who gets to name the generation and define its characteristics', then we now see poets questioning hierarchies that led editors in the past to assume this role.[57] Although it is never fair to judge a project by its press-releases, the expectation that 2014 Next Generation Poets will 'dominate the poetry landscape of the coming decade' or that the generation in the *Salt Book of Younger Poets* will 'dominate UK poetry in years to come' belies the hegemonic designs of that consensus, so out of step with the collaborative and DIY spirit of recent years – and, as it turns out, quite blinkered to online and performance poetry's not-so-sudden 'dominance'. Maybe the most positive conclusion then, is that just a few years on from these more desperate measures, attempting to legislate their visions of the future, contemporary poetry's 'frail citadel' appears not only less frail, but also far too vast and varied to require a citadel at all.

Notes

1. Laura Riding and Robert Graves, *A Pamphlet against Anthologies* (New York: Doubleday, Doran, 1928), 140, 159.
2. T. S. Eliot, letter to the *Times Literary Supplement* (24 November 1921), in *The Letters of T.S. Eliot, Volume I: 1898–1922*, ed. Valerie Eliot and Hugh Haughton, revised edition (London: Faber, 2009), 608.
3. Riding and Graves, *Pamphlet against Anthologies*, 28.
4. Roddy Lumsden (ed.), *Identity Parade: New British and Irish Poets* (Newcastle: Bloodaxe Books, 2010), 17.
5. Originally published in Heaney's pamphlet, *An Open Letter* (Derry: Field Day, 1983), 9.
6. Peter Forbes, 'editorial', *Poetry Review*, vol. 81, no. 2 (Summer 1991), 3.
7. Ibid.
8. Michael Hulse, David Kennedy, and David Morley, *The New Poetry* (Newcastle: Bloodaxe Books, 1993), 25.
9. Ibid.
10. Linda France (ed.), *Sixty Women Poets* (Newcastle: Bloodaxe Books, 1993), 14.
11. Forbes, 'editorial', *Poetry Review Special Issue: New Generation Poets*, vol. 84, no. 1 (Spring 1994), 4.
12. Michael Schmidt (ed.), *New Poetries* (Manchester: Carcanet, 1994), 10. Although Schmidt insists 'the eight poets included here, six of them under thirty, do not constitute a coherent "generation"' (11), the ages of writers included and the premise of introducing 'new voices' belie his resistance to an explicit generational frame.
13. Lumsden, *Identity Parade*, 2010, 17.
14. Ibid.
15. Nathan Hamilton, 'Introduction: Fossils on Mars', in *Dear World & Everyone in It* (Newcastle: Bloodaxe Books, 2013), 29.
16. Clare Pollard and James Byrne (eds.), *Voice Recognition: 21 Poets for the 21st Century* (Newcastle: Bloodaxe Books, 2009), 10.
17. Tom Chivers (ed.), *Generation Txt* (London: Penned in the Margins, 2006), ix.
18. Robert Wohl, *The Generation of 1914* (Cambridge, MA: Harvard University Press, 1979), 5.
19. Jonathan White, 'Thinking Generations', *The British Journal of Sociology*, vol. 64, no. 2 (June 2013), 216–47 (216).
20. Wohl, *Generation of 1914*, 204.
21. Ibid.
22. White, 'Thinking Generations', 229.

23 Chivers, *Generation Txt*, ix; Pollard and Byrne, *Voice Recognition*, 10; Hamilton, *Dear World* cover blurb; Forbes (1994), 6.
24 Peter Riley, 'The Youth Tactic,' *Fortnightly Review* (27 April 2013).
25 Laurie Penny, 'Forget the "baby boomer" debate, says Laurie Penny – this is about cuts and class,' *New Statesman* (29 October 2011); Tom Slate, 'Twentysomethings, call off the generational jihad,' *Spiked* (27 February 2015); and Jennie Bristow, *Baby Boomers and Generational Conflict* (London: Palgrave, 2015), 6. Bristow herself is the author or subject of a number of essays in the loose series *Spiked* has published since 2015 critiquing 'generation wars'. Outside the United Kingdom, bestsellers like Mark Davis's *Gangland: Cultural Elites and the New Generationalism* (London: Allen & Unwin, first published in 1997, revised in 1999 and again 2010) offered an earlier critique of generational narratives in Australian media.
26 Bourdieu, *The Rules of Art: Genesis and Structure of the Literary Field* (Stanford, CA: Stanford University Press, 1996), 126.
27 White, 'Thinking Generations', 238. Indeed, much criticism of Mannheim's founding 'theory of generations' within sociology stems from his own vagueness in defining a generation, and the fact that many (or all) of its social consequences might as readily be attributable to class or other socio-economic differences.
28 Ibid.
29 Sampson, *Beyond the Lyric: A Map of Contemporary British Poetry* (London: Chatto & Windus, 2012), 8.
30 Sampson, 'One Land, Many Voices', *New Statesman* (30 August 2012).
31 Wooten, 'The Hows and Whys of Writing Poetry,' *Times Literary Supplement* (21 November 2012).
32 Sampson, 'Afterward', *Beyond the Lyric*, 283–84.
33 David Wheatley, c, *Beyond the Lyrics: A Map of Contemporary British Poetry*', *Tower Poetry* (September 2012), reprinted in *Tower Poetry Reviews: 2004–2014*, ed. Peter McDonald (Oxford: Tower Poetry, 2015), 240–49 (243, 240). In light of social and political complexities glossed over by Sampson's designation of 'communal truths', Wheatley asks: 'Where is her natural scepticism towards so degraded a word, so degraded a concept?' (243).
34 Donaghy, 'On being a New Generation Poet', *The Shape of the Dance: Essays, Interviews and Digressions* (London: Picador, 2009), 98.
35 Hulse et al., *The New Poetry*, 16.
36 David Herd and Robert Potts, *Poetry Review*, vol. 94, no. 4 (Winter 2004–5), 4.
37 Lumsden, *Identity Parade*, 19–20.
38 Brownjohn, 'Poetry Wars', *Poetry Review*, vol. 97, no. 2 (Summer 2007), 105.
39 Peter Barry, *Poetry Wars: British Poetry of the 1970s and the Battle of Earls Court* (London: Salt Publishing, 2006), 68.
40 Ibid., 181.
41 Barry, *Contemporary British Poetry and the City* (Manchester: Manchester University Press, 2000), 12.
42 France, *Sixty Women Poets*, 16.
43 Forbes (1994), 4.
44 Ibid., 5.
45 Sarah Maguire, *Poetry Review* (Spring 1994), 69.
46 Lumsden, *Identity Parade*, 19. Defending his approach with Carcanet's *New Poetries* series, Michael Schmidt criticises the sheer breadth of *Identity Parade*: 'Lumsden proposes a

triumphal parade of discreet identities, marching obediently forward. A generational victory parade.' (interview with Evan Jones, *Canadian Notes & Queries*, June 2013).
47 Simon Armitage, 'Life on the line,' *The Guardian* (5 June 2004).
48 Stan Smith, *Poetry and Displacement* (Liverpool: Liverpool University Press, 2007), 195.
49 Official press release, reported by various places, including Tim Masters, 'Kate Tempest storms next generation poets list,' *BBC News* website (11 September 2014).
50 Brownjohn, *Poetry Review* (Summer 2008), 107.
51 Sheppard, 'Poets Behaving Badly', *Jacket 31* (October 2006).
52 Tuma, *Fishing by Obstinate Isles: Modern and Postmodern British Poetry and American Readers* (Evanston, IL: Northwestern University Press, 1998), 213.
53 Wheatley, Review of Fiona Sampson', 241.
54 Sampson, 'Introduction', *Beyond the Lyric*, 6.
55 Forbes, *Poetry Review* (Spring 1994), 5.
56 Hamilton, *Dear World*, 19.
57 White, 'Thinking Generations', 238.

Chapter 2

SHORTLISTED AGAINST MY RUINS: THE ECONOMY OF SCANDAL IN THE NEW PRIZE CULTURE

Jeremy Paxman had some choice words for poets in early June 2014. 'I think poetry has really rather connived at its own irrelevance,' he lamented. 'It seems to me very often that poets now seem to be talking to other poets and that is not talking to people as a whole.'[1] Normally, such opinions from a broadcaster and quiz show host who had otherwise shown little interest in the state of contemporary poetry would not have circulated so widely in traditional media outlets, nor, as a result, been criticised so widely on social media. Except in this case, Paxman had been appointed chair of the judging panel for the UK's Forward Prizes, and these statements were made in conjunction with the announcement of its shortlists. The response from the supposedly self-defeating poetry community was better than immediate. Alison Flood, first reporting the story in the *Guardian* newspaper, had already collated responses from eminent poets and critics. Added to Paxman's reproach, however, Flood's mention of poetry's declining sales, alongside a concession by Michael Symmons Roberts, a previous winner and judge, that Paxman's censure was 'not without foundation in terms of the symptoms', had set the charges for an explosive defence of poetry beyond those solicited responses, in the more than 7,500 shares of the *Guardian* article, 428 comments below it (before closed), reprintings of the story in other newspapers, and any number of social media posts, blogs, or comment pieces in those same mainstream outlets.[2] The *Guardian* published a longer response by the poet George Szirtes and a further letter responding to Szirtes that same week, while the awarding of the prizes that September were another occasion for weighing Paxman's comments against the work by winners Kei Miller and Liz Berry.[3]

In his formative study of cultural prizes, *The Economy of Prestige* (2005), James F. English argues that this proliferating commentary and meta-commentary is essential to prizes' function. 'Much of it, indeed,' he writes, 'is simply part of the extra-institutional apparatus of this or that particular prize, part of the prize's undeclared and perhaps unwitting publicity machinery, even and especially when its posture is a scandalized or condescending one.'[4] Paxman's 'posture' was both of these, and the sense of his censure performing this 'extra-institutional' function for the sake of the Forward Prize's visibility was reinforced not only by his visibility as chair of judges and a celebrity outsider to the community he was criticising, but also by the inclusion, in those same official announcement summaries, of approving comments by the director of the Forward Arts Foundation, which administers the prize. For readers first encountering Paxman's provocation, director Susannah Herbert was already on record, welcoming the comments' potential to 'kick start an overdue national debate about the power of well-chosen words, communication and the role of poetry in our collective lives'.[5] Thus, Paxman's officially endorsed rebuke and chorus of responses conform neatly to English's sense that 'the vast literature of mockery and derision with respect to prizes must, in my view, be seen as an integral part of the prize frenzy itself, and not as in any way advancing an extrinsic critique'.[6] As Carcanet founder Michael Schmidt put it in a revised edition of *The Lives of Poets* published later that year, 'Much of what [Paxman] is reported as saying was intended to elicit the outrage that becomes news.'[7] In that sense, it was just the sort of manufactured scandal – someone bemoaning the state of an art form, a rallying of defences, and the prize itself finally taken as proof of its health – that has operated as part of the 'publicity machinery' behind writing awards at least since the Greeks gathered for their Dionysia prize festivals.

What has changed – to an extent that it fundamentally alters the nature of these debates – is the means by which these debates are conducted. Even in the time since English's study of prize culture was published in 2005, the role of social media and participatory journalism has advanced at a rate than can be measured in scandals only a few years apart. For English, the commentary landscape appears much simpler, with clear distinctions between the different parties involved. It allows him to insist that his own

> project, a 'reflexive sociology' of the economy of cultural prestige, diverges sharply from the existing commentary on prizes and awards, a body of discussion that is voluminous but, as a source of critical insight, mostly negligible. Thousands of articles about prizes appear every year in the major newspapers and magazines, and this journalistic literature is what we have in lieu of any real scholarship.[8]

The sharper lines – not only between the 'voluminous' journalistic literature supposedly devoid of 'critical insight' or 'real scholarship', but between official prize rhetoric and the 'extra-institutional apparatus' in his comments above – are blurrier in the Paxman story, where the initial attack is already accompanied by responses from academic critics and the prize's spokespeople.

Across the three further poetry prize 'scandals' examined in this chapter, the breakdown of traditional tiers within commentary and analysis becomes more and more pronounced. While opening these debates to a wider range of voices has been encouraging, the discussion here will point to ways in which the expansion of prizes' 'publicity machinery' also risks absorbing those voices into an 'economy of cultural prestige' and the market logic that comes with it. This chapter, therefore, extends English's analysis of book awards' 'primary function' as 'that of facilitating cultural "market transactions"' to the communal structures that facilitate transactions *beyond* the prizes themselves, in the form of commentary.[9] As Claire Squires writes, 'awarding a prize to a book acts not only to indicate value, but also to confer it.'[10] Across three separate debates around the awarding of the UK's T. S. Eliot Poetry Prize over the past decade, I suggest that these communal structures have widened and adapted to incorporate the prize – and especially debates or scandals around the prize – into an economy that offers individual commentators a greater 'share' in that value, by way of these various transactions. Therefore, this is less a discussion of the value of prizes as such, or the rights and wrongs of individual debates, than a re-conception of the way in which prizes' value is reinforced by the proliferation of commentary and feedback loops.

The T. S. Eliot Prize

In order to promise literary value for their recipients, prizes must also assert their own unique value within the cultural economy. Like many prizes, the T. S. Eliot winner is often announced alongside assertions of its merit as, according to a 2017 *Evening Standard* headline, the 'world's most prestigious poetry prize'.[11] When the Poetry Book Society (PBS), which had administered the T. S. Eliot prize since its launch in 1993, had its funding cut from Arts Council England in 2011, an open letter signed by a number of former judges, winners, and shortlistees made their case for renewed support on behalf of 'the most respected award for new collections of poetry in English'.[12] With an even more circular sense of where the prize's value originates, the most often-repeated tagline in official prize statements or media summaries is former laureate Andrew Motion's description of the Eliot prize as 'the prize most poets want to win'.[13] By aligning the value of the prize with either prestige, respect, or desirability, such rhetoric establishes a symbolic structure through which the prize's cultural capital is linked to that of its 'shareholders', which is to say, those who reiterate those qualities and stand to benefit from its symbolic value in the literary economy. Like world currencies or financial commodities in the absence of a gold standard, the value of a prize – and, in turn, its ability to confer value – is utterly dependent upon interested parties' faith in that abstract prestige. This religious-like belief is what Pierre Bourdieu calls the *illusio* behind cultural practices more generally. If, on the one hand, writers and readers are willing to acknowledge the 'game' of literary prizes – Julian Barnes dismissing the Booker prize as 'posh bingo', for example (before he won it)[14] – such cynicism persists in tension with the *illusio* (from the Latin *ludus*, or game) 'of taking the game seriously' and the collective belief that 'playing is worth the effort'.[15]

It is within these value-games that prizes seem to attract almost perpetual scandal or criticism, and the T. S. Eliot prize not least among these in recent years. For Bourdieu, scandal remains the 'instrument *par excellence*' of symbolic action', since, as English explains, 'there is perhaps no device more perfectly suited than scandal to making things happen on the field of culture.'[16] While newspapers and other mainstream coverage happily perpetuate a narrative in which prizes – like the Booker, with its annual public debates – exist *in spite of* such scandals, English argues that, 'far from posing a threat to the prize's efficacy as an instrument of the cultural economy, scandal is its lifeblood'.[17] Or as Mark Lawson puts it as a former judge, the purpose of the Booker prize is not simply 'to promote the cause of serious fiction', but 'to provoke rows and scandals, which may, in due course, promote the cause of serious fiction'.[18] One might reasonably ask whether the past decade has witnessed a shift towards an analogous relationship between the Eliot prize and 'serious' poetry, in which criticism around the prize is tacitly accepted (or encouraged, even) for the sake of the public visibility it brings to poetry.

But as suggested above, the nature of these scandals and debates has also changed since Lawson's assessment (in 1994), moving away from aesthetic disagreements to more administrative issues. The attention given to the Booker or other fiction awards in recent scholarship on prizes tends to focus on debates regarding the merits of one winning or 'snubbed' novel over another. As English himself attests, 'the most common and generic scandals concern judges, specifically the judges' dubious dispositions, as betrayed by their meagre credentials, their risible lack of habitus, or their glaring errors of judgment'.[19] While the Paxman episode might fit this genre of scandal (despite it concerning a judge's more general comments, rather than the ultimate choice of winner), the debates around Alice Oswald's withdrawal from the 2011 Eliot prize, David Harsent's win in 2014, and Sarah Howe's in 2016 were more focused on reactions than the prize itself. Increasingly, in other words, the commentary *is* the scandal.

2011: Alice Oswald

On 20 October 2011, the PBS announced its shortlist of 10 books vying for that year's T. S. Eliot poetry prize, including Alice Oswald's *Memorial* and

John Kinsella's *Armour*. For many, this was as much an achievement for the Poetry Book Society, an organisation which had been founded by Eliot himself in 1953 and had launched the prize in his name in 1993. After losing its Arts Council funding earlier that year – on the grounds that 'the Poetry Book Society's reach and distribution was not as wide or effective as other applicants', according to the Arts Council's director of literature – the PBS was able to announce, on the same day as the shortlist announcement, 'the new supporter of the TS Eliot Prize', the private investment management firm, Aurum Funds.[20] In their official online statement (since removed), the PBS affirmed the benefits and uniqueness of the sponsorship arrangement:

> The PBS is particularly gratified to have attracted serious support from the financial sector for the Prize and believes that this may be the first time poetry has attracted this kind of backing, showing the growing importance and visibility of the T S Eliot Prize.[21]

Six weeks later, on the sixth of December, the poet Alice Oswald withdrew her book, *Memorial*, from contention with the following statement:

> I'm uncomfortable about the fact that Aurum Funds, an investment company which exclusively manages funds of hedge funds, is sponsoring the administration of the Eliot Prize; I think poetry should be questioning not endorsing such institutions and for that reason I'm withdrawing from the Eliot shortlist.[22]

The following day, the Australian poet John Kinsella withdrew his own collection, *Armour*, in a statement via his publisher: 'I am grateful to Alice Oswald for bringing the sponsorship of the TS Eliot Prize to my attention.' While acknowledging his 'regret that I must do this at a particularly difficult time for the Poetry Book Society,' Kinsella explained that 'the business of Aurum does not sit with my personal politics and ethics'.[23]

Despite speculation about further withdrawals, the shortlist of eight remained, and the prize proceeded without replacements. When it was awarded to John Burnside in January, newspaper accounts could hardly resist reminding readers why it was the 'most controversial TS Eliot prize in decades', according to one headline.[24] Between Oswald and Kinsella's withdrawals and the prize ceremony, however, a flurry of commentary affirmed a general sense of controversy, while displaying a lingering disconnect between traditional media outlets and newer online platforms. The *Guardian* article announcing Oswald's withdrawal embodied this divide in its straightforward account, which stated that Aurum and the PBS had 'declined to comment on Oswald's decision'.

Those commenting below the line, however, soon chimed in to express their support in pithy terms: 'admirable', 'good on her', and 'occupy poetry!'[25] Similar sentiments appeared on Twitter, with links to the article shortly after it appeared: 'good on alice oswald for dropping out of the running for the TS Eliot prize. fuck hedge funds. fuck the rich becoming richer.'[26] While few on social media expressed a directly contrary view, other users that same day began to question the terms of what newspapers had described as a 'protest'. 'So now everyone in my replies is backing Alice Oswald,' the blogger and critic John Self tweeted, 'can we say why? Why are hedge funds intrinsically bad? Even when funding poetry?'[27] The poet Kathryn Maris asked: 'Does Alice Oswald have specific info re Aurum Funds (e.g. wrongdoing?) or does she just believe that hedge funds are inherently evil?'[28] When John Kinsella added his withdrawal, a blog post by Katy Evans-Bush posed similar questions – 'Are hedge funds really any worse than any other corporate sponsor?' – while acknowledging the political atmosphere, and possible links with the Occupy movement then taking hold in London and elsewhere.[29]

Alongside these ruminations among fellow poets and others outside mainstream media, a separate line of commentary interrogated Oswald and Kinsella's stance more pointedly. An article in the *Telegraph* complained that 'neither Oswald nor Kinsella have elaborated on how exactly poetry should question an investment firm' and another in the *Observer* dismissed the poets' appeal to 'an old romantic idea: namely, that art should have no truck with commerce'.[30] 'Neither poet appeared to find anything much out about Aurum. For them, apparently, the dread words "hedge fund" were enough,' it continued, complaining that such vague idealism 'seems self-indulgent and irresponsible'. Less publicly, and without explicitly linking the Eliot prize to another debate regarding British Petroleum's sponsorship of the Tate gallery, culture secretary Jeremy Hunt spoke to the conservative think tank, New Culture Form, the day after Kinsella's withdrawal about the need for the arts to support these sorts of financial relationships, in turn 'encouraging good behaviour by corporations'.[31] Others thought it sufficient to point out the fact that T. S. Eliot himself (like Oswald's father) had worked as a banker.

By the time Oswald expanded on her initial statement in the *Guardian* with 'Why I pulled out of the TS Eliot poetry prize,' the various threads of commentary had little chance of coming back together. The claim that she was taking her cue from the sixth-century poet Thomas Wyatt's notion of 'repining' and simply needed to listen to 'the very faint honest voice at the bottom of the skull' did little to clear up the vagueness Oswald had been accused of. Nor, on the other hand, did her qualified criticisms of Aurum Funds offer much ammunition to her supporters-in-principle. (Having offices in Bermuda, e.g. 'doesn't necessarily mean they pay less tax than they should'.) Finally, whatever steam was left among any of the disjointed commentariat could be relieved by her withdrawal from collective protest. She hadn't signed the petition when the PBS lost its funding ('because it seemed a minor issue compared with the dismantling of the health service') and even now, she added: 'I don't suggest that anyone else should agree with me. I hope my fellow poets will have different opinion and not be afraid to express them.'[32] Ultimately, the brief excitement and confusion were diffused among this series of disjointed takes. Although Oswald and Kinsella's withdrawals had no more immediate effect than John Berger's protest at the Booker's sponsorship in 1972 (when he accepted the prize, but donated half of his winnings to the Black Panthers), the involvement of these disparate feedback mechanisms at least gestured to new means by which future scandals would be conducted.

2014: David Harsent

Three years later, after two relatively uneventful wins by Sharon Olds and Sinéad Morrissey, the 2014 T. S. Eliot prize was awarded to David Harsent for his collection *Fire Songs*. As soon as that year's shortlist was revealed three months before, criticism had begun to simmer. On 23 October 2014, the day of the shortlist announcement, a post asking, 'Who Is the PBS for?' appeared on poet and publisher Todd Swift's *Eyewear* blog. Again linking the prize to wider political contexts with his reference to 'the Poetry 99%', Swift offered a lengthy critique of the poetry's 'inner circle'. 'I'm not saying the TS Eliot Prize shortlist process is fixed,' he writes, but 'it looks to be a closed shop.'[33] While Swift's complaints concerned the prize's general neglect of small presses, the poet and critic David Wheatley, sharing the link on Twitter, added that it was 'Hard to disagree with @eyewearpoetry on the TS Eliot Prize shortlist, with its egregious & hard-to-stomach cronyism'.[34] When queried by the poet Andrew McMillan on the claim of 'cronyism', Wheatley replied: 'The Sampson/Harsent/ Burnside Bermuda triangle of review-/prize-swapping wrongness. Also FS is DH's departmental colleague.'[35] In December, the satirical account 'Rank Formsby' put names to those initials with the tweet: 'I'm shock to the core – to the very core! – that Fiona Sampson has chosen David Harsent in THE GREAT LIST 2014,' with a link to Sampson's year-end book list for the *Independent* newspaper.[36]

The alleged 'cronyism' here concerned various connections between Fiona Sampson, one of the three Eliot judges in 2014, and David Harsent, who won the prize a few weeks later. When the winner was announced on 12 January 2015, the digital murmurs resumed, prompting an article on the *TLS* blog (since removed), outlining links between Sampson and Harsent for the uninitiated. In it, critic Michael Caines not only cites Sampson's glowing reviews of many books by Harsent (including the Eliot-winning *Fire Songs*) but, like Wheatley, points out their professorships at the University of Roehampton, and the fact that Sampson had, in 2012, also been 'one of two judges who awarded the [International] Griffin Prize to Harsent for *Night*, after reading 481 volumes of poets from thirty-seven countries'.[37] Referencing the £20,000 Eliot award (raised that year from £15,000), after the C$65,000 (£40,000) Griffin Prize, Rank Formsby tweeted again: 'Fuck me. Another example of Fiona Sampson giving a fuck-load of money [to] David Harsent. I can hear [David Wheatley] wailing from here.'[38]

The following week, in a gesture connecting the problem with Harsent's poetry, the critic Dave Coates offered a scathing critique of the 'sexualised violence against women' throughout *Fire Songs*. Despite his review's disclaimer that the 'debacle' had been 'well-covered' elsewhere (with a link to Caines's *TLS* article), Coates also advanced the cronyism argument by pointing out that one of the other two Eliot judges, Sean Borodale, was also a recent student of Harsent's.[39] This game of associations was taken still further that week when the Canadian academic David A. Williams shared a series of nodal network graphs, highlighting the connectedness of judges and recipients for UK poetry prizes, including the Eliot, Forward, and Costa book awards.[40]

As with Oswald's 2011 withdrawal, there remained a degree of disconnect between the different modes of commentary regarding Harsent's 2014 win. Fiona Sampson's own response – printed in the *Guardian*, but not online – admitted only that 'the intimacy of the poetry world can make judging feel oddly embarrassing'.[41] Even Caines's *TLS* post, though taken by others on social media as a semi-official record of collusion, concludes that 'others may carp (mainly in the Twittersphere), but it is difficult in the small world of poetry [...] to avoid treading on a colleague's toe, as it were, every now then.'[42] Unlike the 2011 scandal, however, this particular debate had originated on non-traditional media sites, and was sustained there by the interactions between individual commenters. Despite some bewilderment by those commenting on Williams's charts, the controversy around the 2014 Eliot prize had again advanced new modes by which individuals could weigh in.[43]

2015: Sarah Howe

The very next year, the Eliot prize was back at the centre of debate, although this time, the controversy emerged entirely in the wake of its awarding. Like those before, the prize ceremony for the 2015 prize didn't take place until January 2016. That same evening, the *Guardian*'s Mark Brown was first in, publishing his report on Sarah Howe's winning collection, *Loop of Jade*. As with other write-ups of shortlist or winner announcements, coverage in traditional media outlets were padded with repetition of semi-official rhetoric about the prize's prestige and quotes from the judges. In this case, newspapers could fill out their copy by noting Howe's winning of the 2015 *Sunday Times*/Peter Fraser and Dunlop Young Writer of the Year Award the month before, and the fact that *Loop of Jade* was the first ever debut collection to win the Eliot prize. Nearly every summary, echoing the publisher's blurbs and Eliot prize's official statement, also noted Howe's 'dual British and Chinese heritage' and the way 'her poems chart journeys she made back to Hong Kong to rediscover her roots'. As the judges' chair, Pascale Petit, expanded: 'She is exploring the situation of women in China,' in a book that 'really does speak to what is going on today with the status of women in the world'.[44]

A few racist comments appeared below the online *Guardian* article that same evening. Among other gripes and celebrations, the user 'deadgod' commented that 'Straight white bros can't get a break in the prize racket,' and was supported by 'Glozboy,' who added, 'These days you need to be black, have had a troubled start in life, or live in a shitty borough of London to get any recognition.'[45] Where these anonymous posters were easily ignored, more visible reactions that focused on Howe's race and gender prompted wider debate in the week that followed. While the accelerating timelines of the 2011 and 2014 Eliot debates show the challenge in retracing threads of disparate commentary in the days or weeks of a scandal's lifespan, the responses to criticism of Howe show the feedback loops between social media and 'traditional' media turning at an even faster pace.

At 9:42 p.m. on 21 January 2016, the critic Charles Walley tweeted images from a new issue of the satirical magazine, *Private Eye*, which questioned: 'How did Sarah Howe come to win the £20,000 TS Eliot prize for poetry last week with *Loop of Jade*, the first debutant laureate in the prestigious award's history?'[46] *Private Eye*'s anonymous 'Bookworm' columnist wondered whether Howe's 'improbable' victory was

> perhaps, as some suggested, for extra-poetry reasons? As a successful and very 'presentable' young woman with a dual Anglo-Chinese heritage, Howe can be seen as a more acceptable ambassador for poetry than the distinguished grumpy old men she saw off.[47]

Twelve minutes later, the poet Amy Key tweeted: 'The piece Oliver Thring wrote on Sarah Howe in *The Sunday Times* last weekend was a horrid piece of crass & sexist writing.'[48] The following morning, in order to circumvent the *Times*' online paywall, Key shared an image of the article itself, an interview with Howe published a few days before, entitled 'Born in the rubbish tip, the greatest poetry of today'. In it, the interviewer Thring offers lifestyle-like descriptions of Howe's London flat ('a tasteful place of turquoise armchairs, mezzanine bookcases, statement mirrors and walls papered with pages from Shakespeare') alongside backhanded descriptions of her poetry: 'At times her verse pummels the reader with allusion, scholarship and a brusque, sixth-formy emphasis on her own intelligence.' He admits, 'I am baffled by much of it.' Elsewhere, he describes Howe 'bark[ing] a nervous laugh', and suggests that 'to interview this Cambridge English don, whose PhD, she says, was on "visual imagination and visual vividness in language", is to undergo a tutorial sprinkled with wordy phrases'. When discussing the book's racial concerns, Thring includes the word 'hybridity' in scare quotes and concludes that 'what she calls "the fluidity of my racial experience" seems destined to remain the central theme of her work'.[49] The deserved reaction on social media was immediate, and hardly assuaged when Thring himself responded an hour later, baiting followers with a link to the piece: 'This gentle interview with a young leading poet has led various deranged poetesses to call me thick, sexist, etc.'[50] By six o'clock that evening, the Twitter hashtag #derangedpoetess, reclaimed by those criticising Thring's interview, was trending across the United Kingdom.[51]

The next morning, the *Guardian* was ready with a summary of the debate by poet Katy Evans-Bush, entitled: 'TS Eliot prize row: is winner too young, beautiful – and Chinese?' (By comparison, Evans-Bush's thoughts on Oswald's withdrawal, mentioned above, had been posted to her own blog.) 'The boys appear not to be happy,' she began her write-up of 'three dodgy newspaper articles and a trending Twitter hashtag', referencing the *Private Eye* column, Thring's *Sunday Times* interview, and another from the *TLS* about the recent 'series of successes on the British prize circuit for persons of colour'.[52] Further accounts would appear on the *NBC News, The Bookseller, South China Morning Post*, and elsewhere. At last, a debate that had been initiated and sustained on social media had closed the loop with its traditional media forebears.

Towards a Theory of Participatory Poetry Culture

In recounting these episodes, I worry my own historiographic approach to structures and origins of debate online might be mistaken for mere chatter. As Amy Key tweeted amid reactions to the Howe interview, 'it would be easy to dismiss #derangedpoetess as a storm in a twitter teacup'.[53] James English, in the history of modern prizes he introduces as 'one of the great untold stories of modern cultural life', remains clearer in his position among the discrete tiers of commentary.[54] Regarding the 'journalistic literature' he separates from 'real scholarship,' he adds: 'Much of this, moreover, falls well outside the category of reportage or news, consisting rather of deprecating brief-mention paragraphs, catty bits of gossip, or strongly opinionated, and often rather acerbic, byline feature pieces.'[55] As we've seen, the media landscape supporting that endless prize commentary has changed dramatically and permanently since English studied prize culture in 2005. To this end, his most prescient insight regarding prize culture might be that 'no commentator can altogether avoid participating in the very economy of prestige, the very system of valuing and devaluing, esteeming and disesteeming, that he or she undertakes to examine'.[56] After judging the Forward prize in 2014 and winning it in 2016, Vahni Capildeo reflected on these issues in *PN Review*, concluding:

> There is no 'prize culture'. There are numerous, interlinked, imperfect mechanisms for bringing more, and different, poetry to more, and different readers – including those outside these four [UK] nations, who nonetheless happen (who knows why?) to read in English.[57]

But even if the proliferation of 'interlinked, imperfect mechanisms', including the layers of commentary and metacommentary peeled back above, helps to debunk an outdated critique of the 'inner circle' establishment behind these prizes, there remains an even more interwoven structure (whatever we call it) by which access to and authority in these debates is regulated. Making sense of these rapidly changing spaces for commentary might begin with acknowledging the link between English's sense of complicity on the part of those commenting and more recent media theory that contends with the very literal mechanisms of that widening net. On the one hand, English insists the following:

> Arts editors, book reviewers, and authors and academics who write for the newspapers or engage in book chat on radio and TV are by no means perfectly opposed to the sponsors and administrators of prizes, nor, where the two sets of interests do diverge, would the writers stand to gain by driving prizes off the cultural field altogether.[58]

On the other hand, media scholar Henry Jenkins, despite publishing his study of *Convergence Culture* (2006) only a year later, offers a vision of collapsing layers that seems truer than ever:

> Rather than talking about media producers and consumers as occupying separate roles, we might now see them as participants who interact with each other according to a new set of rules that none of us fully understands. Not all participants are created equal. Corporations – and

even individuals within corporate media – still exert greater power than any individual consumer or even the aggregate of consumers. And some consumers have greater abilities to participate in this emerging culture than others.[59]

Among scholars examining these changes in journalism, the breakdown of distinctions between writers, readers, critics, academics, producers, and consumers is manifest in the rise of 'participatory' media or 'citizen' journalism. In a 2017 special issue on the topic for *Journalism Practice*, Nikki Usher offers an account of the 'structural limitations' involved in 'participatory content creation' that extends Jenkins's sense of not all participants being equal. Emphasising the varying degrees of 'appropriation' and 'amplification' involved on the part of outlets and platforms featuring user content, Usher challenges a 'utopian view' of the levelled playing field supposedly enacted by these exchanges between old and new media. The power balance, she argues, is still heavily skewed towards news organisations, partly due to the way web traffic is structured and regulated by Twitter and other user-content platforms.[60]

In working towards an understanding of the distinctive participatory culture around poetry prizes and poetry more generally, Usher's journalistic model might be linked back to English's Bourdieu-inflected understanding of the 'economy of prestige', in which no commentator can avoid participating. Moving away from a top-down model of prize's absolute value, we come to see how the 'numerous, interlinked, imperfect mechanisms' that make up the so-called prize culture are involved in these transactions of cultural capital. Sharing one's own views or links and retweets of others' becomes a means of staking a claim, however small, on a share in that value. As Jenkins and Usher make clear, these claims are never equal. But just as importantly in the case of prizes, we can see how these individual 'shares' inevitably reinforce the value of the prize, even when commenting critically. In Bourdieu's terms, they reassert that the game is worth playing, or worth commenting upon. In something not entirely unlike a hedge fund, these 'shares' in the form of commentary enact the collective faith that supports a prize's own claims to prestige. Even while I've been typing this, another email has arrived asking for recommendations from Poetry Society members for this year's Ted Hughes Award, launched in 2009. Since 2011, the Saboteur Awards have been similarly led by reader input. The Eliot prize 'scandals' discussed above show the growing role of commentary in fortifying the importance of prizes over the past decade. Conversely, the nature of these debates also shows the degree to which the prizes' value is accepted as a central signifier, in order that it might confer a share of that value on those weighing in. For the sake of meta-commentary around reactions and administration, the value of prizes becomes harder to question. In that sense, the potential for a more 'participatory' prize culture to challenge power structures remains in tension with the extent to which all commentary serves to reinforce that regulatory function.

Notes

1. Alison Flood, 'Jeremy Paxman says poets must start engaging with ordinary people', *Guardian* (1 June 2014).
2. Ibid.
3. Szirtes, 'Jeremy Paxman doesn't see that poetry is felt, not fathomed', *Guardian* (2 June 2014); letter from Ralph Windle, 'Jeremy Paxman, elitism, and poetry for ordinary people', *Guardian* (8 June 2014).
4. James English, *The Economy of Prestige: Prizes, Awards, and the Circulation of Cultural Value* (Cambridge, MA: Harvard University Press, 2005), 24.
5. Flood, 'Jeremy Paxman' (1 June 2014).
6. English, *The Economy of Prestige*, 25.
7. Michael Schmidt, *Lives of the Poets*, rev. ed. (London: Head of Zeus, 2014), 3.
8. English, *The Economy of Prestige*, 23–24.
9. Ibid., 26.
10. Squires, *Marketing Literature: The Making of Contemporary Writing in Britain* (Basingtoke: Palgrave, 2007), 97.
11. Jessie Thompson, 'TS Eliot Prize 2017: Jacob Polley Is Awarded World's Most Prestigious Poetry Prize for His Collection Jackself', *Evening Standard* (16 January 2017).
12. Open Letter, 'A defence of poetry', *Times* [London] (1 April 2011).
13. The T. S. Eliot Prize website, tseliot.com/prize.
14. Julian Barnes, 'Diary', *London Review of Books* vol. 9, no. 20 (12 November 1987), 21.
15. Bourdieu, *Practical Reason* (Stanford, CA: Stanford University Press, 1998), 76–77.
16. Bourdieu and Hans Haacke, *Free Exchange* (Stanford, CA: Stanford University Press, 1990), 96; English, *The Economy of Prestige*, 190.
17. English, *The Economy of Prestige*, 208.
18. Mark Lawson, 'Never mind the plot, enjoy the argument', *Independent* (6 September 1994).
19. English, *The Economy of Prestige*, 190.
20. Open letter, 'Arts Council: we support poetry', *Times* [London] (4 April 2011).
21. 'Aurum – the new supporter of the T S Eliot Prize', Poetry Book Society website (20 October 2011) – since removed.
22. Qtd in Florence Waters, 'Poet withdraws from TS Eliot prize over sponsorship', *Telegraph* (6 December 2011).
23. *Qtd in Benedicte Page*, 'Kinsella Joins Oswald in Withdrawing from T S Eliot Award,' *The Bookseller* (7 December 2011).
24. Maev Kennedy, 'John Burnside wins most controversial TS Eliot prize in decades', *Guardian* (16 January 2012).
25. Comments on Alison Flood, 'Alice Oswald withdraws from TS Eliot prize in protest at sponsor Aurum', *Guardian* (6 December 2011).
26. Charlotte Geater (@tambourine), Twitter (12:55 p.m., 6 December 2011).
27. John Self (@john_self), Twitter (11:19 a.m., 6 December 2011).

28 Kathryn Maris (@KathrynMaris), Twitter (10:06 a.m., 6 December 2011).
29 Katy Evans-Bush, 'Occupy Poetry?', *Baroque in Hackney* blog (7 December 2011).
30 Emma Hogan, 'We shouldn't forget that TS Eliot was a banker', *Telegraph* (9 December 2011); William Skidelsky and Geoff Dyer, 'Should the arts be more selective about sponsors?', *Observer* (10 December 2011).
31 Qtd in Alex Needham, 'Tate may not renew BP sponsorship deal after environmental protests', *Guardian* (13 December 2011).
32 Alice Oswald, 'Why I pulled out of the TS Eliot poetry prize', *Guardian* (12 December 2011). Oswald's qualification of Aurum's offshore interests is noteworthy in light of the UK's Forward Prize's sponsorship by Bookmark Content (formerly Forward Worldwide), whose parent company since 2001, the global advertising conglomerate WPP, has been repeatedly accused of exploiting offshore tax structures. After moving to Ireland in 2008, following the introduction of new corporate tax measures in the United Kingdom, WPP is currently registered in Jersey. An SEC report that same year found WPP had more subsidiaries in tax havens (618) than any other FTSE 100 company. See 'Datablog: FTSE 100's use of tax havens', *Guardian* (12 May 2013).
33 Swift, 'Who Is the PBS for?', *Eyewear* blog (23 October 2014).
34 Wheatley (@nemoloris), Twitter (7:09 p.m., 23 October 2014).
35 Wheatley (@nemoloris), Twitter (7:18 p.m., 23 October 2014).
36 Rank Formsby (@hanestulsterman), Twitter (5:53 p.m., 18 December 2014).
37 Michael Caines, 'Sui generous', *Times Literary Supplement* blog (14 January 2015) – since removed.
38 Rank Formsby (@hanestulsterman), Twitter (7:34 p.m., 12 January 2015).
39 Dave Coates, 'David Harsent – Fire Songs', *Dave Poems* site (23 January 2015).
40 David A. Williams, 'Poetry Prize Networks in the UK' (20 January 2015) and 'Now With More Nodes! Updated Prize Network Maps' (23 January 2015), *The Life of Words* blog.
41 Qtd in. 'The Intimacy of the Poetry World,' *Write Out Loud* (17 January 2015).
42 Caines, 'Sui generous,' 14 January 2015.
43 Comments on Williams, 'Poetry Prize Networks' and 'Updated Prize Network Maps' (2015).
44 Qtd in Mark Brown, 'TS Eliot prize: poet Sarah Howe wins with "amazing" debut', *Guardian* (11 January 2016).
45 Comments on Brown, *Guardian* (11 January 2016). Other commenters referenced another prize scandal in the United States a few months prior, in which the white male poet, Michael Derrick Hudson, had poems included in *The Best American Poetry 2015*, after submitting them under the name 'Yi-Fen Chou'.
46 Charles Whalley (@charleswhalley), 'How Did Sarah Howe Win TS Eliot Prize, asks Private Eye', *Twitter* (9:42 p.m., 21 January 2016).
47 'Bookworm', *Private Eye*, No. 1410 (22 January 2016), 23.
48 Amy Key (@msamykey), Twitter (9:54 p.m., 21 January 2016).
49 Thring, 'Born in the rubbish tip, the greatest poetry of today,', *Sunday Times* (17 January 2016).
50 Thring, Twitter (10:08 a.m., 22 January 2016) – since deleted.
51 Trendogate, result for "#derangedpoetess", 5:59:57 p.m., Friday, 22 January 2016.
52 Katy Evans-Bush, 'TS Eliot Prize Row: Is Winner Too Young, Beautiful – and Chinese?' (23 January 2016).
53 Amy Key (@msamykey), Twitter (9:31 a.m., 23 January 2016).

54 English, *The Economy of Prestige*, 1.
55 Ibid., 24.
56 Ibid.
57 Vahni Capildeo, 'On Judging Prizes, & Reading More Than Six Really Good Books', *PN Review* (237) vol. 44, no. 1 (September-October 2017).
58 English, *The Economy of Prestige*, 209–10.
59 Jenkins, 3.
60 Nikki Usher, 'The Appropriate/Amplification Model of Citizen Journalism: An Account of Structural Limitations and the Political Economy of Participatory Content Creation', *Journalism Practice* vol. 11, no. 2–3 (2017), 247–65.

Chapter 3

POETRY AS CONTENT: THE NETWORK VALUE OF LYRICAL THOUGHT

The day after the 2016 US presidential election, media outlets that had gorged themselves on sensational gossip throughout the campaign quickly pivoted into a therapeutic role. By early afternoon on 9 November, *Newsweek* published 'How to Survive a Trump Presidency', and *Teen Vogue* explained 'How to Cope with Fear after the Presidential Election'. Among these remedies, it didn't take long for digital publications to begin prescribing poetry. That same day, *HuffPost* recommended '18 Compassionate Poems to Help You Weather Uncertain Times', *Vox* asked 'Feeling Terrible Right Now? Maybe Some Poetry Will Help', and *BuzzFeed* posted Danez Smith's poem 'You're Dead, America', apparently written overnight in response to the news, and which promptly went viral. The following day, mainstream outlets played catch-up. The *Atlantic* posted an interview with the editor of *Poetry* magazine under the headline 'Still, Poetry Will Rise', the *Guardian* offered 'Words for Solace and Strength: Poems to Counter the Election Fallout', and *CNN* suggested 'Langston Hughes Is Helping People Get through This Election'. The heralding of poetry's resurgence continued through the end of 2016 and into 2017. 'Don't Look Now, But 2016 is Resurrecting Poetry', *Wired* proposed in the weeks after the election, while the *Los Angeles Times* reported that 'Donald Trump has roused the poets to stinging verse'. *ViewPoint* published a longer meditation on 'Poetry after Trump' the following February; in March 2017, the *Guardian* continued to explain 'Why Poetry is the Perfect Weapon to Fight Donald Trump'; and in April, the *New York Times* published 'Poems of Resistance: A Primer'. Speaking from a rally in Washington that month for an article headlined 'American Poets, Refusing to Go Gentle, Rage Against the Right', the poet Jane Hirshfield told the *Times*: 'Poems are visible right now, which is terribly ironic, because you rather wish it weren't so necessary.'[1] In an interview with the London *Times* published on the last day of 2017, the Scottish poet Jackie Kay suggested 'people need poetry even more' in 'these particular times'.[2]

Beyond individual pronouncements, their synchronised spread begs questions about the structural forces behind the phenomenon. Tempting as it is to take poetry's 'resurrection' at face value, I want to suggest that blind faith in poetry's cultural or political value overlooks its network value in a changing media landscape. That's not to say poetry doesn't provide solace and insight, but rather, stating the obvious, that the cultural currency of any art form is subject to many factors. Beyond the political urgency of the headlines above, poetry's broader network value is captured in a very different light by *Teen Vogue*, earlier in 2016, 'These 9 Young Poets Are Actually Making the Genre Cool Again', or by another *Guardian* piece in April 2017 (by a commentator on consumer trends) telling us poetry is now 'the coolest thing', mostly due to Rupi Kaur.[3] In sharp contrast with the political poetry published on the same day, on 10 November 2016, the *Evening Standard* ran a feature on 'London's new generation of poets [...] storming the catwalks at Fashion Week' (with no mention of Trump or Brexit).[4] Any account of poetry's online circulation would have to take in this complex media landscape, in which poetry is absorbed without contradiction into both political commentary and lifestyle consumerism. Poems, after all, provide cheap and plentiful content for internet platforms, with no shortage of producers accustomed to getting little return for their labour. Compared to other text-based content (already the cheapest and most disposable form of online media), poetry is exceedingly portable, shareable, and open to interpretation. Its 'users', in that regard, are free to adapt poetic content to multiple uses or contexts. Above all, compared to prose, much poetry offers a greater compatibility with an increasingly visual web.

There's no harm in sharing poems online, of course. But this chapter aims to show, at the very least, that overstating poetry's inherent virtues risks obscuring the dynamics of its circulation among other marketised content. However well-intended, clickbaiting claims for poetry's coolness or political impact also discourage readers from considering their own role in the sharing of content from commercial outlets on commercial platforms via commercial service providers on commercial devices. From the algorithmic perspective of sites whose business is measured in clicks, a poem is no different from any cat video or Trump tweet. If poetry has a growing *currency* – in the double-sense of timeliness and a value in exchange – it's worth considering how the social values attributed to it are also bound up in the market forces driving the outlets making claims on its behalf. The idea of poetry's direct value for marketing shouldn't be too shocking, given the increasing use of poetry in *actual* advertising – entire campaigns for McDonald's or Nationwide banks in the United Kingdom, among many others. The UK's Forward Prizes and National Poetry Day were both founded and are still sponsored by a subsidiary of one of the world's largest marketing conglomerates (WPP). Even the word 'POEM' turns out to be a prevalent acronym in marketing strategy, helping companies distinguish between Paid, Owned, and Earned Media. This chapter focuses on more indirect links, however – the many thousands of times every day that poems are read and shared through online news sites and social media, with no obvious commercial stake. Before insisting on poetry's autonomy in these digital contexts, it's worth considering how online media is already changing the way poems are written, read, and used.

Converging Content

'Content' is the great levelling concept of our age, collapsing any hierarchies or distinctions we might impose among very different media. As content, a poem online is right there in the mix with any think piece or Tumblr post, and to post or re-post anything online is to be in the content business. As a catch-all term, 'content' is also symptomatic of a new phase in the development of mass communication technologies. Where Marshall McLuhan's famous dictum, 'the medium is the message', might have been incisive in 1964, the convergence of media technologies has rendered it a moot point over the last 50 years. In most contemporary contexts, the universal medium is the internet and the message is 'content' – adaptable in either case to the user's preferred devices. As a category, content now extends to anything that can be digitally encoded, bringing all forms of text, image, audio, video, software, and other material under the same umbrella. The media theorist Henry Jenkins discusses this levelling effect in his 2006 book, *Convergence Culture: Where Old and New Media Collide*, and acknowledges previous formulations by thinkers like Ithiel de Sola Pool, who described a 'convergence of modes' as early as 1983. Pool writes:

> A single physical means, be it wires, cables or airwaves – may carry services that in the past were provided in separate ways. Conversely, a service that was provided in the past by any one medium – be it broadcasting, the press, or telephony – can now be provided in several different physical ways. So the one-to-one relationship that used to exist between a medium and its use is eroding.[5]

Jenkins and others take the story further, following the trajectory of media convergence across the twentieth century – culminating in the iPod on the cover of Jenkins's book or, to even greater extent, the iPhone first sold the year after its publication. Notwithstanding the overhyped battle between e-books and print, the convergence of online media – a context in which the vast majority of poetry is now consumed, one might confidently wager – has reached a point of near-singularity.

For online media platforms, this levelling occurs at the instant of the click and in the wealth of ad-based analytics and profit derived from that innocuous gesture. We might see an instinctive disconnect when poems appear in direct advertising, whether we view it as a sacrilege or a chance for poetry to reach new audiences. But the beauty of 'content', as any marketing blog will tell you (before asking you to sign up for their newsletter), is that the power of these clicks means this work is no longer confined to advertising proper. In fact, most guides to creating 'effective' content are adamant that online marketers should refrain from treating content as directly promotional. 'Have empathy,' Jennifer G. suggests in the article, 'How to Market Yourself on Facebook without Annoying Your Fans': 'Try to come across as a person, rather than an office or organization. This gives the users confidence in you and instead of getting annoyed they will welcome any new content from you.' Jennifer's guide is a case in point, obviously cobbled from tens of thousands of similar articles, in order to draw Google-optimised traffic to the website for BleuPage, in this case, a company specialising in 'creative innovative softwares [*sic*] that could help marketers and entrepreneurs execute their daily chores with stellar efficiency'.[6] In other words, the same 'softwares' that generated Jennifer G. and this very guide. This is the automated world of twenty-first-century media, commoditised at every level. And this is the convergent context in which the click to view or a share a poem is rendered fundamentally equivalent to the click to view any other online content. The only value that matters is how many of those clicks there are.

Accompanying these enormous changes to mass media consumption has been the long evolution of what Jenkins first dubbed 'participatory culture', often associated with 'Web 2.0' or the rise of social media. For Jenkins and others, it figures in a narrative of progress – 'a cultural shift as consumers are encouraged to seek out new information and make connections among dispersed media content', moving beyond what he describes as 'older notions of passive media spectatorship'.[7] We can accept new possibilities for the way content is encountered while at the same time acknowledging the extent to which the often-utopian rhetoric of user agency and freedom now forms part of new media's content strategy. This valued sense of individual ownership can also be taken into account when considering 'user' engagement with poems as they circulate in this online landscape.

A Bit of History

Working towards a better understanding of the way poems work online, a more detailed sense of changes in the means of consumption becomes essential. A potted history of new media platforms over the past two decades might be insultingly familiar to many, but helps to reframe a related history of online poetry outlets. One way to think about these developments is in waves. When the World Wide Web first became widely accessible in the mid-1990s, initial experiments with online magazines began in earnest with sites like *Wired*'s HotWired, launched in 1994, or stand-alone magazines like *Salon* and *Slate*, launched in 1995 and 1996, respectively. Being run by former staff from the *San Francisco Examiner* (in the case of *Salon*) and a former *New Republic* editor (in the case of *Slate*) helped to legitimise these early sites as credible outlets for online journalism. Over the next 10 years, a second wave of more participatory or 'community' models gained traction, amid the rise of Web 2.0, as christened at a San Francisco conference in 2004. The *Huffington Post* and *BuzzFeed* were launched in 2005 and 2006, expanding the content aggregator model of sites like *Gawker*, launched in 2002. The shift towards user-generated content also included the launch of YouTube in 2005, and Facebook and Twitter in 2006. When the dust settles, a third decade-long wave of online media platforms might be characterised by sites like *Vox* – combining traditional journalistic pedigree in its founding by former *Washington Post* staff in 2014, with more dynamic technologies in its 'explainer' cards or bespoke content management system – or by sites like Medium, launched by one of Twitter's co-founders in 2012, and functioning primarily as a platform for other publications, rather than its own.

Against this timeline, we can map a parallel evolution of online poetry in English. Again, a complex story is exemplified by a few key sites in a few major waves. In terms of dedicated poetry content, the Academy of American Poets' Poets.org was quick out of the gate, launching in 1996 with an aim to promote poetry more generally. *Poetry* magazine's relaunch of the Poetry Foundation website and the UK's Poetry Archive followed in 2005, and similarly distinguished themselves from commercial magazine platforms in their emphasis on education and poetry-awareness. (Hence '.org', not '.com' domain suffixes.) Meanwhile, sites like *UbuWeb* (launched in 1996), *All Poetry* (1999), and *Poem Hunter* (2004) cater to the general interest in reading poems online, with now enormous archives combining previously published poems (with sometimes questionable copyrights) and those submitted by users.

For commercial media, the predominant online business model – from smaller independent publications to major newspaper websites – has been to offer 'free' content subsidised by targeted ad content. Nicholas Carr, in a blog post from 2006 republished in his 2016 book *Utopia is Creepy*, describes the effect this has had on content production and consumption with a striking metaphor:

> It's a modern kind of sharecropping system. Like plantation owners in the American South after the Civil War, a social network gives each

member a little plot of virtual land on which to cultivate an online presence, through the posting, for instance, of words and pictures, and then the social network collets the economic value of the member's labor through advertising [...] The digital sharecroppers are generally happy, because their interest lies in self-expression or socializing, not in making money, and, besides, the economic value of each of their individual contributions is trivial. It's only by aggregating those contributions on a massive scale – on a web scale – that the business becomes lucrative. To put it a different way, the sharecroppers operate happily in an attention economy while their overseers operate happily in a cash economy.[8]

In this context, online poetry outlets – including any number of smaller individual sites and journals, as well as those named above – might feel very disconnected from major global media conglomerates, with their billions in capital investment and clickbait frenzy for ad revenue. To no small degree, the philanthropic or state funding models behind Poets.org, the Poetry Foundation, Poetry Archive, and similar sites have not only shielded those particular platforms from commercial compromises, but also have fed into a wider and long-standing rhetoric regarding poetry's market autonomy, making it possible to adapt the myth of poetry's free and independent labour from print to digital contexts.

Put another way: while critics like Carr and others have become increasingly sceptical about claims for the participatory internet utopia awaiting us in McLuhan's 'global village' – partly owing to the exploitative content-harvesting or sharecropping models of sites mentioned above – the transmission of online poetry has retained its independent, share-for-share's sake sheen. Conversely, this sheen is clearly part of what gives poetry such currency in commercial outlets in times of political and economic despair. In Carr's terms, poetry's perceived autonomy is the means by which its 'attention economy', as a mode of self-expression or social good, is integrated into online media's 'cash economy'. In the terms of Pierre Bourdieu discussed in my Introduction, poetry's symbolic capital is being converted by these sites into economic capital. This exchange likely accounts for the growing entanglement of poetry and online media: The Poetry Foundation has been one of the main contributors to the *Huffington Post*'s 'HuffPoetry', mirroring content from its own site. *BuzzFeed* launched BuzzFeed Reader in March 2016, under the editorship of poet Saeed Jones. Sites like *Vox* and *Vice* regularly post poetry-related articles, while Medium hosts a number of poetry journals and collectives. Without negating its political capital, poetry's 'renaissance' in the wake of Trump's election also attests to the poetry world's and the media world's shared investment in getting as many poems on as many screens as possible.

The Viral Poem

At the same time, no two poems are alike, either in substance or the paths they take when shared online. Understanding the impact of new media contexts on the reading and writing of poems depends on a more practical consideration of the way individual poems function online. It might help to think about what happens when a poem goes 'viral', starting with the paradoxical term itself. The metaphor of 'going viral' seems straightforward enough, capturing the sense by which a poem, in this case, 'infects' a given medium and replicates itself. Yet, the positive connotations of internet popularity are strangely at odds with the harmful effects of biological or software viruses. This more negative sense was what Douglas Rushkoff, the media theorist most often credited with coining the term, had in mind in his 1994 polemic, *Media Virus! Hidden Agendas in Popular Culture*. 'This term is not being used as a metaphor,' he tells us. 'These media events are not *like* viruses. They are viruses.'[9] To some extent, Rushkoff's conception (and fear) of viral media is a throwback to older theories of mass media, such as the 'hypodermic needle model', infecting consumers without their knowledge. Yet the evolution of participatory media over the two decades since Rushkoff's coinage has left the passive metaphor of 'going viral' feeling more and more anachronistic. It persists, I would argue, precisely because its implied passivity so effectively obscures the actions and actors involved. We prefer to think of things (e.g. poems) going viral of their own accord.

A few brief case studies might reveal some of the machinery. They also show how the context of other online content affects the reading of viral poems. In the absence of an official definition or threshold for what constitutes 'viral' status, most commentators work from a more circular notion, by which viral content is content that has been said to have gone viral. (Reflexively, of course, it also benefits commentators to be in a position to confer viral status.) Poetry's viral potential was already well established when the *Atlantic* published 'Still, Poetry Will Rise' on 10 November 2016, initially with the more clickbait-y title: 'Why Poetry Is Viral in the Aftermath of Trump's Election' (still visible as the page title in web browsers). Neil Hilborn's spoken word piece 'OCD', for example, had gone 'viral' after appearing on Button Poetry's YouTube channel in July 2013. In September 2013, *Thought Catalog* published an interview with Spencer Madsen after a poem about his cat 'went really viral' on Tumblr.[10] But when *Time* asked poet and *BuzzFeed* editor Saeed Jones, 'Does poetry have a capacity to go viral?' in a 2014 interview, the question is prompted by Patricia Lockwood's poem, 'Rape Joke'.[11]

The publication of Lockwood's poem on *The Awl* on 25 July 2013 marks an undeniable tipping point in the mass consumption and sharing of online poetry in English. Within hours of its appearance, other magazines were analysing its performance. Later the same day, a summary with excerpts of the poem appeared on *Salon*.[12] The following day, the *Guardian* published an article entitled, 'What Is Patricia Lockwood's Poem Really Saying?'[13] In terms of clicks, 'Rape Joke' was quickly proving poetry's capacity not just for reproducing itself, but for generating further content, in the form of these cobbled summaries, substantiating what *Coldfront* magazine calls the poem's 'serious crossover appeal'.[14] Most pieces mention the 10,000 'likes' the poem had on Facebook within hours of publication. But the impulse to paraphrase or to tell us what the poem is 'really saying' overlaps with an impulse to incorporate 'high-performing' online poetry into frameworks more accustomed to prose commentary. As the spread of secondary content around 'Rape Joke' shows, essays *about* a poem can encourage us to read the poem as a kind of essay.

For some, this feels reductive. Adam Plunkett's sneering *New Yorker* review of 'Patricia Lockwood's Crowd-Pleasing Poetry' suggests the poem 'probably wouldn't have been written if Twitter hadn't been around', and he laments the influence of online spaces, where 'the lowest common denominator feels provoked to respond'. Plunkett admits that 'Lockwood fits uncannily well on social media, especially on Twitter', but says 'I worry that she fits herself to it.'[15] All this patronising worry fails to account for the poem's particularities, however: not only the way it 'fits' itself to the medium, with long lines of prose-form stanzas looping to fill different screen sizes and the conventional paragraph spacing of online prose, but also the extent to which its length, structure, and tone fit inclusively and memorably within a commentary culture – to which the *New Yorker* is central, of course. By suggesting that 'the source of [Lockwood's] fame is almost entirely owing to her tweets and not to her poetry', without taking seriously the relationship between these forms, Plunkett makes the mistake advised against by online marketing gurus like 'Jennifer G' – focusing so much on analytic strategies he forgets that content's content matters. Of course, Plunkett nevertheless feeds the bigger cycle with his 'crowd-pleasing' condescension for a *New Yorker* audience.

If, as commentary, Lockwood's 'Rape Joke' found an audience by addressing a subject of sadly perennial 'relevance', it's worth comparing its reception with that of a poem which circulated in a more particular news context. Maggie Smith's 'Good Bones' was first published on 15 June 2016 in the online magazine *Waxwing*, three days after the nightclub shooting that killed 49 people in

Orlando, Florida. Although the poem cites no specific events that make the world 'at least / fifty percent terrible' and which the speaker admits to keeping from their children, the internet content machine was quick to make the link. Within days, the writer herself was being interviewed for *Slate*, under the headline, ' "Good Bones" Poet Maggie Smith on Watching Her Poem Go Viral in the Wake of the Orlando Shooting'.[16] The *Guardian* was ready again with a summary of the poem, but broadened its applicability 'in the wake of this week's tragedies', when the MP Jo Cox was murdered the day after the poem was published.[17] By December, the *Washington Post* was hailing 'Good Bones' as 'the poem that captured the mood of a tumultuous year'.[18] Compared to Lockwood's poem and its more direct title and content, 'Good Bones' shows the extent to which a lyrical poem with no obvious subject or commentary can be incorporated into content networks, and reframed as valuable and timely commentary.

The reception of these two poems also demonstrates the changing relationship between commercial publications and poetry platforms, and their shared, insatiable need for content. If the *Guardian* write-ups seem slightly redundant, adding little to the conversation, but amplifying and piggybacking onto the poems' viral spread, the Poetry Foundation's *Harriet* blog is even more transparent in its 'signal-boosting' approach. Using the blog's typical form of reposting, 'Patricia Lockwood "Rape Joke" Poem Is World-Famous' was published anonymously by 'Harriet Staff' under the category 'Poetry News' the week after the poem's appearance, with excerpts and links to the *Coldfront* and *Guardian* articles. The mode of content recycling is even more direct in the case of Smith's 'Good Bones', where the poem itself was reprinted (with permission, and without comment) on both the Poetry Foundation and Academy of American Poets websites.

Together, these examples show the degree to which poetry's function as online content is inextricably linked to its perceived currency, in that double-sense of relevance and transactional value. But they also raise the question: to what extent is a poem's currency in online networks contingent on its reframing as essayistic commentary – in terms of its discursiveness, timeliness, a sense of argument, 'serious' subject matter, or personal interest? A final example seems to throw a great spanner into the apparent alignment of currency and these features. Hera Lindsay Bird's poems 'Monica' and 'Keats Is Dead So Fuck Me from Behind' were published separately on the New Zealand website *The Spinoff* in May and July of 2016, respectively. Both went 'viral', despite ostensibly working against the triangulation of poem-as-commentary-into-content described above. Having been published and widely shared in the weeks immediately before and after Maggie Smith's 'Good Bones' was made to speak to some of 2016s darkest events, the humour and irreverence of

Bird's poems seem all the more incongruous with the totalising narrative of that 'tumultuous' moment.

As Stephanie Burt writes of Bird's work in the *London Review of Books* (*LRB*), 'The poems refuse not only family traditions of craft but also serious Public Speech on Big Issues, of the kind that poets on the political left have long offered as alternative to craft.'[19] One view is that Bird's poems turn to the flip side of all this gloom, and that their much-needed levity is part of what struck a nerve. Having distinguished the poems from the essayistic premise of 'serious Public Speech', Burt suggests a kind of counter-relevance: 'Hilarity in Bird,' she writes, 'may tip over into the kind of anything-goes despair at the fragility of all human constructions (this even though the collection went to press before Brexit, before Trumpism, before the 2016 round of New Zealand earthquakes).'[20] Like 'Good Bones', even Bird's work is made to speak to its moment by Burt's critical content, with 'important' and 'political points' to make about sexuality, the claiming of language, the state of poetry, and other 'Big Issues' after all. And like 'Good Bones', which doesn't seem to have been written in the three days between the Orlando shooting and its publication, the lack of direct connection between Bird's poems and events of summer 2016 when they went viral is neither here nor there. What matters is the potential for currency. The attention of an *LRB* review essay (in late 2017) itself confers on Bird's writing a degree of essay-like urgency. Commentary inflects (or infects) its subjects. Content begets content.

Conclusion

In a world of levelled content, commentary projects its nature onto other texts, with the same self-replicating impulse by which viral status is conferred by sites desperate for their share of clicks. Articles, summaries, or interviews on a range of online outlets cumulatively determine the poems' value as content in the attention economy, measured above all by a text's ability to generate (and withstand) further content. This circular process was repeated at a greater scale in December 2017 (the very same week, for what it's worth, that I delivered a version of this chapter at a conference in New Zealand), when Kristen Roupenian's short story 'Cat Person' went viral after its publication in the *New Yorker*. Here, the transfiguration of imaginative writing into commentary was even more forceful, without the formal barrier of readers having to reimagine verse as something like a prose essay. The *Atlantic*'s Megan Garber (who penned 'Still, Poetry Will Rise' a year before) considers the extent to which Roupenian's story was misread as an 'essay' or 'think piece', despite its third-person narration and 'fiction' label on the *New Yorker* site. The 'mistake is revealing,' Garber concludes. Readers of 'Cat Person', she suggests, 'looked at the story and saw – not because of malice, but because of the stubborn inertias of cultural assumption – not a story at all, but something else entirely. An essay. A memory. A woman, dreamy and sad, telling the internet about her bad date.'[21]

If any of this implies that we've reached a point of happy convergence, in which reader-users are free to consume writing as best suits the occasion – commensurate with the passive sense by which Roupenian's story 'went viral' – that assumption again deflects from click- and profit-driven structures at work. As Garber puts it, 'the internet is its own framing device'. Its automatic and unconscious levelling deliberately inhibits readers' ability to make meaningful formal distinctions and, therefore, their sense of the impact convergent online media has on the work itself. Tracing the ways in which 'Good Bones' might be linked to any number of world events needn't preclude a practical analysis that acknowledges the smartphone-friendly shape of Smith's poem, which enabled its initial sharing as a screenshot on Facebook. Likewise, the influence of Patricia Lockwood on Hera Lindsay Bird might be extended to practical analysis of the long-line poetics and mock-clickbait titles now prevalent in recent anglophone poetry. These superficial observations show how much more work there is to be done, reading beyond the mere fact of a poem's online publication, taking screen formatting and shareable features into account, considering the effect of forced line-breaks, scrolling and specific site functionality, or even how other 'paratextual' content (e.g. ads) on the same page might affect individual readings.

News in 2017 of Roupenian's 'seven-figure book deal', signed off the back of her story's viral spread, might seem detached from the financial stakes of viral poetry, but it reminds us of the relationship between 'attention' and 'cash' economies, in Carr's terms, for *all* online content. Again, there is no point condemning the commercial realities of online poetry. Nor, on the other hand, reverting to naïve claims of market autonomy, without acknowledging the paradoxical value of this myth for its network currency. There is a sense in which overstated defences of poetry's virtue in disastrous political contexts work to legitimise a kind of 'sharecropping' for the benefit of participatory platforms that are ultimately dependent on enormous amounts of good will and free labour. There is a sense, in other words, in which presumptions of poetry's political power become self-defeating. Yet, despite the apparent inescapability of these mostly invisible structures, readers and producers of poetry (and any content) still have some say in how their labour and resources are offered. As fake and non-fake news and media increasingly converge with content marketing and marketised content across our screens, the greater danger lies in rationalising little moments of exploitation in the name of an attention economy, which may have the cumulative effect of making poems as indistinguishable, re-applicable, and finally disposable as any other content.

Notes

1. Qtd in Alexandra Alter, 'American Poets, Refusing to Go Gentle, Rage against the Right', *New York Times* (21 April 2017).
2. Qtd in Stephen McGinty, 'Now we need poetry more than ever', *Sunday Times* [London] (31 December 2017).
3. Rob Walker, '"Now it's the coolest thing": rise of Rupi Kaur helps boost poetry sales', *Guardian* (7 October 2017).
4. Samuel Fishwick, 'Meet London's new generation of poets: from Caleb Femi to Greta Bellamacina', *Evening Standard* (10 November 2016).
5. Pool qtd in Jenkins, *Convergence Culture: Where New and Old Media Collide* (New York: New York University Press, 2006), 10.
6. BleuPage Ultimate website, no title or author.
7. Jenkins, *Convergence Culture*, 3.
8. Carr, 'Digital Sharecropping', in *Utopia is Creepy: And Other Provocations* (New York: W.W. Norton, 2016), 31. The original essay is also available on Carr's blog, Rough Type (posted 19 December 2006).
9. Rushkoff, *Media Virus! Hidden Agendas and Popular Culture* (New York: Ballantine Books, 1994), 9. Later in the book, Rushkoff directly compares the rise of MTV and meme culture to poetry, using a pre-social media conception of 'memes': 'That a genre like poetry can develop to the point where a single phrase intentionally evokes the imagery of a dozen other poems is not lamentable but laudable. That the nature of the relationship between MTV and its viewers is comparable to an organism and its genes only attests to the network's ability to transmit lots and lots of memes' (148).
10. Adam Humphreys, 'My Poem Went Really Viral: An Interview with Spencer Madsen', *Thought Catalog* (18 September 2013).
11. Nolan Feeney, 'Saeed Jones: "No One Is Safe" In These Poems', *Time* (29 September 2014).
12. Prachi Gupta, 'Patricia Lockwood's "Rape Joke" Should End the Rape Joke Debate', *Salon* (25 July 2013).
13. Viv Groskop, 'Rape Joke: what is Patricia Lockwood's poem really saying?', *Guardian* (26 July 2013).
14. 'Lockwood's "Rape Joke" Goes Viral' [no author], *Coldfront* (26 July 2013).
15. Adam Plunkett, 'Patricia Lockwood's Crowd-Pleasing Poetry', *New Yorker* (29 May 2014).
16. Katy Waldman, '"Good Bones" Poet Maggie Smith on Watching Her Poem Go Viral in the Wake of the Orlando Shooting', *Slate* (17 June 2016).
17. Alison Flood, 'Poem about struggle "to love this world as it is" goes viral', *Guardian* (17 June 2016).
18. Nora Krug, 'Maggie Smith and the poem that capture the mood of a tumultuous year', *Washington Post* (23 December 2016).

19 Stephanie Burt, 'On Hera Lindsay Bird', *London Review of Books*, vol. 39, no. 23 (30 November 2017).
20 Ibid.
21 Megan Garber, '"Cat Person" and the Impulse to Undermine Women's Fiction', *Atlantic* (11 December 2017). As the title and quote above implies, Garber suggests the misreading of Roupenian's short story stems partly from gendered stereotypes, a sentiment shared on (after a mistake perpetuated by) social media.

PART II

NEW PRODUCTS

Chapter 4

FULL-LENGTH: THE INVENTION OF THE MODERN POETRY COLLECTION

1

Writers, readers, and critics have debated the history of the novel at least as long as the form has existed. In this century, the two-volume English edition of Franco Moretti's *The Novel* (first published in five Italian volumes between 2001 and 2003), offering a number of new histories, advertises itself as 'a watershed event in the understanding of the first truly planetary literary form'.[1] Variations on the novel's origin story were already rife by the late eighteenth century, however, with early attempts to distinguish it from other narrative modes. Among these, Clara Reeve's *The Progress of Romance* (1785) depicts a group of friends discussing the history of literary forms, one of which proposes 'to trace Romance to its Origin, to follow its progress through the different periods to its declension, to shew how the modern Novel sprung up out of its ruins'.[2] Amid rapid changes in print technologies and readerships changing as a result of major socio-economic developments, a retrospective fantasy was emerging, reimagining that complex cultural shift as a specific traceable point in which the modern novel had 'sprung up'.

Three centuries investigating the novel's advance as both a literary form and a literary commodity beg the question addressed by this chapter: Why hasn't there been similar interest in an analogous history of the modern poetry collection? One reasonable response is that the forms are hardly analogous. The novel has an inherent formal integrity that might be shared by some published volumes of poetry, but thematically or narratively cohesive book-length poems or sequences are still a minority among more miscellaneous collections of discrete short lyrics. And if the individual poem remains the basic unit of most contemporary poetry, we have plenty of histories of 'the lyric', which correspond in many ways to the novel's ascendance in the seventeenth and eighteenth centuries.[3] Yet, the poetry book – as both an immaterial conceit and physical object – is as codified as ever, both for poets and for poetry's circulation in contemporary culture. Exerting something like the pressure short story writers might feel towards the novel, the so-called full-length collection remains, in Joel Brouwer's words, 'the coin of the realm in the poetry world'.[4] The focus of prizes on collections, both before and after publication, show to extent to which the print book still embodies poetic achievement for many readers, even amid the growing visibility of online platforms and spread of poetry for performance over the past decade.

2

Debate regarding 'the modern novel' shows the futility of rigid histories or definitions, but also the usefulness of questioning a form's development in ways that acknowledge both writerly and material aspects. As Albert Thibaudet's oft-quoted mantra reminds us, 'Literature takes place as a function of the Book, and yet there are few things to which a man of books gives less thought than the Book.'[5] While there is no shortage of writerly advice regarding the arrangement of poetry books, these reflections rarely connect the notional 'book' in progress with the physical product. Among the very small body of scholarship on the book as a poetic form, Neil Fraistat's edited volume, *Poems in Their Place: The Intertextuality and Order of Poetic Collections* (1986), promotes what he calls 'contextual poetics', extending analysis of individual poems to the book as a whole. But like essays and blog posts written from an authorial perspective, formalist scholarship (including that in *Poems in Their Place*) has tended to foreground choices at the writing stage. Writers naturally focus on their part in collaborative book production. Fraistat insists that 'contextual critics ought to prefer over other arrangements an authorially sanctioned ordering'.[6]

Where histories of the novel situate literary content within socio-economic contexts which very literally shape the form, the relationship between the poetry book's artistic and material substance has only lately been called to attention.[7] Joel Brouwer's 2009 essay for *Harriet* acknowledges the tension in a question regarding the popularity of 'project books': 'Is this a hardware problem (money or distribution issues) or a software problem (received notions about book length as it relates to "seriousness") or both or other?'[8] William Kuskin, in a new entry for 'Book, Poetic' in the *Princeton Enyclopedia of Poetry & Poetics* 2012 edition, spells out the duality:

> On one hand, books are simply material objects, vehicles for the ostensibly more primary artistic and intellectual works they contain. On the other, their format implies a poetic dimension, a trope for writing, a shaping force, and a silent collaborator in reading.[9]

A history of the modern poetry collection might begin to connect these material and poetic dimensions through points of intersection around the ambiguous label 'collection', the length of 'full' collections, or their inherent 'wholeness'. Interrogating this creative-commodity hybrid, in turn, offers practitioners and readers a greater sense of the extent to which, paraphrasing Thibaudet, *poetry takes place as a function of the collection.*

3

For Marcus C. Levitt, the lack of an 'historical typology' – labels differentiating single-author volumes of new poems from anthologies, for example – is an immediate hurdle to 'even a simple history of the poetry book as a phenomenon in the Western tradition'.[10] In Reeve's *The Progress of Romance* and other early uses, the word 'novel' clearly marks a new evolutionary phase for long-form narrative as a named species, distinct from forbears in the romance, epic, saga, or tale.[11] The new term marks a further distinction between the novel in English, along with a material history linked to publishing industries in the United Kingdom and North America, and developments in other European countries, which still refer to these same texts as 'romances' in their respective languages. (Moretti's study, for instance, is published in Italian as *Il Romanzo.*) By comparison, the use of the term 'collection' to refer to author-composed poetry books – as opposed to anthologies or 'collected' editions reprinting work from several 'collections' – appears to be a much more recent designation within that same transatlantic network of anglophone writing.

Well into the twentieth century, 'collection' retains a more general, literal usage in reviews, more often denoting volumes collected by an editor. Reviews of anthologies in *Poetry* magazine, for example, call them 'collections' throughout the first half of the century.[12] As late as 1964, Louis Untermeyer's review of 'Three Notable Collections' considers collected or selected poems of Mark Van Doren, Babette Deutsch, and Stanley Burnshaw. While single-author volumes were labelled 'poetry collections' in *New York Times'* lists of 'Books Published Today' as early as 1941 (seemingly for reasons of space), the first equivalent use of the phrase in the UK's *Guardian* is as recent as 1988.[13] Other UK and Irish newspapers use the term in this way from the 1970s.[14] These archival appearances are also consistent with Google Ngram results, showing a steep rise for instances of 'poetry collection' (as well as indicative terms like 'first' or 'second' or 'latest collection') across its searchable texts, from the 1950s onwards.[15]

Where use in periodical reviews or advertisements shows the collection's emergence as a practical designation, its spread in the second half of last century also coincides with that of poetry prizes (especially 'first book' prizes in the United States) and creative writing degrees in what Mark McGurl has dubbed the 'program era', in which the book-length collection becomes the standardised currency of an increasingly institutionalised field.[16]

4

On the one hand, terms differentiating the poetry 'collection' from anthologies or collected editions, emphasising the authorial impetus of the former, emerge in a period when poets are having to work harder to differentiate themselves in a crowding arena. On the other hand, the difference between full poetry collections and pamphlets or chapbooks (as respective UK and US terms) stems from an older and more material distinction between published products. And in this case, we can see how traditional definitions for pamphlets have also instilled a hierarchical, professional trajectory in recent decades, by way of contrast with the full-length collection.

As early as 1716, Myles Davies's *Critical History of Pamphlets* defines its subject as a 'stitch'd' rather than bound printed form.[17] The pamphlet's stitch-binding remains both a distinguishing feature and excuse for its lesser commercial status. As an article from the British Library explains matter-of-factly, 'Very few bookshops take poetry pamphlets, partly because, without a spine, they are not suited to being displayed on shelves.'[18] The poet and bookseller John Clegg concurs: 'Due to their utter spinelessness, there's always a risk of poetry pamphlets getting lost on the shelves – which is a real shame.'[19] In turn, the pamphlet's material impracticality for sales contributes to its perceived status as a stepping stone for emerging authors. The UK Society of Authors, for instance, advises: 'A lot of poets will publish at least one pamphlet before putting out a full collection, allowing you to experiment with curating a smaller body of work and (hopefully) gaining attention for it.'[20]

As the emphasis on a book collection's 'fullness' implies, the pamphlet has also been increasingly differentiated by its page count, rather than binding. Publication contests for chapbooks or pamphlets in the United States and the United Kingdom stipulate maximum submission lengths anywhere between 12 and 48 pages.[21] Although those competitions are for poets typically submitting on page sizes larger than what will be published, the guidelines for the UK's Michael Marks and Sabotage Awards – two of the very few prizes honouring pamphlets already published – specify a comparable upper limit of 36 and 40 pages, respectively.[22] Despite variations among prizes and publishers, these all fall within the length-bound definition agreed by UNESCO in 1964: 'A pamphlet is a non-periodical printed publication of at least 5 but not more than 48 pages, exclusive of the cover pages.'[23] In this way, the shorter pamphlet helps codify the 'full' collection beyond that 48-page boundary.

5

Joel Brouwer's 'hardware' and 'software' distinction raises questions of 'received notions about book length as it relates to "seriousness"'. Centuries-old received notions of the pamphlet as an ephemeral form, or contemporary associations of it with either new poets or side projects between book collections – a kind of poetry EP in relation to LP album releases – suggest a cultural identification of length with literary value. Yet, the past decade has also tested the upper limits of this equation, with some stark deviations among major prizes on either side of the Atlantic. The UK's Costa Award for Poetry provides the most consistent benchmark, with winning books between 1999 and 2008 averaging 83 pages, and 82 pages between 2009 and 2018. The average length for all winners of the UK's three major prizes – the Costa, TS Eliot, and Forward Best Collection – are nearly as consistent, at 90 pages in the earlier decade and 92 pages in the most recent one. As an exception that proves the rule, Michael Symmons Roberts's 176-page *Drysalter* (2013) was the only winner of either the Eliot or Costa prize in the last decade to weigh in at more than 96 pages. Such regularity can be compared with the US Pulitzer Prize for Poetry, whose winning books averaged a similar 91 pages between 1999 and 2008, but grew to an average 121 pages in the decade since 2008. The cultural gap implied by this 30-page (or 34 per cent) expansion in the received notion of 'serious' (or at least Pulitzer-worthy) US collections, while British winners remained roughly the same, is also suggested by the fact that the only UK prize with notable growth in the same period – the Forward Best Collection prize, lengthening by 16 per cent to an average 109 pages – was awarded to US poets three times in the decade.[24]

The increased length of US prize-winning collections in the past decade has been matched by page guidelines for US book publication contests, typically for first or second collections. Brouwer (a US poet and critic) laments 'the tyranny of the technology of the book, which seems to want to be 48–64 pages long', implying the root of this tyranny lies in such contests: 'Why? Because Yale says so?'[25] And as it turns out, the Yale Series of Younger Poets is the only US major book publication prize that maintains a 64-page upper limit, while most others have extended to 90 or 100.[26]

6

A third defining feature of the book-length collection is its projection of unity. Like the shifting typology around single-author volumes and emphasis on 'fullness' of length, the collection's internal cohesion has both creative and material dimensions. At a glance, its wholeness might be equally construed by the presence of a title and set of covers.[27] From the writer's perspective, David Morley's sentiment is typical: 'I see a poetry book as a form, not as a collection of various writing.'[28] It also chimes with Robert Frost's often repeated, possibly apocryphal advice: 'if you have a book of twenty-four poems, the book itself should be the twenty-fifth.'[29] In recent years, however, the insistence on conceptual integrity has prompted debate around a perceived fashion for so-called project books.

In a 2003 article, Beth Ann Fennelly first raised concerns about increasing 'pressure for a poet to display a unified style' in first book contests.[30] Among many sympathetic responses, Joel Brouwer's essay, cited earlier, spells out the potential problem:

> I think poets more and more these days conceive of writing projects and then write poems to fulfill those projects, as opposed to writing poems and later attempting to discern what projects, if any, the poems have made manifest.[31]

This scepticism towards the collection as preconceived project is expressed most forcefully in Dorothea Lasky's pamphlet, *Poetry Is Not a Project* (2011). 'Projects are bad for poetry,' Lasky argues, suggesting 'that a poet with a "project" might not be a poet at all'.[32] Although she admits that 'perhaps nowadays a poet who wants to make a living as a poet needs to have a project to survive', ultimately 'what most poets do is not a project but is an act of *intuition*.'[33] Finally squaring the two positions, after publishing an article in 2012 bemoaning the project book as 'a product of this system' and maybe 'a regrettable creature of the time', Jake Adam York tempered his view a week later, suggesting every collection, 'even in what appears to be a miscellany', strives towards a natural unity. 'A good, well-developed book,' York concludes, 'whether seemingly more organic or not, whether "project-y" or not, will carry that kind of resonance.'[34] Two years later, the new *Princeton Encyclopedia* entry for 2012 points similarly to the collection's 'ability to span these contradictions, to figure paradox as unity and thus to sustain the fragmentary, fissured nature of representation as a coherent whole'.[35]

7

Within discussions of the novel's history, attempts at definition often rely on possible prototypes. Although Michael McKeon suggests that 'there is little sense in seeking the identity of "the first novelist"', the second half of his own study of *The Origins of the English Novel* is structured around discussions of texts by Miquel de Cervantes, Daniel Defoe, and others 'which are themselves traditionally accorded a central role in the origins of the novel'.[36] If William Wordsworth and Samuel Taylor Coleridge's *Lyrical Ballads*, first published in 1798, has been 'traditionally accorded a central role' within the poetry collection's parallel history, it does at least exemplify a key moment of transition in its form and contents. The title *Lyrical Ballads* is poised between connotations of earlier anthology collections and the distinctiveness implied by its coinage, combining the two traditional genres.[37] The 'Advertisement' at the start of the 1798 edition (later replaced by the longer preface) famously advertises this novelty in its expectation that readers might 'struggle with feelings of strangeness and aukwardness' [*sic*].[38] But it also, pointedly, affects the cohesiveness of non-anthology collections in its statement of purpose and repeated references to 'the author' in singular throughout those prefaces.

In the parlour game of naming still earlier precedents for the modern collection, another unsurprising, but instructive candidate might be William Blake's *Songs of Innocence* (1789), first printed nine years before *Lyrical Ballads*, then combined with *Songs of Experience* in 1794. The poetic title is again a rarity among the eighteenth-century single-author collections of short poems, which tend towards more straightforwardly descriptive names (e.g. *Poems*). Lori Emerson, in her contribution to the *Princeton Encyclopedia's* 'poetic book' entry, describes the 'monumental' *Songs of Innocence* as 'a turning point in British letters', towards a unity of design that would develop towards William Morris's late nineteenth-century editions or the 'artist's book' tradition emerging in the twentieth century.[39] Compared to the initial 224-page single-volume edition of *Lyrical Ballads*, produced in standard type by a Bristol printer, the 19 'illuminated' poems of Blake's hand-painted and hand-bound *Songs of Innocence* show two extremes by which a collection might be either entirely produced by one person or in collaboration both at the writing and printing stages – exemplified by the *Songs* title-page attribution to 'The Author & Printer W Blake' and *Lyrical Ballads* unnamed 'author'.[40] Somewhere between these practices, a basis for the 'full-length', single-author, mass-producible, and conceptually unified modern collection has emerged.

8

Another obvious, but informative influence on the development and received notions of the modern collection is Walt Whitman's *Leaves of Grass*, from its 1855 original to the ninth 'deathbed' edition of 1892. The production of the 1855 volume sits squarely between those of *Lyrical Ballads* and *Songs of Innocence*, with its unusually collaborative printing process. As Ed Folsom explains, Whitman was not only 'clearly present while Andrew Rome ran his hand-inked iron-bed press' in Brooklyn – editing individual poems in the midst of printing 800 copies – but also 'clearly calculating on the run, rearranging his poems to accommodate the size' of the book.[41] In this way, *Leaves of Grass* epitomizes the complex relationship between the 'book' as it exists in an author's head or hand and the material, mass-produced object, in this case funded and sold by Whitman himself.

The overlap between authorial and published 'collections' also makes factors like length more immediate than where a sharper division of labour exists. The 1855 edition is shaped in every sense by economic constraint, with its 12 poems arranged for maximum content over 96 pages, omitting their individual titles entirely and losing the 'Leaves of Grass' at the top of each page halfway through to save space. The book's gradual expansion to a final edition of 389 poems on 438 pages, also shows the extraordinary identification between the author and his nearly 40-year project, as well as the profound commitment to its unity. The word 'whole' or 'wholeness' appears 17 times in the 1855 *Leaves of Grass* (notably, perhaps, the same number as 'book'), after a preface that describes the ideal poet as 'complete in himself'.[42] 'I take part,' we read in 'Song of Myself', 'I see and hear the whole.' It affects an organic whole as well, in its green binding, with leaves both embossed in the cover and interwoven with the gold-leaf title of the 1855 edition. The absence of Whitman's name from that cover and title page only makes its appearance in 'Song of Myself' more remarkable. While contemporary poets might come to see their collections as calling cards out in the world, Whitman's 'So Long' (added to the 1860 edition) makes this book-author metonymy complete:

> This is no book,
> Who touches this, touches a man,
> (Is it night? Are we here alone?)
> It is I you hold, and who holds you,
> I spring from the pages into your arms.[43]

9

A final, perhaps less conspicuous archetype for the modern poetry collection extends these self-reflexive senses of unity and the book as material commodity, but also opens the scope of this history beyond the English language and 'Western' traditions. In May 1814, Johann Wolfgang von Goethe's publisher sent him a copy of the fourteenth-century Persian poet Hafez's *Divan*, in its first German (and first European) translation by Joseph von Hammer-Purgstall. Having read 'translations of this magnificent poet when they had appeared piecemeal in journals here and there,' Goethe recalled, 'now *as a whole* they had all the more lively an effect upon me'.[44] More than an incidental fact of his delayed access to the complete book, this emphasis on wholeness is fundamental to Goethe's philosophy, politics, and conception of nature throughout his life. Our entire well-being depends, he insists repeatedly, on becoming 'unaware of our parts and conscious only of the whole itself'.[45] It was this principle of cohesion that he found so inspiring in Hafez's collection.

Almost immediately, Goethe began a new sequence modelled on its structure. In a letter a few months later, he writes excitedly of new poems already forming 'a little whole, which can probably expand'.[46] When the book-length sequence in 12 parts was published as *West-Östlicher Divan* (*West-Eastern Divan*) in 1819, a composer asked for a short lyric to set to music. Goethe found himself unable to extract one, as 'every member is so penetrated with the sense of the whole'.[47] In the divan, a traditional Persian form of thematically linked lyrics, he had found a frame for faith in unity. As the poem 'Summer-Night' puts in (in John Weiss's 1877 first English translation): 'For to God the whole is lordly.'[48]

The divan as a form also projects a sense of its materiality, both in its literal meaning as 'a bundle of sheets' (not a world away from the many page-puns of Whitman's 'leaves') and, for Goethe, the sense of it as a commodity passing between cultures. In his *Divan*, according to Daniel Purdy, 'Goethe raises the question of how to treat foreign treasures, literary and material, as he formulates an aesthetic that intertwines the public presentation of poetry with luxury consumption.'[49] The endnotes to Goethe's *Divan* make this explicit, where he imagines the poet assuming 'the role of a merchant who lays out his wares pleasingly while trying through various means to make them seem agreeable'.[50]

10

These examples show how a history of the collection might approach the book as a material whole, bound by productive tensions between its creative and material parts. It becomes clear where Goethe's image of the merchant poet 'laying out their wares' anticipates the spirit of most guidance on arranging a collection, just as the Romantic fixation with wholeness anticipates debates around predetermined or organic unity, and the wider rhetoric of 'full'-ness regarding texts of a certain length. A more direct legacy of these principles could also be traced in more detail. Whitman's debt to Hafez' faith in 'the central urge of every atom […] to return to its divine source', for instance, is detailed in 'The Persian Lesson', one of the last poems added to his last edition of *Leaves of Grass*.[51] Whitman's mentors Henry David Thoreau and Ralph Waldo Emerson had been similarly inspired by Hafez's divan, the latter reading it in the same German translation as Goethe and reading Goethe's *Divan* before attempting his own versions.[52] It was Emerson who praised Wordsworth and Hafiz together, as poets who 'believe' in their poetry to a religious degree.⁵³ Just as Edward Everett had led Emerson to Goethe at Harvard, the scholar Edward Dowden would stimulate William Butler Yeats's engagement with the poet whom Yeats thought had achieved a 'Unity of Being'.⁵⁴ Such ideas were carried into the twentieth century by neo-Romantics like Wallace Stevens, whose first collection, *Harmonium*, nearly became a life project comparable to *Leaves of Grass* with its expanding editions and Stevens's hope of titling his collected poems *The Whole Harmonium*.⁵⁵

This historical account of the modern collection's 'rage for order' also helps supplement debates that often regard the contemporary project book as derived primarily from conceptual or visual art traditions. Likewise, this materialist approach to the collection as a composite production might help reassess recent book-objects by writers like Anne Carson or experiments by others that blur whatever lines persist between the collection and artist's book.⁵⁶ A broader history would recognise the collection's cultural specificities in different markets as well – the relative status of US hardback collections, for example, or the influence of European publishing traditions on UK presses' tendency towards uniform design, or the very different funding structures behind either. Analysis of sales and marketing could be balanced with the extent to which book contests and the word 'collection' have standardised its currency in recent decades.

11

While poetry books have a long history of spoofing the collection's relationship to other book products – the titles, for example, of Mina Loy's *Lost Lunar Baedeker* (1923), Elizabeth Bishop's *Geography III* (1976), or Jericho Brown's *The New Testament* (2014) – they have also increasingly functioned as a single node within a network of activity off the page. Understanding the collection as a creative commodity depends as much on rethinking its changing role for writers working in more diverse modes, involving performance, film, and digital spaces. Although Chapter 5 will examine the new (and old) technologies enabling this shift, it is worth considering its specific impact on the collection here.

Rebecca Watts's essay, 'The Cult of the Noble Amateur', prompted widespread debate on social media, soon covered by traditional media outlets, after appearing in *PN Review* in early 2018.⁵⁷ Denouncing the general rise of 'amateurism' and what she calls 'personality poets', Watts offers extended critiques of Rupi Kaur, whose bestselling verse initially found an audience on Instagram, and Hollie McNish and Kate Tempest, whose performance have garnered millions of YouTube views. Although their work is scrutinised directly, Watts's polemic is prompted less by the existence of such 'ignorant' writing than the attention given to these writers by the poetry 'establishment', including 'publishers, editors, reviewers, and awards administrators'. Therefore, in a sense, the problem is their collections. The traditional conception of the print book's legitimising or gatekeeping function has a clear force in Watts's complaint that these poets are 'dragging their significant and seemingly atypical followings into the arena of establishment-endorsed poetry'. Elsewhere, specific criticism of their book editors reinforces this sense of the collection having failed to maintain previously separate 'arenas' (or 'scenes').

Whatever one thinks of these poets' work or Watts's attack, the interest from all sides suggests an awareness of the collection's evolving remit. 'Establishment' prizes like the Ted Hughes Award for 'new work in poetry' (launched by the UK's Poetry Society, Poetry Book Society, and poet laureate Carol Ann Duffy in 2009) are a further acknowledgement, as Watts admits. In its first decade, the award has been won for live performance, sound works, multimedia productions, radio programmes, and only three times for printed books.[58] The subsequent release of several Hughes-winning performances in the form of books shows both that the print collection still provides an important point of access, though perhaps as only one part of a larger whole.

12

A weirdly persistent inversion of the novel's many origin stories is the repeated pronouncement of its death. Among the (almost exclusively white male) handwringing over the last century, recent iterations have focused on technologies supposedly endangering print books in general.[59] Kathleen Fitzpatrick's *The Anxiety of Obsolescence* explains this 'cultural pose' as an attempt to create 'a protected space within which a threatened form might continue to flourish,' but which does so 'in highly suspect ways, ways that reveal a certain desire to submerge questions of social hierarchy within a more comfortable cultural framework'.[60] Although the poetry collection's cultural or commercial status might not warrant sensational claims of its demise, anxieties about career pressures behind 'project' books or prejudices towards books by writers better known through performance or online work show a similar impulse to preserve the collection as an *intuitive* or *organic* form. However, just as new or newly visible forms of poetic production might appear to threaten the print collection's primacy as 'coin of the realm' (in Brouwer's words), this widening field might equally be said to have bolstered its status within a hierarchy regulated by prizes before and after publication. As poetry appears on pages, stages, and screens in more varied forms, the pessimists might argue, the more readers should be able to rely on the print collection as validating currency.

But like the novel, the collection's survival depends on its adaptability. As the sections above suggest, it also depends on reassessing its material composite of writerly and published incarnations, as 'a poetic and temporal form' operating (in Kuskin's words) 'at a literary level beneath authorial intention'.[61] The relatively recent standardisation of naming, tautological definitions of 'full-length', or various conceptions of unity are all points at which the written, printed, and read book meet. Celebrated experiments in book form – from Anne Carson's box fold-out *Nox* (2009), the lyric essayism of Claudia Rankine's *Citizen* (2014), to the historical rigour of Tyejimba Jess's *Olio* (2016) – might be considered alongside the bestselling volumes of 'Instagram poets', often produced by publishers with little regard for traditional collection formats. The idea that prize panels and readers share an interest in books that surprise them physically as well as poetically should only encourage new possibilities. In whichever origin myth best serves the modern collection, the examples of Blake, Whitman, or countless others reveal a form that has always been as much made as written.

Notes

1. Princeton University Press webpage for *The Novel, Volume 1: History, Geography, and Culture*, no author.
2. Reprinted in *Novel Definitions: An Anthology of Commentary on the Novel, 1688–1815*, ed. Cheryl L. Nixon (Peterborough: Broadview, 2009), 351.
3. For recent lyric history and theory, see especially Paul Allen Miller, *Lyric Texts and Lyric Consciousness: The Birth of a Genre from Archaic Greece to Augustan Rome* (London: Routledge, 2005); Scott Brewster, *Lyric* (London: Routledge, 2009); Marion Thain (ed.), *The Lyric Poem: Formations and Transformations* (Cambridge: Cambridge University Press, 2013); Virginia Jackson and Yopie Prins (eds.), *The Lyric Theory Reader: A Critical Anthology* (Baltimore, MD: Johns Hopkins University Press, 2014); and Jonathan Culler, *Theory of the Lyric* (Cambridge, MA: Harvard University Press, 2015). G. Gabrielle Starr's *Lyric Generations: Poetry and the Novel in the Long Eighteenth Century* (Baltimore, MD: Johns Hopkins University Press, 2004) also explicitly connects the histories of the lyric and the novel.
4. Joel Brouwer, 'Boox', *Harriet* blog, Poetry Foundation (8 September 2009).
5. Albert Thibaudet, *Physiologie de la critique* (Paris, 1930, p. 141) qtd and trans. Culler, *Structuralist Poetics* (London, Routledge, 2002), 154.
6. Neil Fraistat (ed.), *Poems in the Place: Intertextuality and Order of Poetic Collections* (Chapel Hill, NC: University of North Carolina Press, 1986), 9.
7. The influence of studies like Ian Watt's *The Rise of the Novel* (1957), Michael McKeon's *The Origins of the English Novel* (1987), and many others have been essential to this foregrounding of material and social histories.
8. Brouwer, 'Boox' (2009).
9. William Kuskin, 'Book, Poetic', in *The Princeton Encyclopedia of Poetry and Poetics*, 4th edition, ed. Roland Green and Stephen Cushman (Princeton, NJ: Princeton University Press, 2012), 154.

10 Marcus C. Levitt, *Early Modern Russian Letters: Texts and Contexts* (Boston, MA: Academic Studies Press, 2009), 219. In lieu of an accepted typology, critics often offer their own designations: where Levitt resorts to specifying 'unified poetry collection', for example, Fraistat refers to 'the poetic collection as an organized book' (3), and Earl Miner offers a schema of 'integrated' versus 'ordered' collections (ed. Fraistat, 18).

11 Elsewhere in *The Progress of Romance*, Reeve relies further on this distinction: 'No writings are more different than the ancient *Romance* and modern *Novel*, yet they are frequently confounded together, and mistaken for each other.' (ed. Nixon, 351). The *OED* lists similar examples from as early as 1711: 'I am afraid thy Brains are a little disordered with Romances and Novels.' (*Spectator*)

12 See, for instance, editor Harriet Monroe's anthology round-ups from the magazine's first decade, or a typical example of the interchangeable labels where Morton Zabel says of the two-volume, 3,000-page *The Book of Poetry*, that 'the collection has no character as an anthology, but may be found useful as a book of reference' (vol. 32, no. 2 (May 1928), 96–101 (98).

13 Carol Ann Duffy, 'Poison on the gravel' (review of George Macbeth's *Anatomy of a Divorce*), *Guardian* (6 May 1988), 27.

14 See 'Programme Announced for Writers' Week', *Irish Times* (12 April 1975), 6; and ('John Avon's Diary', *Coventry Evening Telegraph* (28 April 1972), 18.

15 Whatever the limitations of Google's Ngram, which reports the frequencies of search terms in Google's digital library, the sharp mid-century rise of these terms can be measured against the fairly steady occurrence of phrases like 'collection of poems' since 1800 (Google's early search limit), which are likely to be used in the more literal sense for anthologies or complete oeuvre collections.

16 Mark McGurl, *The Program Era* (Cambridge, MA: Harvard University Press, 2011). The later establishment of creative writing programmes in the United Kingdom (with MA programmes at the universities of East Anglia and Lancaster from the 1970s, as opposed to Iowa's MFA from 1922) might partly account for the delayed appearance of the term there.

17 Joad Raymond, *Pamphlets and Pamphleteering in Early Modern Britain* (Cambridge: Cambridge University Press, 2003), 7.

18 Debbie Cox, 'Shining a Light on Poetry Pamphlets for National Poetry Day', *English and Drama* blog, British Library website (8 October 2015). Even in 1703, Thomas Bodley, founder of Oxford University's Bodleian library, dismissed pamphlets as 'not worth the custody in suche a Librarie' (qtd in Raymond, *Pamphlets and Pamphleteering*, 5).

19 John Clegg, 'Poetry Pamphlet Round-Up', *London Review Bookshop* blog (24 June 2015).

20 'Making a Living as a Poet,' The Society of Authors printed guidesheet (available online to members).

21 e.g. Button Poetry Chapbook Contest (20–30 pages), Tupelo Press Sunken Garden Chapbook Contest (20–36 pages), Poetry Business Pamphlet Competition (20–24 pages), and Rialto Open Pamphlet Competition (18–24 pages). UK competitions tend to specify a lower maximum due to the larger standard A4 vs US Letter page.

22 'Michael Marks Awards submission rules', Wordsworth Trust website (2017), 'About the Saboteur Awards', Saboteur Awards website (2019).

23 'Recommendation concerning the International Standardization of Statistics Relating to Book Production and Periodicals,' *UNESCO Constitution* (19 November 1964).

24 Data based on listed page counts. The US National Book Award for Poetry is also consistent with the trend towards longer collections in the last decade (averaging 124

pages, compared to the Pulitzer's 120), although it proves more difficult to compare with previous winners, since seven of the ten winning books between 1999 and 2008 were for editions of 'new and selected poems'.

25 Brouwer, 'Boox' (2009).
26 Printing processes (and therefore costs) are a factor often overlooked in poets' discussion of book lengths. For centuries, almost all mass-produced books are printed with groups of pages on single large sheets (known as signatures), which are then folded and cut. The process requires these to be done in multiples of 8, 16, 32, or 64 pages – hence the 48-page lower limit and tendency towards page counts of 64, 96, or 128, and so on. This is particular true in the United Kingdom, where production costs and retail prices for poetry books are generally lower – and may or may not account for the trend towards slightly shorter books overall.
27 'Do-si-do' bindings, with two collections bound back-to-back (and flipped), such as Eileen Myles, *Snowflake/Different Streets* (Seattle, WA: Wave, 2012), or Michael and Matthew Dickman's *Brother* (London: Faber, 2016), play pointedly with this physical sense of unity. *The First 4 Books of Sampson Starkweather* (New York: Birds LLC, 2013) is another recent collection that challenges this unity, leaving *HuffPost*'s reviewer Seth Abramson unsure about the verb tense, and whether it 'is (are) rife with the sorts of gestures […]' etc.
28 'David Morley on writing' (interview), *The Word Factory* website (16 June 2017).
29 Most frequently cited from 'James Wright, The Art of Poetry' (No. 19), interview with Peter Stitt, *Paris Review*, Issue 62 (Summer 1975), online.
30 Beth Ann Fennelly, 'A Winnowing of Wildness: Style and First Book Contests', *Writer's Chronicle* vol. 36 (2003), 53–54.
31 Brouwer, 'Boox' (2009). Also see Katrina Vandenberg, 'Putting Your Poetry in Order: The Mix-Tape Strategy', *Poets & Writers* website (May/June 2008) and Erika Meitner, 'In the Poetry Contest Gulags: Project vs. Mix-Tape Books', *About a Word* blog (6 November 2011), among others.
32 Dorothea Lasky, *Poetry Is Not a Project* (Brooklyn, NY: Ugly Duckling, 2010), 10.
33 Ibid., 8. Emphasis in original.
34 Jake Adam York, 'Poems : Books :: Trees : Forests?' *Kenyon Review* blog (24 January 2012) and 'Forests of Trees: More on the Book as a Form (for Poets)', *Kenyon Review* blog (4 February 2012).
35 Kuskin, 'Book, Poetic', 154–55. It's worth noting that pamphlets (or chapbooks) are perhaps even more often defined by their conceptual unity. A guide on Ireland's *Writing.ie* website, for instance, advises: 'When selecting these poems you need to concentrate on both the quality of your work and how the poem relates to the other ones you have selected. Do your poems have a clear theme, or common elements that will serve to unify the pamphlet?' (Victoria Kennefick, 'Poetry Pamphlet DIY: How to Create Your Own Chapbook', *Writing.ie* 'Resources for Writers' website, 2 July 2014).
36 Michael McKeon, *The Origins of the English Novel, 1600–1740: 15th Anniversary Edition* (Baltimore, MD: Johns Hopkins University Press, 2002), 257.
37 In one of many critical interpretations (including objections when first published), John Jordan's *Why the Lyrical Ballads?* (Berkeley: University of California Press, 1976), suggests the title poses 'one of the interesting and probably finally unanswerable questions of literary history' (172). The books unstable subtitle – '*with a Few Other Poems*' in 1798, '*with Other Poems*' for the 1800 edition, and '*with Pastoral and Other Poems*' for 1802 – only adds to its tenuous presentation as a unified whole.
38 *Lyrical Ballads, with a Few Other Poems* (London: T. N. Longman, 1798), ii.

39 Kuskin and Emerson, 'Book, Poetic', 157.
40 The most comprehensive critical accounts of the production of *Songs of Innocence* and *Lyrical Ballads* can be found in Joseph Viscomi's *Blake and the Idea of the Book* (1993) and James A. Butler and Karen Green's edition of *Lyrical Ballads and Other Poems* (1982), respectively. *Songs of Innocence (*and *Experience*) can be viewed online at the William Blake Archive.
41 Ed Folsom, *Whitman Making Books, Books Making Whitman: A Catalog & Commentary* (Iowa City: Obermann Center for Advanced Studies, University of Iowa, 2005), 12.
42 Walt Whitman, *Leaves of Grass* (Brooklyn, NY: Self-published, 1855), v. (NB: Text and page images of all editions published in the author's lifetime are available on *The Walt Whitman Archive* website at whitmanarchive.org.)
43 Whitman, *Leaves of Grass* (Boston, MA: Thayer & Eldridge, 1860), 455.
44 Qtd in Siegfired Unself, *Goethe & the Ginkgo: A Tree & A Poem*, trans. Kenneth J. Northcott (Chicago, IL: University of Chicago Press, 2003), 22. Emphasis in original.
45 Goethe, 'Observation on Morphology in General', in *The Essential Goethe*, ed. Matthew Bell (Princeton, NJ: Princeton University Press, 2016), 950.
46 Qtd. in Unself, *Goethe & the Ginkgo*, 31.
47 Qtd in *Goethe's West-Easterly Divan*, trans. John Weiss (Boston, MA: Roberts Brothers, 1877), xxvi.
48 Weiss (trans.), *Goethe's West-Easterly Divan*, 158.
49 Daniel Purdy, '*West-östliche Divan* and the "Abduction/Seduction of Europe": World Literature and the Circulation of Culture', *Goethe Yearbook 22*, ed. Adrian Daub and Elisabeth Krimmer (Rochester, NY: Boydell & Brewer, Camden House, 2015), 203.
50 Qtd. and trans. Purdy, '*West-östliche*', 208.
51 Whitman, *Leaves of Grass* (Philadelphia, PA: David McKay, 1891–92), 419.
52 Paul Kane, 'Emerson and Hafiz: The Figure of the Religious Poet', *Religion & Literature* vol. 41, no. 1 (Spring 2009), 111–39.
53 'Poetry and English Poetry,' *The Selected Lectures of Ralph Waldo Emerson*, ed. Ronald A. Bosco and Joel Myerson (Athens, GA: University of Georgia Press, 2005), 207.
54 Marjorie Perloff, 'Yeats and Goethe,' *Comparative Literature* vol. 23, no. 2 (Spring 1971), 125–40.
55 Paul Mariani, *The Whole Harmonium: The Life of Wallace Stevens* (New York: Simon & Schuster, 2016), 376. Richard Allen Blessing also appropriates the unused title for *Wallace Stevens' "Whole Harmonium"* (Syracuse: Syracuse University Press, 1970).
56 See Anne Carson, *Nox* (New York: New Directions, 2009), *Antigonick* (New York: New Directions, 2012), or *Float* (New York: Knopf, 2016). The following chapter discusses the New Directions volumes in greater detail.
57 Perhaps relevant to this particular subject: although the print issue of *PN Review 239*, vol. 44, no. 3 (January-February 2018) appeared in December 2017, it wasn't until the following month that a link to its online version was widely shared on Facebook and Twitter.
58 'Ted Hughes Award', *Poetry Society* website.
59 Among many others, on this particular point see Will Self, 'The novel is dead (this time it's for real)', *Guardian* (2 May 2014) and again, 'Will Self: "The novel is absolutely doomed"', *Guardian* (17 May 2018).
60 Kathleen Fitzpatrick, *The Anxiety of Obsolescence: The American Novel in the Age of Television* (Nashville, TN: Vanderbilt University Press, 2006), 47.
61 Kuskin, 'Book, Poetic', 155.

Chapter 5

POETIC DEVICES: TECHNOLOGIES OF A RETRO-FUTURE

In the *Oxford Handbook of Contemporary British and Irish Poetry* and the *Cambridge Companion to American Poetry Since 1945*, both published in 2013, Salt Publishing is held up as a success story, a small poetry press that survives by making the most of newly available technologies. Since its start in 2000, Matthew Sperling writes in the Oxford volume, 'Salt dramatically expanded its poetry list, keeping large numbers of titles available using print-on-demand technology, and rivalling presses such as Bloodaxe and Carcanet as one of the major independent poetry publishers.'[1] In the Cambridge book, Hank Lazer also describes Salt as a 'leader' in the use of 'the small-batch print-on-demand model, which allows a publisher to create many titles per year'.[2] In hindsight, the relationship between Salt's growth and its use of print-on-demand offers a dramatic example of the conflicting ways in which old and new technologies have been regarded by poetry communities in recent years. As just one of these technologies, print-on-demand – used to produce single copies of a book at relatively low cost – allows small publishers to expand their catalogues without having to estimate the right size for traditional print-runs or bear the costs of storing inventory. But like other technological developments, print-on-demand has also become a short-hand for more complex structural changes by those either optimistic or wary about its implications.

When Salt suddenly announced the closure of its poetry list in May 2013, the same year these positive accounts were published, the news was generally received as another sign of poetry's commercial downturn, in the face of funding cuts and declining sales. Media coverage cited falling trade for UK poetry books in each of the previous three years, including 'a major drop of 18.5% volume and 15.9% value in 2012'.[3] Salt's director, Chris Hamilton-Emery, emphasised the market's 'sharp decline' in his own statements. 'As a very small, nice commercial publisher,' he explained, 'we can't possibly sustain what we have done in the past.'[4] For others, however, Salt's fate was less a problem of being stuck in the past than it confirmed suspicions towards the new technologies that Salt had led the way in adopting. In one widely shared response, Neil Astley, director of Bloodaxe Books, blamed print-on-demand specifically, for creating a publishing model that 'isn't compatible with promoting poetry to a wider readership'. 'If you can only afford to use print on demand,' Astley insists, 'you're never going to be able to promote your books effectively to a readership of more than a few hundred people.'[5] Already in 2010, in an article marking the press's 10-year anniversary, John O'Donoghue had voiced related concerns about Salt's growth: 'To some,' he writes, 'Salt now feels slightly supersized – as if its ambition has led not just to global reach but also to overreaching; to a sense that Hamilton-Emery's big-publisher background has made it the first small-press corporation.'[6] The coded reference to Hamilton-Emery's previous work as production director at Cambridge University Press (where he also introduced print-on-demand in 1999) connects these perceived divisions between 'big' and 'small' press publishing models with the imperatives of 'wider readership' in Astley's comments.

As this chapter shows, these big–small hierarchies have been increasingly complicated by technological trends and developments. To a more circular extent, a given press's readership and ambitions, however notionally 'big' or 'small', have come to determine and be determined by its approaches to design and production. Broadly speaking, small presses might retain a greater flexibility and motivation to experiment with print methods or DIY aesthetics more suitable to shorter print-runs, while larger presses still have greater resources for material or design improvements within the constraints of industrial printing. But as a press 'somewhere in the middle', in Clare Pollard's words, Salt's abandonment of (and very recent return to) single-author poetry collections is just one of many instances where tensions between size and 'ambition', old and new print technologies, or print and online media have challenged such distinctions, requiring presses to re-examine their own place within various traditions.[7] Beyond such binaries, my discussion focuses on the ways in which poetry producers combine new and old technologies in order to project both continuity and innovation. Therefore, this chapter is not about publishing as such. It argues that any discussion of technological developments affecting poetry production over the past 10 years must also follow this story beyond the printed book and consider print's relationship to online platforms that have supported the expansion of performance-based writing and new creative forms made possible by digital media. The examples below highlight a tendency towards layering and blended technologies in each of these areas, with poets, publishers, and other producers working to balance their individual sense of digital possibilities with traces of the material artefact.

The Temptations of Booklust

The simplest and perhaps most typical way of telling this story has been to characterise publishing in the first two decades of this century as a battle between the physical and digital – a kind of good versus evil, depending on one's stake in the fight. One front has been sales outlets, given the domination of Amazon since the late 1990s, the subsequent demise of large chains like the Borders Group (closed in 2009 in the United Kingdom and in 2011 in the United States), and the fate of independent 'bricks-and-mortar' bookshops generally. For consumers, this is linked to another, similarly moralised dilemma occasioned by the rise of e-books. Following the introduction of Amazon's Kindle in 2007, Apple's iPad in 2010, and less successful devices like Kobo, Barnes and Noble's Nook, or Sony's Reader, mainstream news sites soon filled with apocalyptic predictions for the printed book. A *Telegraph* article from 2009, whose headline suggests 'Ebooks will make authors soulless, just like their product,' explains matter-of-factly: 'The end, therefore, is nigh for the standalone book. The single physical text won't be able to survive the growing e-book storm.'[8] A long 2008 *New York Magazine* feature on 'the waning era of print', simply titled 'The End', warns: 'the book business as we know it will not be living happily ever after.'[9] And yet, a decade later, this bedtime story had taken a crowd-pleasing twist. Sales of ebooks fell in each consecutive year from 2015 (and by as much as 10 per cent in 2017), while sales of print books have been on the rise.[10] Newspapers, caught in their own conflicts between print and digital platforms, again made clear which side they were on. In a 2017 *Guardian* article shared online more than 25,000 times, Sian Cain reassures us that 'readers committed to physical books can give a sigh of relief'.[11]

In nearly every telling, this oversimplified drama has been a means for reasserting not only the printed book's commercial robustness, but also its continuing appeal on more humanistic terms. The look, feel, and even smell of print books are often cited among un-digitisable features. As the Publishers Association's chief executive, Stephen Lotinga, accounts for the resurgent sales: 'Physical books have become celebrated again as objects of beauty and publishers invest a lot of time and thought into making their print books beautiful.'[12] Continuing fascination with print books' physicality is further born out in the efforts of e-reader manufacturers to simulate the experience of virtual page-turning, 'e-ink', or Kindle's 'paperwhite' format. For the columnist Simon Jenkins, the interaction with physical books remains a fundamental 'human experience', drastically underestimated by 'hysterical cheerleaders of the e-book'. And as with many book-lovers, his attraction veers towards the ineffable: 'Just buying, handling, giving and talking about a book seems to have caught the magic dust of "experience". A book is beauty. A book is a shelf, a wall, a home.'[13]

Many of these print proponents happily admit that the backlash against changing technologies is nothing new. With that in mind, it might be useful to sketch some lines of historical thought beyond the digital/physical divide before considering examples from contemporary poetry publishing. The recent wave of booklust in all its ironically Instagrammable forms is undeniably part of a more specific contemporary nostalgia for non-digital cultural objects – as Jenkins maintains, 'People want a break from another damned screen' (in a *Guardian* article shared more than 112,000 times online).[14] But wider twenty-first century anti-digital sentiments, typified by the proliferation of 'artisanal' or 'handmade' products, are equally informed by reactions to industrial-scale production from the nineteenth century onwards. Defences of pre-industrial craft traditions by John Ruskin or William Morris, for instance, have found recent support in writers like Richard Sennett, who draws on Ruskin's rejection of mechanical production and Morris's emphasis on embodied labour.[15] In the early twentieth century, the privileging of unique handmade work over industrial manufacturing is also prominent in the philosophy of Martin Heidegger, who pre-empts Sennett's focus on 'the intimate connection between hand and head'.[16] Heidegger's stark comparison of 'things' and 'objects' is summarised by Bruno Latour:

> The handmade jug can be a thing, while the industrially made can of Coke remains an object. While the latter is abandoned to the empty mastery of science and technology, only the former, cradled in the respectful idiom of art, craftsmanship, and poetry, could deploy and gather its rich set of connections.[17]

Beyond its philosophical implications, Heidegger's admiration for the handmade jug's 'thingness', as a more authentic or even 'poetically' crafted product, is alive and well for bibliophiles who insist that the 'handling' of physical books or filling houses with them is an essential part of their magic. On the other hand, very few books are actually handmade. In the 570 years since Johannes Gutenberg's innovations in metal type methods or the 1,000 years since moveable type was first used in China, the direct traces of human hands on book manufacture have been reduced in inverse proportion to more efficient and consistent reproducibility, to the point that an infinitely and perfectly duplicated e-book might have been entirely written, typeset, published, distributed, and read without ever leaving the digital realm. Following the spread of digital design in the 1980s and digital printing in the 1990s, most physical books' only claim to distinction is in the final step, when the digital file is sent to a printer. Thus, while it is important to recognise the wider nostalgia for pre-industrial commodities as a context for defences of the physical book, the radical potential of book production, as a mechanical process for many centuries, has always rested in the extent to which its material form facilitates access to content.

The potential for a less romanticised engagement is examined by Walter Benjamin, a contemporary of Heidegger, in his often reproduced and endlessly influential essay, 'The Work of Art in the Age of Mechanical Reproduction' (1935, revised in 1939). Although Benjamin is mostly concerned with the historical shift from painting and live theatre to photography and film, the applicability of his critique to debates around digital literature begins with his notion of the *aura*, an indescribable and unreproducible quality supposedly possessed by the singular work or performance, which 'even the most perfect reproduction of a work of art is lacking'.[18] Like the apparent 'soullessness' of digital texts, this aura is often defined by its absence or by the way it 'withers in the age of mechanical production'.[19] Yet, unlike the champions of craft above, Benjamin does not lament the new technologies of mass culture for propagating 'the social bases of the contemporary decay of the aura'.[20] Rather, he celebrates the degree to which, 'for the first time in world history, mechanical reproduction emancipates the work of art from its parasitical dependence on ritual'.[21] By freeing the work from its aura and from the 'fabric of tradition' in which the auratic art is embedded, 'the total function of art is reversed': 'Instead of being based on ritual, it begins to be based on another practice – politics.'[22] By destroying the 'cult value' of the art object, the mass reproduction 'put[s] the public in the position of the critic'.[23] Benjamin, building up to the impact of film and photography in the early twentieth century, begins his essay by acknowledging the 'particularly important' precedent of 'the mechanical reproduction of writing' in print.[24] These same tensions between the tradition-bound 'aura' of the handmade 'thing' and the urgency of access that again define the priorities of poetry publishers in the early twenty-first century.

New Directions and Old

In terms of the economic and aesthetic constraints involved in making the aura of print books accessible *and* profitable, no contemporary publisher of poetry in English offers a more pertinent case study than New Directions. Their recent series of collaborations with gallery director Christine Burgin, for instance, incorporating full-colour facsimiles of handwritten work by Emily Dickinson and Robert Walser, are advertised as 'books that are for reading, looking and touching in equal measure'.[25] The press's longer tradition is also defined by what might be called its archival ethos:

> Although New Directions started in the service of verbal revolution, it also reprinted Henry James, E. M. Forster, Ronald Firbank and Evelyn Waugh when other publishers would not; when no one would print F. Scott Fitzgerald's *The Crack Up*, ND did; when *The Great Gatsby* was out of print, New Directions brought it back.[26]

As Eliot Weinberger adds, 'because of [founder James] Laughlin's belief that a writer of "serious literature" takes twenty years to be discovered, [New Directions] keeps most of its books in print forever.'[27] Twenty years after Laughlin's death, this legacy can be found in recent books whose status as mass-produced commodities is complicated by their 'aura' as objects that retain or even foreground traces of their transmission from archive to market.

Among these, perhaps no other New Directions publication has ever married an archival impulse with material form as strikingly as Anne Carson's *Nox* (2009). The publisher describes it as 'an epigraph in the form of a book, a facsimile of a handmade book Anne Carson wrote and created after the death of her brother.'[28] In its purchasable form, *Nox* comes housed in a sturdy printed box that opens to reveal its nearly 200 pages, folded concertina-style, with full-colour reproductions of photographs, handwritten notes, sketches, and even the stitched seams from Carson's handmade original. In this digitally printed replica, we encounter an immediate and uncanny conflict between the singularity of the original and the access made possible by mechanical reproduction. *Nox*'s simulation of a unique, handmade object implicitly appropriates the tradition of artist's books, or what Garrett Stewart has called 'bookworks', for a mass-produced item that not only bears traces of but makes a USP of its ghostly aura. For all the emphasis on touching and handling, the virtual tactility of its high-quality images also reinforces the distance from the original. It is in these contradictions that Stewart diverges from Benjamin, locating the disruptive potential of bookworks like *Nox* in their resistance of the readerly expectation that books will function as a simple content-delivery system. By 'demediating' and 'rematerialising' itself, Stewart argues, the bookwork's 'easily recognized forms give way instead to the formative stuff and structure of its transmission'.[29]

Such disruption can be witnessed, of all places, in the mixed reviews that *Nox* has received on Amazon. Many readers are as enthusiastic as the user Yasue, who describes it as 'more than a poetry book due to the format – it's a 3D work of art', giving it 5 stars, along with 71 per cent of reviewers. Others are less convinced. 'I am amazed that this project was brought out by a major publisher,' writes Steven A. May. 'It's not a book. It's a text which is interestingly displayed' – 2 stars. BrianAloha reports:

> I have discussed 'Nox' with another interested friend and we both agree that this is not in any way a real book. It's an experimental piece of art [...] like a big paper Slinky that is very difficult to hold, read or put away. [1 star][30]

Such gripes return us to a defining tension between availability and materiality throughout New Directions' history – a tension recognisable in other debates regarding the economics and production of contemporary poetry, like that around Salt's decision. According to Gregory Barnhisel, James Laughlin was initially 'convinced that consumers should want to own books that were finely made as well as finely written'.[31] 'In the 1930s,' Barnhisel points out, 'Laughlin had most New Directions books printed by small craft printers across the United States.'[32] In a postscript to their first book publication, William Carlos Williams's novel *White Mule* (1937), Laughlin makes clear his own feelings regarding the balance of art and commerce:

> It is time I think to damn the book publisher as hard as you can damn them. They're traitors and enemies of the people. They have made literature a business. They have made the writing of books the production of cheap-goods. They have made a book a thing no more valuable than an automobile tire.[33]

By the 1950s, New Directions' more specific dilemma, which lingers in these Amazon complaints, centred on the rise of trade paperbacks as a cheaper alternative to hardcovers. When Laughlin eventually relented, New Directions reaped the benefits, massively expanding its business and profits across the decade.[34] Yet recent projects like *Nox* or Carson's follow-up, *Antigonick* (2012) – bound in 'real book' format, but with handwritten text and illustrations by Bianca Stone on tracing paper – revive the debate. Of *Nox*, the Amazon user 'An Ordinary Man in New Haven' writes:

> My 'review' is mostly an entreaty. To Anne Carson, to New Directions. Though I completely understand the necessity of the folding structure of this work, I long for a 'reading copy'. A paperback – even, heaven help us, a Kindle edition – so that I might more easily take it with me when I go.[35]

Not only has New Directions failed to oblige 'Ordinary Man' with a Kindle edition, but when they first posted photos of *Antigonick* on Twitter, the publisher quipped: 'As we like to say, they're anti-ebooks.'[36] Echoing Laughlin's paperback acquiescence 60 years before, *Antigonick* was eventually republished in softcover and Kindle formats in 2015, though differences in the editions drew complaints that might seem to justify their reticence. While Ordinary Man in New Haven longed for a 'reading copy' of *Nox*, Amy M. Dunlap is 'very disappointed this paperback version [of *Antigonick*] does NOT include the illustrations as described' – 2 stars.[37] An anonymous user broaches the digital dilemma: 'I'm really upset that the Kindle version does not have the pictures and the original print style of the actual book [...] those things are just as much a part of the book as the writing itself, so it's like I got an incomplete book' – 1 star.[38]

Despite such contradictory demands – some of which we can imagine finding sympathy in Laughlin – New Directions' current president, Barbara Epler, remains optimistic about the future of print, partly because, as she put it in 2013, 'real literature seems to be having a "retro chic" phase.'[39] It is in this framing that we see Laughlin's preciousness about material form dovetailing with the print book's renewed aura in the digital age. Epler attempts to square those needs, explaining: 'A book is like a bowl, a cat, or a spoon. We will try to make the most beautiful physical object we can, and also offer a digital version.'[40] For a relatively prolific, commercial press like New Directions, the desire to produce beautiful physical objects will always be subject to the economics of larger print-runs. Although Laughlin founded the press with an inheritance from his family's steel fortune, Weinberger suggests this privilege 'let New Directions survive as a money-loser into the 1960s [...] It is an old-fashioned, patrician way of doing business – the long-term investment.'[41] Long after moving away from small specialist printers to mass production, Epler puts the continuing predicament concisely: 'The tricky thing is we need to make more money, and yet keep the quality up.'[42] A sense of compromise arises when a *New Yorker* interviewer says she felt 'a sort of reverse sticker shock' on seeing the price of a Robert Walser collection: 'You can do tipped-in art and sell this for a profit for twenty-five dollars?!' Epler admits they saved with cheaper printing: 'It went to China [...] true confessions. Not something we love to do, but it feels necessary with these books including art.'[43]

Although the degree to which 'books including art' are compromised by economic necessities will vary according to the scale and resources of individual presses, the falling costs of lithographic and digital printing has given larger and smaller presses shared options in recent years. In the United Kingdom, presses as diverse in size and style as Cape, Faber & Faber, Valley Press, Penned in the Margins, and UniformBooks have used the Cornwall-based printer TJ International, for example. To some extent this levelling of costs, along with the now logistically feasible option of using cheaper printers overseas, appears to have encouraged a greater emphasis on design. This can be seen with larger presses like Manchester's Carcanet – who, in 2015, relaunched a redesigned *PN Review* alongside new cover designs for their collections – or smaller presses like London's Test Centre – who work with a range of independent artists, designers, and print co-operatives for their limited editions. Test Centre and other UK micro-presses like Sad Press, Girasol, Spirit Duplicator, and clinic have also incorporated risograph or other older technologies into productions, linking DIY zine aesthetics with a British avant-garde tradition. At the digital end, the latter tradition has also been invoked by presses like Shearsman and

Reality Street, whose use of print-on-demand (unlike Salt's, perhaps) can be placed in a lineage with the use of duplicator presses or early photocopiers by experimentalists like Bob Cobbing, printing books for Writers Forum in the basement of the Poetry Society in the 1970s.[44] Collectively, these digital, retro, and hybrid approaches have had the effect of both scrambling and preserving material aura of traditional print production, in a period when online ephemera has inspired a renewed public interest in the labour and provenance behind all sorts of commodities. Again though, these trends in the manufacture of books must be interpreted in relation to the rise of online platforms which, in most cases, now provide the most important shopfront for print products. In other cases, print books might be seen as optional merchandise, like a physical album of music, for new poetry consumers whose primary access is provided by 'free' posts on social media. Perhaps surprisingly, these digital spaces also reveal an equally complex blend of new and old technologies in service of the material trace.

The Accessible Aura

The fetishisation of print books tends to disregard the benefits of digital technologies for readers with different needs. This includes readers with print disabilities, for whom the ability to change the size, colour, and contrast of text or text-to-speech support are essential.[45] In an era of funding cuts to public libraries and stagnant wages for many consumers, the material cost of print books becomes a socio-economic issue as well. Another risk of heartfelt booklust lies in the extent to which it has encouraged a tiered economy in which limited or hand-printed editions drift towards the status of luxury items. An extreme, but hardly unique example can be found in Susan Howe's recent publications with New Directions. Howe's *Spontaneous Particulars: The Telepathy of Archives* (2014) is another product of the collaboration with Christine Burgin, which again includes full-colour facsimiles of archival material alongside a text adapted from a lecture given at Harvard, on thick card paper in clothbound hardcover (and again printed in China). Among its images, *Spontaneous Particulars* – which has a suggested retail price of £22 in the United Kingdom and $29.95 in the United States – includes a number of text collages that previously appeared in Howe's collection *That This* (2011) – a New Directions paperback, retailing at £12.99 and US$16.95. This price difference is negligible, however, compared to the US$7,500 price for The Grenfell Press's limited letterpress edition of Howe's *Frolic Architecture* (2009), in which collages reprinted in both of the New Directions books first appeared. At the start of *Spontaneous Particulars*, Howe admits that 'electronic technologies are radically transforming the way we read, write, and remember'. These technologies, she writes, 'offer new and often thrilling possibilities for artists and scholars'.[46] But in describing the archival meditations of the book as 'a collaged swan song to the old ways', there is also a more practical sense in which new possibilities for *readers* remain ignored.

As discussed in Chapter 3, poetry was shared and read online since well before the rise of social media. Yet, the popularity of sites like Tumblr and Instagram, launched in 2007 and 2010, respectively, together with the introduction of smartphones and faster internet service, has prompted the spread of more visually oriented poetry, increasingly incorporating text into digital images in ways that emphasise a paradoxical sense of physicality. In the early 1990s, more than a decade before the panic over ebooks, the advent of digital photography had prompted a similar crisis regarding its ontological status. Art historians like William J. Mitchell argued that the difference between digital and analogue (or 'true', i.e. chemical-based) photography was 'grounded in fundamental physical characteristics that have logical and cultural consequences'.[47] The theorist W. J. T. Mitchell disputed this 'prevailing myth', arguing that 'the authenticity, truth value, authority, legitimacy of photographs […] is quite independent of their character as "digital" or "chemical analog" productions'.[48] From either side, this sense of digital artefacts' 'ambivalent ontology', in Jannis Kallinikos's term, figures heavily into the layered aesthetics of recent online poetry, typified by the efforts of so-called Instapoets to foreground material traces of their craft by digital means.[49] As with Carson's recent books, a new sort of virtual aura is made possible by transmitting embodied work via new technologies.

As the audience for image-based online poetry has grown, poets working in this medium have had to find new ways to distinguish their work through its virtual-material presentation. The Canadian poet Rupi Kaur, by far the best known of this first generation of poets who first found success on social media, provides a much-imitated model for integrating the physical and digital. Simple, hand-drawn sketches accentuate her poems' corporeality, contrasted, in her case, by text rendered in a plain digital typeface on unmanipulated white backgrounds. Across her Instagram feed with its 3.7 million followers, the productive tension between digital text and physicality is borne out by the meticulous alternation of poems with photos of the poet. That embodied link is also present in the fact that Kaur's poetry first came to many readers' attention in 2015, when one of her self-portraits was removed from Instagram for showing the poets' menstrual blood.[50] With a curiously gendered regularity, well-known male poets on Instagram, like Tyler Knott Gregson, r. h. Sin, Robert M. Drake, and Christopher Poindexter, seem more likely to give handwrought and mechanical substance to their poems by photographing them as rendered on a manual typewriter, self-conscious double-keystrokes and all.

Others bear out the guidance in the 'Instagram Poets Toolkit' published on the community website *Her Heart Poetry*, where advice on choosing backgrounds also notes that 'many poets are creating an aesthetic for their page around handwritten poetry'.[51] Typewritten or handwritten texts are often given further layers of material content in their framing, presented as hand-torn scraps within domestic or natural scenes, in situ on a wooden desk or with flowers, writing utensils, cigarettes, rings, or other invocations of the writer's hand. Even where the text is seemingly produced by a digital printer, materialising effects are achieved by combining lighting filters with textured paper – or in early posts by the poet Nikita Gill, for instance, pages with text showing through from the reverse. Perhaps most pointedly in the wider context of contemporary poetry's print problem, the social media feeds of 'successful' online poets inevitably include images of their print collections. In this dynamic loop, the material presence of these books – often held in hands or stacked together to imply mass production and physical mass – clearly offers a crucial substantiation for both author and reader of formerly 'digital' words (or digital images of words) made flesh.

The cultural assumption that poetry is a form of writing especially dependent on its embodied form helps to account for its popularity in a digital age. In print, digital images, and performance, traces of the poet's body offer points of reorientation amidst layers of mediation. If the advent of digital reproduction is a crisis met by presses working to imbue their wares with 'touchable' value and by poets working to infuse their digital output with visual substance, either might learn from the other's intricate fusions of old and new technologies. The commercial success of 'Instapoets' over the past decade helped make 2013 a low point followed by five consecutive years of rising poetry sales. It was the same year Salt announced its retreat from poetry publishing, but also when Kansas City-based Andrews McMeel published their first bestselling collection, re-releasing Tumblr-poet Lang Leav's previously self-published *Love & Misadventure*. The coincidence is a salient marker on poetry's shifting landscape. It's difficult to imagine how online poets could have found such enormous readership without the legitimising effect of Andrews McMeel's intervention – publishing five further bestselling collections by Leav, Kaur's multimillion-selling collections, and bestsellers by Amanda Lovelace, r. h. Sin, and many others. The publisher's previous history as the world's largest syndicator of comic strips (*Calvin and Hobbes*, *The Far Side*, *Garfield*, and more than 80 others), meant the press was uniquely sensitive to poetry's visual orientations, while earlier successes with photo-humour anthologies like *Cake Wrecks* (2009) had shown the potential for converting social media audiences to print sales.

To dismiss these sales as proof of their 'consumer-driven content', full of 'amateurism and ignorance' (in the terms of Rebecca Watts's hotly debated critique) is to ignore the challenge of producing poetry that responds to the material experience of its readers.[52] Such categorical resistance to new possibilities for poetry publishing – or its dissemination more generally, where 'publishing' proves too narrow a term – returns us to the quaint fear of ebooks or the dismissal of presses making use of print-on-demand as 'virtual publishers'.[53] Of course, the use of vintage typewriters or risograph duplication is no less nostalgic for Benjamin's always-lost aura. But their use in conjunction with digital technologies demonstrates meaningful negotiations with new media's complex ontological status, as well as prompting important questions about access. It might not be long before these hang-ups appear as futile as James Laughlin's against paperbacks. The fact that he was finally persuaded that they would help New Directions make headway into the student market (the 'academic stock exchange', as he called it) points to ways in which poetry publishers might also look to debates and opportunities regarding 'open access' around academic scholarship. In any of these contexts, as readers, our consumption of new poetry cannot be materially disentangled from that of any Instagram follower or any 'Ordinary Man in New Haven'.

Notes

1. Matthew Sperling, 'Books and the Market: Trade Publishers, State Subsidies, and Small Press,' in *Oxford Handbook of Contemporary British and Irish Poetry*, ed. Peter Robinson (Oxford: Oxford University Press, 2013), 191–212 (208).
2. Hank Lazer, 'American Poetry and Its Institutions', in *Cambridge Companion to American Poetry since 1945*, ed. Jennifer Ashton (Cambridge, UK: Cambridge University Press, 2013), 158–72 (162).
3. Alison Flood, 'Salt abandons single-author collections amid poetry market slump', *Guardian* (24 May 2013).
4. Qtd in Flood, 'Salt Abandons' (24 May 2013).
5. Neil Astley, comment on Clare Pollard, 'The Health of Poetry', Pollard's personal website (20 May 2013). These comments were also copied and shared on Astley's Facebook account.
6. John O'Donogue, 'Ten Years of Publishing Worth Its Salt', *Guardian Books Blog* (30 July 2010).
7. Pollard, 'The Health of Poetry' (2013).
8. Andrew Keen, 'Ebooks will make authors soulless, just like their product, *Telegraph* (17 September 2009).
9. Boris Kachka, 'The End', *New York Magazine* (14 September 2008).
10. Adam Rowe, 'Traditional Publishing Ebook Sales Dropped 10% in 2017', *Forbes* (29 April 2018), citing data from PubTrack Digital; and Sain Cain, 'Ebook sales continue to fall as younger generations drive appetite for print', *Guardian* (14 March 2017), citing data from Nielsen, the Publishers Association, and *The Bookseller*.

11 Cain, 'Ebook sales', *Guardian* (14 March 2017).
12 Qtd in Rhys Handley, 'Printed Books Turn a New Leaf as Digital Sales Decline', *PrintWeek* (27 July 2018).
13 Simon Jenkins, 'Books are back. Only the technodazzled thought they would go away', *Guardian* (13 May 2016).
14 Ibid.
15 See Richard Sennett, *The Craftsman* (London: Allen Lane, 2008), and Chapter 10 here for further discussion of the ethical and creative implications of 'craft' labour.
16 Ibid., 9. And Heidegger, *What Is Called Thinking?*, trans. J. Glenngray (New York: Harper, 1976).
17 Latour, 'Why Has Critique Run out of Steam? From Matters of Face to Matters of Concern', *Critical Inquiry* vol. 30, no. 2 (Winter 2004), 225–48 (233). Latour's critique of reductive fetish or anti-fetish: those 'who associate criticism with antifetishism'. For such interpreters, the role of the critic is to reveal this fetish to its 'naïve believers' (237).
18 Walter Benjamin, 'The Work of Art in the Age of Mechanical Reproduction', in *Illuminations*, trans. Harry Zorn, ed. Hannah Arendt (London: Pimlico, 1999), 214.
19 Ibid., 215.
20 Ibid., 219.
21 Ibid., 220.
22 Ibid., 218.
23 Ibid., 233–34.
24 Ibid., 213.
25 'Christine Burgin,' New Directions website, no author or date.
26 'History,' New Directions website, no author or date.
27 Eliot Weinberger, 'At the Feet of Ezra Pound,' *New York Review of Books* (1 March 2007).
28 '*Nox*,' New Directions website, no author or date.
29 Stewart, *Bookwork: Medium to Object to Concept to Art* (Chicago, IL: University of Chicago Press, 2011), 168.
30 Yasue, 'An Experience [...]' (16 April 2013); Steven A. May, 'Interesting Idea, but' (17 December 2010); and BrianAloha, 'Not in Any Way a Book' (29 July 2010) – reviews from Anne Carson, *Nox* (2009), hardcover format, posted to Amazon.com.
31 Barnhisel, *James Laughlin, New Directions, and the Remaking of Ezra Pound* (Boston: University of Massachusetts Press, 2005), 167.
32 Ibid., 240.
33 Qtd in Barnhisel, 64.
34 Barnhisel notes monthly grosses between $4,000 and $10,000 in the early 1950s, compared with $23,000 in 1960 and $38,000 the following year (166).
35 An Ordinary Man in New Haven (user), 'Her glory, if only [...]' (24 April 2018), review on Amazon.com.
36 New Directions (@NewDirections), Twitter (5:18 p.m., 29 March 2012).
37 Amy M. Dunlap, 'Two Stars' (24 February 2018), review on Amazon.com.
38 Amazon Customer (anonymous user), 'Don't Get the Kindle Version!!!!!' (24 April 2017), review on Amazon.com.
39 'Pub Talk: Fiona McCrae Interviews Barbara Epler', *Graywolf Press* blog (14 November 2013), since removed.
40 Epler, Graywolf interview.
41 Weinberger, 'At the Feet of Ezra Pound' (2007).
42 Epler, Graywolf interview.

43 Qtd in Maria Bustillos, 'How Staying Small Helps New Directions Publish Great Books', *New Yorker* (16 February 2016).
44 See Ken Edwards, 'Writers Forum Live', *Reality Street* website (1 April 2010) or a 2006 interview with Shearsman's Tony Frazer on The Argotist Online.
45 According to Alistair McNaught and Huw Alexander's report on 'Ebooks and Accessibility' (2014): 'The term print disability refers to any disability that hinders an individual's ability to access hard-copy printed text. It is more than visual difficulty, and includes those who have difficulty decoding printed text – for example dyslexic people. Equally, spinal injury or involuntary muscle spasms may hinder someone from physically holding a book. Ebooks can potentially transform access to content for these very varied users.' (McNaught and Alexander, 'Ebooks and Accessibility', in *Ebooks in Education: Realising the Vision*, ed. Hazel Woodward (London: Ubiquity Press, 2014), 39–45).
46 Howe, *Spontaneous Particulars: The Telepathy of Archives* (New York: New Directions, 2014), 9.
47 William J. Mitchell, *The Reconfigured Eye: Visual Truth in the Post-Photographic Era* (Cambridge: MIT Press, 1994), 4.
48 W. J. T. Mitchell, 'Realism and the Digital Image', in *Critical Realism in Contemporary Art: Around Allan Sekula's Photography*, ed. Jan Baetens and Hilde Van Gelder, Lieven Gevaert Series, vol. 4 (Leuven: Leuven University Press, 2012), 12–27 (15).
49 Jannis Kallinikos, Aleksi Aaltonen, Attila Marton, 'The Ambivalent Ontology of Digital Artifacts', *MIS Quarterly* vol. 37, no. 2 (June 2013), 357–70.
50 The image, part of Kaur's photographic series 'period', was posted on 23 March 2015 and removed two days later, before eventually being reinstated. The story, including Instagram's explanation of the 'community guidelines' violation and Kaur's response, was widely covered in mainstream news outlets. The series can be viewed on Kaur's website.
51 No author, 'The Instagram Poets Toolkit', *Her Heart Poetry* website (8 December 2016).
52 Watts, 'The Cult of the Nobel Amateur', *PN Review* (2018).
53 Frazer, The Argotist online interview (2006), in reference to Shearsman's use of print-on-demand: 'I've heard cheap shots being taken at Salt and Shearsman by one of the Big Publishers, with the throwaway line that we're "virtual publishers". Which is of course a misunderstanding of the way we operate.'

Chapter 6

DEBUT FEVER

When Hannah Sullivan's *Three Poems* was published by Faber & Faber in 2018, the jacket blurb began: 'Hannah Sullivan's debut collection is a revelation – three long poems of fresh ambition, intensity and substance.' When the book was awarded the TS Eliot Prize in early 2019, Sinéad Morrissey, chair of the judging panel, echoed this sense of discovery:

> A star is born. Where has she come from? […] I don't know her personally, I hadn't read her in magazines or anywhere else before. She has not come through the usual creative-writing, pamphlet route. She has just arrived, and it is breathtaking. I couldn't be more delighted if I had won it myself.[1]

Although she goes on to praise the Sullivan's 'formal mastery' and 'fresh and observant' approach to 'our mortality, our sexuality, our gender and our movement through time and place', it is obvious that Morrissey's delight also lies in the book's appearance, seemingly from nowhere. Not having seen Sullivan's work in magazines and not having come through the 'usual' routes all figures into the feeling of a poet having 'just arrived'. As much as these details call attention to the standardisation of this trajectory, they also highlight the novelty of such 'revelations' – in order words, the rarity of a debut actually being the poetry community's first impression of a poet – to which Faber's promotional rhetoric is similarly attuned. In considering the state of what I call 'debut culture' in recent years, the language around a book like Sullivan's is an exception that helps us understand the accepted rules regarding debuts, as well as the first book's broader regulatory function. Such language, together with remarkable prize successes for first collections on both sides of the Atlantic in the past five years, calls for a reassessment of the effects this debut culture has had on writers both before and after publishing their first book-length volume, along with repercussions for established publishers looking to keep their lists 'fresh' or newer presses building their lists amid this zeitgeist celebration of 'new voices'.

My conception of debut culture specific to contemporary poetry stems from a wider sense of its historical specificity and its part in the professionalisation of poetry over the past century. Jesse Zuba's recent study of *The First Book: Twentieth-Century Poetic Careers in America* (2016) helpfully reconsiders the poetic debut as a key structuring device for poetic careers in the United States, as well as 'a unique form of literary production that comes to be endowed with its own tradition, conventions, and prestige as it assumes an increasingly prominent role in the way poetry is written, published, marketed, and read'.[2] Beyond poetry, scholars of fiction like Marius Hentea also provide useful models for exploring the debut's social history in relation to first novels.[3] Within a contemporary frame, this backdrop brings into relief a twenty-first century moment characterised by what might be reasonably called 'debut fever', in which more debuts are being published and celebrated than possibly any point in anglophone poetry's modern history, and in which the pressures and possibilities for writers and publishers are therefore more acute than ever. In its handling of these tensions, this chapter brings the discussions of 'generationalism' and prize culture in the first two chapters together with the history of the collection as a form and its recent technological iterations in Chapters 4 and 5. First books are necessarily bound up in these generational discourses, both in the practical sense by which publication and any prizes will usually be conferred, blurbed, or reviewed by 'established' poets and in the degree to which the word *debut* implies entry into an established social order. But I also consider ways in which the hierarchy and trajectory evoked by debuts has been increasingly challenged – by first collections like Sullivan's, surprising a contemporary audience by returning the debut to its introductory premise, and conversely by collections whose author's established presence online or in other published forms means that a so-called debut can justifiably be advertised as 'long-awaited'. Finally, this discussion is underpinned by ways in which poetry's unique debut culture continues to be informed the language of debuts in other art forms and by wider cultural obsessions with 'the next big thing'. Poetry's debut fever, I argue, is not entirely separable from the spread of aspirational celebrity culture across the creative industries in the age of social media.

So Many

In the past five years, first poetry collections have been afforded an unprecedented level of attention and acclaim. As I suggested above, one of the most visible and easily quantifiable aspects of this phenomenon has been the success of debuts in major national and international awards. Even before Sullivan's win, the 2018 TS Eliot Prize made headlines for its inclusion of five debut collections on its shortlist of ten. Comparing this across the decade since 2008, the only year where more than one debut collection made the shortlist (and there were several where none did) was 2015, when Sarah Howe was the first ever debut winner with *Loop of Jade*, and Rebecca Perry's *beauty/beauty* was shortlisted. The year 2015 was also noteworthy for the first ever poetry winner of the *Guardian*'s First Book Award (Andrew McMillan's *physical*) and the first debut to win the US National Book Award for Poetry since 1975 (Robin Coste Lewis's *Voyage of the Sable Venus and Other Poems*). Fiona Benson and Liz Berry's sharing of the 2014 Geoffrey Faber Prize were also the first debut winners since 2002. Just as Howe's 2015 Eliot win seemed to blaze the trail for further debut winners with Ocean Vuong's *Night Sky with Exit Wounds* in 2017 and Sullivan's *Three Poems* the year after, the Geoffrey Faber Prize was again awarded to a debut in 2016 for Kim Moore's *The Art of Falling*, and the 2018 US National Book Award went to Justin Phillip Reed's *Indecency*. In the Costa Book Awards' poetry category, Adam Foulds's *The Broken Word* in 2008 was followed by Jonathan Edwards's *My Family and Other Superheroes* in 2014 as the only two debut winners in the prize's long history. Likewise, in 2016, the prestigious Griffin Prize went to a debut for the first time ever, for Liz Howard's *Infinite Citizen of the Shaking Tent*. Alongside the Eliot's debut-laden 2018 shortlist, the Costa shortlist that year featured an unprecedented three debuts on its shortlist of four. From this staggering account, we can either infer that the generation of poets publishing first books in the past five years are either self-evidently superior to any previous generation, or that a variety of social, industrial, and perhaps political factors have contributed to an atmosphere of debut-mania, prompting publishers' and prize-judges' extraordinary response to an extraordinary level of interest and accomplishment among new writers.

The sense of writers and publishers jointly contributing to this flood of strong debuts is also captured in Sinéad Morrissey's comments on the 2018 Eliot prize:

> There is such tremendous energy coming from people writing their first books right now. So many of the debuts were not only accomplished, but testing the boundaries of their fields. It is a really exciting moment for poetry, because it feels like publishers are taking more chances, and we're now reading a more diverse and experimental field.[4]

To some extent, the notion of 'tremendous energy' and 'testing the boundaries' might be substituted for any of the platitudes that define the debut as a kind of genre in its own right, with expectations of experimentation and chance-taking. Even Morrissey's emphasis on the uniqueness of 'right now' as a 'really exciting moment' invokes the 'double bind' Zuba describes as 'an unavoidable pitfall of contemporary first-book prize culture', in which judges of awards for first collections find themselves having to celebrate 'exceptional' talent year after year.[5] And yet, the context of the Eliot prize, an award that had until recently given little attention to debuts, marks a difference. Morrissey's parallel emphasis on diversity and experimentation pointedly aligns the work of poetry with ongoing cultural conversations, and implies in turn that the three Eliot-winning debuts between 2015 and 2018, the five shortlisted in 2018, or the publication of debuts in general might offer a means of addressing poetry's historical biases. Morrissey had already stressed diversity and timeliness when the Eliot shortlist was announced, saying that the process of reading 176 collections that year made her feel 'privileged to be able to listen in to such a lively, diverse and urgent conversation'.[6] Even before that, the link between debuts and diversity is explicit in the marketing language around Faber's unusual publication of four debuts in 2018, including Sullivan's. Again, by way of comparison, it is worth bearing in mind that Faber had not published more than one debut per year (and often zero) at any time in recent decades. Faber's poetry editor Matthew Hollis conflates the unusual number and their diversity in a press release: 'Perhaps at no time in the company's history has Faber brought forward so many talented and diverse new voices to publication.'[7]

References to 'diversity' often sit ambiguously in such statements, blurring reference to identity and representation with possible artistic meanings. Its repeated use in relation to the 2018 Eliot prize, for instance, seems all the more pointed in light of criticism the prize received in previous years for its lack of ethnic diversity – most prominently in Sandeep Parmar's 2017 *Guardian* article, 'Why the TS Eliot prize shortlist hails a return to the status quo' and responses to it.[8] Morrissey's slippage between 'more diverse and experimental' and Hollis's 'so many talented and diverse' both imply syntactically that its definition might be broadened to include, for instance, a plurality of poetry 'fields' (in Morrissey's term), in the manner suggested by Maurice Riordan's editorial for a 2016 issue of *Poetry Review*:

> We inherit inequities not only of race and gender, but also of education, geography, age, looks, so many indeed that an effective logarithm of fairness seems impossible. And every individual who takes to writing poetry is, in any case, a minority of one.[9]

This questionable rationale of 'so many' diversities, to the point of seeing everyone as a 'minority of one', sits in the background of much debut celebration wherever its marketing-speak implies that career status might be recognised as another inequity. In this way, every debut comes to signify the possibility of diversity as such, and debut-filled shortlists like those of the 2018 Eliot prize or Costa prize (which, in nearly 35 years, has only ever been won by white poets) provide a distraction from further criticism.

On the other hand, it's no coincidence that a year in which these prizes were dominated by debuts is one in which Faber, the most prestigious publisher in the United Kingdom, released more first collections than any time in its history, with three of those four new Faber authors making both the Eliot and Costa shortlists. After spacing its four previous debuts annually from 2012 to 2015, the burst of four in 2018 might be seen to compensate for what David Wheatley (writing in 2014) describes as 'the slowness of larger poetry publishers to address their demographic base', singling out the company: 'While Bloodaxe, Anvil and Carcanet made significant strides in the 1980s, Faber's publication of Daljit Nagra's debut collection in 2007 made him only the second non-white poet on their list after Derek Walcott.'[10] Although statistics are difficult to pin down (for important reasons I'll address shortly), Wheatley's observation connects with the corresponding tendency for smaller presses to publish more debuts while building up their lists – and even these numbers have been growing. While Faber published only nine debuts in the decade after 2008 (including the four in 2018), mid-sized UK presses Bloodaxe, Carcanet, and Seren each published more than 20, with a fairly steady 2–3 each year. Salt and Eyewear each published at least as many in the same period, despite Eyewear only being founded in 2012 and the closure of Salt's list in 2014. Other newer presses, like Penned in the Margins (which began publishing in 2006) and Nine Arches (since 2012) have published as many as five to six per year. Others, like CB Editions, Peepal Tree, and Liverpool's Pavilion have focused on fewer debuts each year, but with greater prize results by proportion. Overall, by the best possible estimate, there were as many as four times the number of debuts published by UK presses in 2018 as there were in 2008.[11] Although it will be left to publishers, readers, and later critics to gauge the sustainability of such expansion, the sheer volume and the unprecedented prize successes have already made this a historic decade for debuts.

Coming Out

With or without its French accent, the word *debut* comes with all sorts of baggage, partly through its practical application in poetry promotion and the pressures related to that potentially career-defining first impression, and partly through its historical connotations and wider cultural use. Semantically, a subtle, but important historical shift over the past century has converted *debut* from a general term for a writer's 'arrival' or 'coming out' into a more specific label for a first full-length print collection, so that the book now encapsulates that more general arrival. In the same way that 'collection' was shown in Chapter 4 to have been standardised only quite recently as a denomination for single-author volumes of new poems, the linguistic shift from a process to product – or in typical use, from 'making one's debut' to the 'debut collection' – seems to have occurred over the past 50 years. In *Poetry* magazine, for example, the first unambiguous use of *debut* to refer to a first book comes in the mid-1970s, before which it either referred to a writer's first appearance in *Poetry* or their 'public' or 'literary debut' more broadly.[12] The phrase 'debut collection' enters wider use in newspaper reviews and other poetry magazines in the 1980s, in parallel with the emergence of 'debut novel' as a standard designation.[13] Of course, the existence of first books precedes the 'debut' label, and as Zuba and others have shown, the commercial attention and professional anxieties around those books have been growing since the early twentieth century. But the transition of 'debut' to a more commodity-oriented definition suggests an accompanying psychological shift, in which 'coming out' refers to the thing more than the act. On the other hand, its contemporary use allows us to consider the extent to which its former connotations are also transferred from the person to the book.

The *Oxford English Dictionary* includes only single definitions for either the English noun or verb form of *début*, as adapted from the French. As a verb, it refers to the act as described above: 'to make one's début; to "come out"'. As a noun, the *OED* acknowledges only its reference to the person: 'Entry into society; first appearance in public of an actor, actress, or other performer.' The emphasis on the person's introduction into either society or public links the two parts of this definition and suggests that artistic debuts might be conceived just as hierarchically as social ones. The latter has a longer history perhaps, codified in a debutante tradition beginning in sixteenth-century England and persisting in various communities. Mary Michaels O. Estrada describes historical debutante practice as 'a rite of passage whereby an aristocratic young girl of marriageable age, about fourteen or fifteen, was presented to society with the expectation that a suitor and, with luck, a husband, would manifest himself shortly thereafter'.[14] Although Elizabeth II discontinued royal court debuts in 1958, the custom is still widespread in the United States, where Estrada says 'every major southern city has its debutante ball and society', and in Central and South American or Filipino coming-of-age rituals for young women.[15] As with the dictionary definitions above, the legacy of this background for cultural debuts – whether in music, dance, theatre, or literature – is in the notion of a person's entry and acceptance into a community. In this way, fixation on the moment of 'coming out', either in social or artistic contexts, reinforces both the standards of acceptability and the adjudicating role of an establishment into which one enters.

These implications are made explicit in the language regarding poetry debuts. Poets who have succeeded in publishing their debut often regard their first book, like Anna Leahy, as 'a distinct career accomplishment, a benchmark of sorts'.[16] Publishers, like those who prepared Arts Council England's 2010 *Mapping Contemporary Poetry* report, are also apt to emphasise presses' central role in debut culture, whereby a first collection 'appears with the imprimatur of a publishing house which is a species of "guarantor", providing a "license" authorising the poet'.[17] In this way, as Zuba puts it, the debutant poet 'resembles nothing so much as a professional who has just passed the examination that assures her of a career'.[18] The perception of publishers as gatekeepers or 'guarantors' makes the debut an extremely effective tool for regulating entry to what Charles Bernstein famously described as 'official verse culture'.[19] While the recent upsurge in debut publishing and acclaim has clearly been an opportunity for diversifying that culture, it is simultaneously an opportunity for greater policing of the boundary that debuts seem to mark and for re-affirming pecking orders inherent to debut-speak. More visible debuts necessarily lead to more debutantism.

The marketing blurbs, reviews, and judges' comments for first collections are rife with debut-speak cliché. As Zuba observes, words like 'groundbreaking' and 'dazzling' crop up in endless permutations.[20] Some first books are 'thrilling' or 'stunning', others 'unflinching' or 'luminous'. Jacket copy for five of the nine Faber debuts since 2008 use the word 'inventive'. Beyond the lack of inventiveness in these banal descriptors, promotional language also amplifies the debut's regulatory function in its praise tinged with condescension. Frequent emphasis on formal achievement – the 'high-wire act of verbal dexterity and inventive syntax' or 'formally adventurous and wide-ranging' work of Toby Martinez de las Rivas's *Terror* (2014), for example – reassures potential readers that a poet has met an approved craft standard, while reinforcing the authority of that approval. As Zuba observes, 'the technical mastery of a poetic debut' can 'serve as evidence of "promise"', while marking implicitly the debutant's distance from fulfilling it just yet. In this way, technical accomplishment serves 'as both the basis for [a poet's] achievement and its limitation'.[21] The Yale Younger Poets series, the oldest of many dozen first-book competitions in the United States, institutionalised this sense of anticipation in its original statement of purpose, as a series meant to 'include only such verse as seems to give the fairest promise for the future of American poetry'.[22] 'Impressive' is another common and equally backhanded substitute for 'promise'. Even where it isn't intended to patronise, such language circumscribes debut status. While review 'round-ups' qualify opinions by comparing first books as a separate category, the Eliot judges pronounce the respective debut winners in 2015, 2017, and 2018 as 'very erudite', 'compellingly assured', and 'fully-formed'.[23] Elsewhere, hollow comments on a debut poet's 'significance' or 'substance' play their part in the coded ritual by which poetry society welcomes new members. Well before this current wave of debut fever, W. H. Auden aired his own suspicions of debut-speak, upon taking up the Yale Younger Poets editorship in 1947: 'These introductions always sound awful, and the whole idea that a new poet should be introduced by an older one as if he were a debutante or a new face cream, deplorable and false.'[24] Auden's fear that first collections would be treated like debuts now seems prophetic to the point of inevitability, speaking from a time before that label had taken hold. In the past few decades, in blurbs, reviews, and judges' comments, the 'deplorable and false' introduction of new poets by established ones has become as formalised as any debutante ball.

Emerging: Before and After

For writers themselves, the growing pressures of debut culture often stem from the perceived boundary embodied by the first book. While later collections might come to define a career, Zuba suggests, 'the first settles the question of whether the poetic career will exist at all'.[25] And the rigidity of this line between having published one's debut or not is experienced by poets on either side of it. Before the debut, orientation towards that goal has been instilled by the century-long spread of writing programmes and first-book competitions in the United States. Although prizes that lead directly to debut publication are rare in the United Kingdom, the growth of writing programmes in the past 50 years has also been supplemented by the Eric Gregory Awards for pre-debut poets (established in 1960) and various mentorship schemes (discussed in detail in Chapter 12). Although these structures are undoubtedly successful in the training and encouragement they aim to provide, they often cannot avoid complicity in debut fixation, in so far as the desire for publication drives the market for their tuition and – in the case of masters' degrees, especially – provides an easy model for a 'book-length' final assessment. The risk of a kind of debut grooming is spelled out in Peter Riley's critique of what he calls the 'Gregory Trail' for young British poets: 'it generally starts from a magazine which carries some prestige, goes into the [Eric Gregory] award, and, for some, on to greater things, such as Faber and Faber and/or top prestige in general. It is a career boost.'[26] Whether or not a poet aims consciously (or self-consciously) for 'greater things', these institutions are sustained by their desirability.

Beyond the debut, poets are often no less sensitive to its force, though the passing of that milestone is frequently accompanied by mixed feelings. As Chase Twichell reflects in *The Handbook of Creative Writing* (2014):

> When your work begins to be accepted by magazines, and when you publish a first book, it's a heady time. What happens next? Well, actually, that's about it. What happens after publication is nothing much. It's all a big let-down. Poets are often surprised to find themselves a bit depressed.[27]

Others articulate this tension through the sort of labels used to categorise debutantes. As Nancy Kuhl puts it (in the conversation on first-book culture with Anna Leahy cited above):

> It might be said that we are all always emerging, but at what point has one *emerged*? And after emerging, then what? Has Nicole [Cooley], with her third collection now forthcoming, slipped or propelled herself into that other dubious category: *mid-career*?[28]

In many cases, writers' frustration in the mid-career no-man's-land is linked to disproportionate support for debut writers through the structures discussed above. In the funding context of the United Kingdom, Clare Pollard's call for 'art bodies to start supporting "emerged" poets as actively as those who are "emerging"' is echoed in David Wheatley's sense of the problem:[29]

> The writing of poetry by apprentice writers as a vocational exercise is one that grant-aiding bodies may wish to subsidise, but the underwriting of a poet's fortunes once we reach the afterlife of literary history is beyond the power of any Arts Council. It is the awkward stage of 'emergence' midway between these poles, that is the problem.[30]

At the same time, well-meaning analysis like that of 'Mapping Poetic Emergence 1.0', produced in 2013 by Aberystwyth University, also highlights the extent to which career trajectories appear standardised around key 'stages'. Although the authors of this study stress that 'poetic emergence is distinct from poetic development', the three 'bands of emergence' they identify are that of 'pre-collection poets', 'first-collection poets', and 'multi-collection poets'.[31] While Zuba is obviously right in suggesting that 'career is never more at issue than in the first book', this debut dogma maintains its force through constant reiteration by poetry's institutions and by poets themselves.[32]

Making It New

The growing symbolic power of the debut collection is also symptomatic of wider cultural obsessions with newness and innovation. As noted earlier, debut rhetoric has a longer history in relation to performing arts – dance, theatre, and music especially. For the latter, the importance of 'debut' albums for marketing and career trajectories prefigures in many ways the expectations placed on a poet's first major release. In their study of contemporary music economies, Hugh Dauncey and Philippe Le Guern warn of the 'obsession with the "unsigned"' and 'damaging practices' that lead record companies to 'go on signing and dropping acts and having "hits" with a tiny percentage'.[33] This vicious cycle, with labels hedging their bets in hopes that some new artist will justify such speculation, offers a striking analogy for those concerned by the number of debut collections rushed out by some presses, and the general lack of support for writers who might not have a 'hit' with their first attempt. For record labels or poetry publishers susceptible to this debut culture, as Dauncey and Le Guern put it, 'there is almost more to be gained from being associated with the "next big thing" than there is from being associated with existing stars.'[34]

Beyond the creative industries, such fixations are even more rampant among tech and finance, in frantic speculation over new gadgets, new start-ups, or stock market 'debuts'. Few organisations are immune to the obsession with newness that André Spicer describes as 'neocracy', in which 'a steady stream of new structures, new policies, new initiatives, new strategies, new people, new anything' means that individual 'neocrats' increasingly 'gain authority by having some special connection with the new'.[35] As with poetry, much of this neocratic posturing occurs rhetorically, in 'innovation talk', where, according to Evgeny Morozov, 'all innovation is treated as inherently good in itself, regardless of its social or political consequences. After all, innovation is progress – and how can progress be bad?'[36] Online media platforms, as discussed in Chapter 3, provide essential tools and incentives for the spread of such discourse. Quickening news cycles, meme culture, virality, and the clout of obscure metrics like Twitter 'trends' translate the ad-driven demand for clicks and views into an addiction with finding or attaching oneself to the next big thing. In their recent survey of *Celebrity, Aspiration & Contemporary Youth* (2018), Heather Mendick, Kim Allen, Laura Harvey, and Aisha Ahmad identify the problems created by 'entrepreneurialism success discourse' in the context of austerity.[37] Although such language will be the focus of Chapters 11 and 12, it is worth acknowledging here the particular pressure it creates for young people and aspiring poets among them. Like the preoccupation documented by Mendick et al. of young people with online celebrity breakthroughs, the apparently absolute boundary of the poetic debut and its status as a marker of individual achievement risks putting more strain on writers 'who experience constraints in their life but feel that they must rely on themselves to overcome them'.[38]

The End of Beginnings?

These challenges return us to the example at the start. The 'revelation' of Hannah Sullivan's *Three Poems* shows, in its treatment as an anomaly, the degree to which debut culture has been systematised. Poets in the 'pre-collection' stage are advised incessantly to accumulate a 'track record' of magazine publications, prizes, an online presence, or performance experience before approaching publishers. Once the debut debuts, the rhetoric of discovery and approval is extended in ways that also confirm the authority of an established community accepting its newly credentialed member. The debut's speculative value is then inflated (or not) by any who wish to invest their personal enthusiasm. Old and new media benefit, in turn, from these layers of official and unofficial comment. At last, the machine sets its sights on the next 'next big thing'. Rather than disproving these rules, the reception of Sullivan's book demonstrates the extent to which the debut system reconfigures itself to accommodate novelty. And yet, Zuba remains positive about poets' agency within this system, as evident in the negotiations of insider/outsider status he reads in many debuts:

> Many beginning poets on both sides of the divide grapple in interesting, and interestingly similar, ways with the problem of vocational integrity at a moment so dominated by institutional literary practice that opposition to it is often indistinguishable from the central forms it takes.[39]

In other words, there is a sense that debut culture might be equally defined, for poets at least, by resistance to it. As Zuba puts it, the imperative of that debut moment is strong enough to refigure such 'opposition' (or exceptions like Sullivan) as 'indistinguishable' from its institutionalised forms. If there is a quintessential narrative of debuts, it is of the poet styled as 'outsider' coming in. As the metaphor of debutantism implies, debut culture is driven by the twin impulses of regulation and assimilation.

Although I am wary of concluding with speculation on the future of poetry debuts, their unprecedented prize success in recent years raises practical issues that make such a feverish pitch hard to sustain. Most immediately, the debut wins of prizes like the Eliot, Griffin, and Costa, which hadn't previously been awarded to first books, create a conundrum for prizes specific to debuts. The fiction side of the Costa Awards is a case in point, with separate 'novel' and 'first novel' winners that both compete for the overall 'book of the year'. As Claire Squires points out, 'the very idea of having a separate category for the novel and the first novel starts to unravel if the first novel section winner goes on to win the main award' – as it has done, three times now.[40] The Forward Prizes of the United Kingdom are in a similarly strained position, awarding separate prizes for 'the best collection of poetry' and 'the best first collection of poetry'. Although debuts are not specifically excluded from the 'best collection' prize, in practice the distinction has been easier to accept without books from the Forward 'first collection' shortlist winning the TS Eliot's overall 'best collection' prize. More concerningly for other debut awards, and for the assumptions of debut culture more widely, the FAQ section of the Forward Prizes' entry guidelines also suggest a growing instability for the category itself. Questions about the eligibility of a 'first collection' after previous publications of a 'very short poetry book/pamphlet/chapbook' are answered easily enough with a page-count boundary of 40 (though see Chapter 4). Other submissions, however, by writers with previous books of poetry for children or previous books that combined poetry with other genres, will be 'considered on a case-by-case basis'.[41] The rise of self-publishing and online poetry platforms have required similar contortions by other prizes, which collectively suggest the debut boundary may be blurring.

Ten years ago, an article in the *Guardian/Observer* could credibly state that 'getting a first novel published – and publicised – is harder than ever before'.[42] While this might still feel true for writers in an ever more crowded field, the argument that publishers (in 2007) were more risk-adverse and less willing to take a chance on new writers seems harder to justify amid the media frenzy around recent fiction and poetry debuts. By 2016, the interest in debuts was such that Bloodaxe, the most prolific poetry publisher of the United Kingdom, quietly added a clause to their submissions page, explaining that they were 'no longer able to take on poets who have already published book-length collections with other publishers'.[43] Across a decade in which publishers went from neglecting new writers to this opposite extreme, the language of contemporary debut culture has heightened both the possibilities and pressures for debut poets. This double edge is clear in the redressing of historical biases being followed by claims of more generic 'diversity' or in the extent to which debut's presumed innovations come at the expense of longer-term support. Of course, there's no sense arguing against the publication of first books as such, but the way they are promoted and discussed could be more aware of the tendencies noted above and of the burden that debut culture places on poets before and long after. A greater emphasis on the collaborative nature of publishing and the complex realities behind seemingly overnight successes might also help. For now, the only certainty is poetry's stake in future debuts, whatever they bring.

Notes

1. Quoted in various media reports, including Sian Cain, '"A star is born": TS Eliot prize goes to Hannah Sullivan's debut', *Guardian* (14 January 2019).
2. Jesse Zuba, *The First Book: Twentieth-Century Poetic Careers in America* (Princeton, NJ: Princeton University Press, 2016), 2.
3. See Hentea's 'Late Modernist Debuts: Publishing and Professionalizing Young Novelists in 1920s Britain', *Book History* vol. 14 (2011), 167–86.
4. Cain, 'A star is born', *Guardian* (14 January 2019).
5. Zuba, *The First Book*, 163.
6. 'T. S. Eliot Prize Shortlist Is Announced', *Poetry Society* website (18 October 2018).
7. Joanna Lee, 'Faber Poetry Debuts 2018', *Faber & Faber* blog (13 December 2017).
8. Sandeep Parmar, 'Why the TS Eliot prize shortlist hails a return to the status quo', *Guardian* (20 October 2017).
9. Spring 2016, 5. Riordan's comments in *Poetry Review* are offered in the context of announcing 'a series of joint editorships, which *per se* involve a degree of diversity', as opposed to magazines that might actively seek out more diverse submissions ('Such "soliciting" of contributions is fine at creating a semblance of diversity, of the kind readily recognised by funding bodies.' (6)
10. David Wheatley, *Contemporary British Poetry* (Basingstoke: Palgrave, 2014), 65.
11. Since 'debuts' aren't registered as a separate category for sales, these estimates are based on the identifying language of individual presses' catalogues. Again, the challenge with definitively categorising individual books as a 'debut' is taken up later in this chapter.
12. See, for instance, Gerrit Henry's review article 'Starting from Scratch', *Poetry* vol. 124, no. 5 (August 1974), 292–99; or Sandra M. Gilbert's 'Out of the Women's Museum', *Poetry* vol. 127, no. 1 (October 1975), 44–55. Of the 167 items (including articles, reviews, or poems) in which the word has occurred in *Poetry*, which began in 1912, 142 of them (or over 85 per cent) have been since 1974.
13. Data from newspaper and journal archive searches, also corroborated by Google's Ngram Viewer, which charts the frequency of occurrences across a broad English corpus.
14. Estrada, 'Debutante', *The Companion to Southern Literature*, ed. Joseph M. Flora and Lucinda H. MacKethan (Baton Rouge: Louisiana State University Press, 2002), 198.
15. Ibid.
16. Anna Leahy, Kate Greenstreet, Nancy Kuhl, and Nicole Cooley, 'A Conversation on the (Re)Emerging Poet: First Books and What's Next', *Bookslut* (January 2009).
17. Simon Thirsk, Michael Schmidt, and Jeremy Poynting, *Mapping Contemporary Poetry* (London: Arts Council England, 2010), 9.
18. Zuba, *The First Book*, 8, 77.
19. Bernstein, 'The Academy in Peril', *Content's Dream: Essays 1975–1984* (Evanston, IL: Northwestern University Press, 1986), 246.
20. Zuba, *The First Book*, 163.
21. Ibid., 83.

22 Qtd in Kevin Larimer, 'A Culture of Competition: Some Notes on Writing Contests & Literary Publishing', *Literary Publishing in the Twenty-First Century*, ed. Travis Kurowski, Wayne Miller, and Kevin Prufer (Minneapolis, MN: Milkweed Editions, 2016), 203.
23 Pascale Petit on Sarah Howe (qtd in Mark Brown, *Guardian*, 11 January 2016); Bill Herbert on Ocean Vuong (qtd in Sian Cain, *Guardian*, 15 January 2018); and Sinéad Morrissey on Hannah Sullivan (qtd in Sian Cain, *Guardian*, 14 January 2019). Among the pandering language of debut 'round-ups', *Poets & Writers*' lists are published annually with headlines like 'That Glittering Possibility' (2005), 'First Things First' (2009), and 'Breaking Through the Noise' (2013).
24 Letter to Eugene Davidson, qtd in George Bradley (ed.), *The Yale Younger Poets Anthology* (New Haven, CT: Yale University Press, 1998), lix.
25 Zuba, *The First Book*, 8.
26 Peter Riley, 'The Youth Tactic', *Fortnightly Review* (27 April 2013).
27 Chase Twichell, 'American PoBiz', *The Handbook of Creative Writing* (Edinburgh: Edinburgh University Press, 2014), 437.
28 Leahy et al., 'A Conversation on the (Re)Emerging Poet', *Bookslut*.
29 Clare Pollard, 'The Health of Poetry', personal website (20 May 2013).
30 Wheatley, *Contemporary British Poetry*, 168.
31 Peter Barry, Matthew Jarvis, Kathryn Gray, and Bronwen Williams, 'Mapping Poetic Emergence, Discussion Document: Version 1.0', *Devolved Voices: Welsh Poetry in English since 1997* (March 2013).
32 Zuba, *The First Book*, 8.
33 Hugh Dauncey and Philippe Le Guern, 'Conclusion', *Stereo: Comparative Perspectives on the Sociological Study of Popular Music in France and Britain*, ed, Hugh Dauncey and Philippe Le Guern (Oxford: Routledge, 2011), 87.
34 Ibid., 87.
35 André Spicer, *Business Bullshit* (Oxford: Routledge, 2018), 104.
36 Evgeny Morozov, *To Save Everything, Click Here: Technology, Solutionism and the Urge to Fix Problems that Don't Exist* (London: Allen Lane, 2013), 167.
37 Heather Mendick, Kim Allen, Laura Harvey and Aisha Ahmad, *Celebrity, Aspiration & Contemporary Youth: Education and Inequality in an Era of Austerity* (London: Bloomsbury, 2018), 93.
38 Ibid., 93.
39 Zuba, *The First Book*, 70.
40 Claire Squires, *Marketing Literature: The Making of Contemporary Writing in Britain* (Basingstoke: Palgrave, 2007), 99. The three winners of the 'first novel' and overall prize have been Kate Atkinson (1995), Stef Penney (2006), and Nathan Filer (2013).
41 'Forward Prizes FAQ', Forward Arts Foundation website.
42 Kate Kellaway, 'That difficult first novel', *Guardian/Observer* (25 March 2007).
43 'Contact / Editorial' page, Bloodaxe Books website.

PART III

NEW POLICY

Chapter 7

CREATIVE CAPITALS: THE PLACE OF CITIES IN GLOBAL POETRY NETWORKS

Poetry's sense of place is often in tension with claims for its universality. Someone as deeply concerned with geographical particulars as William Wordsworth also insists that poetry's 'object is truth, not individual and local, but general, and operative'.[1] In contemporary debates, the abstract relationship between universals and particulars takes on new material dimensions in the relationship between local and global politics, economics, and culture. One curious consequence of this legacy is a latent continuity between the idealism of Romantic era poets or philosophers and utopian claims for global connectedness in recent decades. In his foundational survey, *The Rise of the Network Society* (first published in 1996), Manuel Castells describes the impact of then-emergent technologies:

> The new communications system radically transforms space and time, the fundamental dimensions of human life. Localities become disembodied from their cultural, historical, geographical meaning, and reintegrated into functional networks.[2]

Frances Cairncross's *The Death of Distance: How the Communications Revolution Will Change Our Lives* (1997) also finds wireless technologies 'killing location, putting the world in our pockets'.[3] Beyond the technological emphasis, Thomas Friedman's bestselling *The World Is Flat: A Brief History of the Twenty-First Century* (2005) argues that 'the global competitive playing field was being levelled' through a process 'connecting all the knowledge centers of the planet together into a single global network'.[4] Behind this proliferation of millennial forecasts lingers the media theorist Marshall McLuhan's famous declaration, in 1962, that 'since the telegraph and radio, the globe has contracted, spatially, into a single large village'.[5]

Whatever specific developments are responsible for these supposedly fundamental shifts, the dream (or nightmare) of a global network made up of 'disembodied' or 'killed' localities cannot be disentangled from a history of universalist ambitions in Western philosophy – ambitions which have often been articulated in relation to poetry. In its most direct expression, Aristotle's sense of poetry's distinctive concern with the 'universal' is expanded by Percy Bysshe Shelley's insistence in *The Defence of Poetry* (1840), for example, by which 'a poet participates in the eternal, the infinite, and the one; as far as relates to his conceptions, time and place and number are not'.[6] In various contemporary guises, these sentiments persist intact. Suggestions that 'when you read literature, you enter a republic of the imagination that transcends time and space' (from a 2014 *Atlantic* article) or that in reading lyric poetry 'the human being becomes a set of warring passions independent of time and space' (in Helen Vendler's *Soul Says*, from 1995) not only echo Shelley's idealism, but dovetail with some of the more poetic claims of globalisation evangelists.[7] The 'radical transformation' described earlier by Castells means that 'the *space of flows* and *timeless time* are the material foundations of a new culture'.[8] More often, perhaps, recent poetry discourse tempers such hyperbolic language into, on the one hand, cosy re-assertions of poetry's generic humanistic value, and on the other, more practical affirmations of its accessibility. An advertisement for a community workshop called 'Poetry for Anyone and Everyone' taught at the barter-based Trade School, Indianapolis, for instance, tells potential students that 'poetry happens to be the cheapest, most portable art form'.[9] From this more pragmatic angle, poetry's apparent boundlessness is also easily linked to technological developments that have opened worldwide markets. 'In our present age of multimedia entertainment, poetry is an art form nearly free of materials,' writes Rachel Galvin on Poets.org.[10] Or for social media contexts specifically, an article for *Kickstarter*'s online magazine is hardly alone in suggesting that 'poetry, with its intensity, portability, and succinctness, seems like a natural fit for our 140-character attention span'.[11]

This chapter considers the changing role of cities within these widening networks, in relation to claims for poetry's geographical accessibility. If the parallel narratives of globalisation and poetry's availability to 'anyone and everyone' are linked by new technology, the status of cities as traditional sites of culture would appear to be at stake. In the supposedly 'level playing field' of the digital age, to what extent does poetry as an industry still depend upon the physical infrastructure and face-to-face interactions that cities provide as traditional centres of culture? Any attempt to answer requires a fresh examination of the political and commercial repercussions for poetry's urban preoccupations, in terms of progressive traditions as well as economic constraints. Where previous chapters examined the effect of online platforms on poetry production, distribution, and reception, the discussion here focuses on the ways in which cities have consolidated their cultural capital through physical institutions, funded resources, and other real-world platforms. In this way, the relationship between poetry and cities returns us to broader questions regarding its material contexts. Exploring 'the city' through five prevalent conceptions – the poetic city, the networked city, the virtual city, the radical city, and the creative city – I suggest ways in which these imbricated layers provide new spaces (and time) for contemporary poetry culture. Rather than viewing the global reach of online poetry communities as a threat to cities' function as creative hubs, the advantages they offer poets and publishers are, like cities themselves, likely only to keep growing.

The Poetic City

I begin with a potted, well-known history – since understanding the relationship between contemporary poetry culture and the city begins with acknowledging the role that poetry has long played in defining urban experience. Despite its rural focus, the pastoral tradition might be the first and most enduring mode by which European writers approach city life, primarily by way of rural–urban antithesis. Early bucolic models by classical Greek poets in Hesiod and Theocritus establish this binary premise implicitly, offering unrealistic images of rural life to mostly urban audiences, while the Roman poet Virgil introduces more direct and politically charged comparisons. The first of his *Eclogues*, for instance, enacts a conversation between shepherds complaining about having to leave their flocks to conduct business in 'the thankless town' and the shame in appealing to Rome (the 'god' of cities) for their livelihood.[12] In modern verse, this city-centric dichotomy survives in British poetry especially, setting rural landscapes against visions of London. From the nineteenth century onwards, as Terry Gifford writes, 'there can be no doubt that, for the largely urban readers of these representations of English countryside, they acted as a form of pastoral escape from their own urbanised realities.'[13]

Cities became a more direct concern for poets of the Romantic period as they responded to the effects of urbanisation and large-scale industrialisation. For Londoner William Blake, the rural–urban divide is mapped pointedly across *Songs of Innocence and Experience* (1789), from the pastoral 'innocence' of the first volume – which begins with 'The Shepherd', 'The Ecchoing Green', and 'The Lamb' – to the gritty 'experience' of poems like 'London' in the second sequence, where the cries of infants, chimney-sweepers, and 'young Harlot[s]' mingle in 'each charter'd street'. Moral implications are preserved in the distinction between 'England's pleasant pastures' and the 'dark Satanic mills' in Blake's poem that became lyrics for 'Jerusalem', the unofficial national anthem. From a rural perspective, Wordsworth's fraught relationship with the capital is similarly framed by an attention to class and labour conditions, summarised in the 1800 Preface to *Lyrical Ballads*, with its lament for 'the encreasing [*sic*] accumulation of men in cities, where the uniformity of their occupations produces a craving for extraordinary incident which the rapid communication of intelligence hourly gratifies'. While the 'rapid communication' and associated cravings connecting city-dwellers are an early recognition of the networked city and virtual city, discussed in those sections below, Wordsworth's emphasis on 'uniformity' points to more intangible forces of alienation. Like Blake's 'charter'd' streets, Wordsworth's conception of the modern city is overlain with new abstractions of economic capital. Among these, E. P. Thompson's classic essay, 'Time, Work-Discipline, and Industrial Capitalism' (1967), highlights the degree to which cities were transformed in the nineteenth century not only by material expansion and population growth, but also by the standardisation of clock times and world time zones. Thompson concludes with Wordsworth's attack in *The Prelude* (from Book V in the 1805 edition) on 'watchful men / And skilful in the usury of time'.[14] Again, Thompson shows the poet's awareness of the effect these changes would have on waged labour and awareness of the extent to which the growth of modern cities depended on chartered and time-bound uniformity.

As European cities continued to develop, abstract (and mostly negative) perspectives on urbanisation gave way to more concrete depictions of lived experience in the modern metropolis. Charles Baudelaire's *Les Fleurs du Mal* (1857) provided perhaps the most influential template, with poems immersed in city nightscapes sordid enough for French courts to ban publication of six of them until 1949. In the meantime, several generations of symbolist and modernist poets adapted Baudelaire's urban gaze to new poetic forms. Hope Mirrlees's *Paris: A Poem* (1919) and T. S. Eliot's *The Waste Land* (1922) are just two prominent multilingual long poems bringing Parisian influence to London, where both volumes were published by Virginia and Leonard Woolf's Hogarth Press. While Baudelaire and Eliot's dark flora and fauna or Guillaume Apollinaire's 'Shepherdess O Eiffel Tower' (from *Zone*, 1913) brought city poetry full circle to an alternative version of 'counter-' or 'urban pastoral', the concentration of publishing activity in these cities provided the infrastructure to ensure their self-conscious urban lyricism would remain a conspicuous mode throughout the twentieth century. More generally, these 2,000 years of poetic urbanity have bolstered the effects of what Jack Halberstam has dubbed 'metronormativity'. For Halberstam – writing in the context of queer histories that closely connect with notions of the poetic or artistic city – the 'locational rhetoric' of a rural–urban divide and 'the metronormative story of migration from "country" to "town"' regulates access to ways of living and being, while rendering 'nonmetropolitan' subjectivities less visible.[15]

The Networked City

Theories of a globally networked society around the turn of the millennium were preceded from the 1980s onwards by urban historians applying network models to modern industrial cities. A network, in its broadest definition, comprises a set of connections and control points, making it possible for systems to run efficiently and at scale. At the city scale, networks mean infrastructure. Urban planning and new technologies in the late nineteenth and early twentieth century made it both possible and necessary to approach urban development in a more holistic way. In turn, these 'networked infrastructure systems' became, according to Oliver Coutard and Jonathan Rutherford, 'at once a site, an instrument, and an outcome of urban economic production and expansion, increasing social inequalities, and environmental transformation.'[16] For good and ill, these city networks have only been more deeply embedded since.

Baron Georges-Eugène Haussmann's reconfiguration of Paris boulevards from the 1850s is a well-known example, not least because Baudelaire's poetic response to these changes captured so immediately the sense of disruption they posed to urban experience. Other new transport networks changed the space of urban poetry as well, including underground systems in London (opened in 1863) and Paris (from 1900) – the latter featuring most famously in Ezra Pound's 'In a Station of the Metro' (1913). Mirrlees's *Paris: A Poem* also begins on a metro line opened just a few years prior. Other infrastructural developments would have a more indirect but undeniable impact on poetry production, from modern sewer systems to communication systems, to lighting and electricity more generally. Into the early twentieth century, the 'garden cities' movement and post-war 'new towns' showed the extent to which urban network ideology might go beyond specific technologies to planning and zoning initiatives on a large scale.

These city-wide developments provided an essential foundation for what we might think of as the modern poetry infrastructure emerging in the same period. Although cities had long offered significant cultural networks in the form of publishers and booksellers or through coffee house and pub connections for writers in previous centuries, the developments above were crucial to the proliferation of 'little magazines', small press publishing, and the rise of poetry performance across the twentieth century. Today, the robustness of this poetry infrastructure helps to account for the disproportionate visibility of city-based poets and publishers. Since 2008, 27 per cent of shortlisted poets for the four major UK poetry book prizes (Costa, Eliot, and Forward Best Collection and First Collection) have been London-based. Given that London's population makes up only 12 per cent to 13 per cent of the country, this means the capital is represented by more than double its proportion. In terms of concrete infrastructure, this disparity is compounded by the fact that nearly 60 per cent of the shortlisted books (and 64.4 per cent of winning books) in this period were from London publishers. Press coverage, moreover, suggests the concentration has grown in this period: in 2008, only 9 of the 52 poets with work reviewed in the *Guardian* were based in the capital. By 2018, more than half of reviews (14 of 27) focused on Londoners. Beyond publishing and reviews, the National Poetry Library, Poetry School, Poetry Translation Centre, British Library, Free Word Centre, performance networks, national events, contemporary versions of modernist café culture in the Troubadour Café or Poetry Society's Poetry Café, and countless other organisations provide London with unique and indispensable resources.[17]

Comparable poetry infrastructures in US metropolitan areas over the twentieth century show the extent to which these networks quickly connect poetry resources between cities. Respective mid-century 'renaissances' in Chicago, San Francisco, or New York highlight the dependence of poetry communities on a combination of non-poetry-specific amenities and local cultural resources, sympathetic bookshops, performance venues, and universities for poetry movements or communities that have thrived in these and other urban hubs. While the so-called Chicago or New York School poets developed in ways specific to their historical and urban contexts, Beat writers congregating in San Francisco's City Lights Bookstore, Six Gallery, or Kenneth Rexroth's apartment included writers who had already connected in New York's Greenwich Village and who depended on links with Chicago, where Rexroth was from and where controversy around publication in the *Chicago Review* brought these writers to national attention.

The global shift towards a service economy in recent decades, as Jefferey M. Sellers writes, has only exacerbated the extent to which any city now 'operates as a node in vast networks of translocal markets, organizations, communications, and distribution'.[18] A parallel drive towards strengthening these metropolis-noded global networks from the perspective of a poetic economy can also be traced across the past 10 years. In 2009, Stephanie Burt's lecture on 'Transatlantic Disconnections' at the University of Glasgow (later reprinted in *PN Review*) called for improved links between UK and North American poets, acknowledging the effect of infrastructure, in so far as 'altered, sometimes reduced, circumstances in the publishing world have also diminished the transatlantic element in the business of poetry'.[19] Since then, *Poetry Review* (founded in London in 1912) and *Poetry* (founded in Chicago the same year) have had an ongoing exchange of material reprinted in the magazines. Since 2014, *Poetry* has also published a series of special issues focused on UK (2014), Irish (2015), and New Zealand poets (2018), the latter co-edited by Burt herself. Through this range of physical and textual means, contemporary poetry's infrastructure supports a global network within which city hubs are often better connected with each other internationally than they are with closer rural regions.

The Virtual City

On the other hand, online networks have increasingly been expected to compensate for the historical centralisation of material resources. Cairncross's 'death of distance' or Friedman's promise of a levelled playing field have led to a prevailing sense that online sales, marketing, and distribution, along with online social networks and other communication technologies, now make it possible for artists to develop careers regardless of location. While the conception of poetry as an especially 'portable' art form ought to be undermined by the measurable benefit of real resources and support networks for poets in major cities, there are also ways in which the rise of virtual communities contributes to the consolidation of resources and cultural capital in the real world. Like the new urban transportation networks mentioned above, communication technologies have played a key role in urbanisation and the shaping of cities, since well before fast and reliable internet access. Older modes of transmission – from landline telephony to early fax and cellular technology – encouraged remote working and suburban flight, which left many city centres culturally desolate by the later twentieth century. By the end of the century, in the contexts of economic globalisation and several years before the explosion of mainstream social media platforms, this left many regions with a sense of community disconnect and loss of social capital, as documented in Robert Putnam's seminal account, *Bowling Alone: The Collapse and Revival of American Community* (2000). At the same time, the first iterations of what would become the early twenty-first century's social media explosion were already emerging. More importantly, these new virtual spaces were modelling themselves explicitly on urban networks.

Geocities was the most successful web-based social platform in the late 1990s. After launching with a Beverly Hills focus in 1995, the online realm quickly expanded to include twenty-nine 'cities' (many named after actual cities), within which 'homesteaders' could choose the location for their personal websites. Users interested in poetry, for example, might find a welcome home in 'Paris', 'Athens', or 'Soho', which listed the arts and writing among communal interests. When Yahoo purchased (and controversially reconfigured) Geocities for $3.57 million in 1999, the network had grown to the point of dividing these virtual cities into suburbs and even individual blocks. One immediate legacy of Geocities was the model's extension to even more literal simulations of city networks, like Amsterdam's popular 'Digital City' (De Digitale Stad, or DDS, 1994–2001). More generally, the metronormative impulse to create virtual spaces in an urban image was manifest in the enormous popularity of urban planning games like *SimCity* and especially the increased scope of *SimCity 2000*, launched in 1993.[20] In other genres, action games like the *Grand Theft Auto* series (launched in 1997) are set in fictionalised versions of New York, Miami, or other US cities, while car-based games like *Driver* (1999) and *Getaway* (2002) or later adventure series like *Assassin's Creed* (from 2007) pushed technology with large-scale recreations of actual cities. Remote as these cultural texts might seem from poetry production, from Geocities to *Minecraft* to the online cities of *Second Life*, they show the extent to which virtual spaces are consistently oriented towards the urban centres where their studios and designers are based. In more recent years, the advent of location-based applications using smartphone GPS has closed this loop, augmenting real cities with new virtual connections, and with Google Maps or *Pokémon Go* showing as great an urban bias in their availability as Airbnb or Uber. Since 2010, those visiting large cities for their cultural resources might had the strange experience of being 'welcomed' by Facebook with a list of places their 'friends' had already been.

Another overlooked reality behind claims of a virtual level playing field is the persistent disparity in basic internet access for rural versus metropolitan users. A 2017 study of broadband use by professional artists in rural Scotland highlights a 'penalty of distance' (contradicting the 'death of distance' above) in terms of both reliability and speed, which might be twice as fast in cities.[21] The paradoxically greater need for access for professional use outside cities is acutely felt by the artists interviewed in the study: 'Broadband connectivity is essential given they may not be able to network in person in the way their urban counterparts can by, for example, attending industry events and exhibitions.'[22] The study also notes the heightened dependence on broadband in areas with limited cellular data coverage. Contrary to the open online global community touted by technology providers, the inability to view or upload media files, take part in video calls, or reliably use other online tools only adds to practitioners' sense of disconnectedness from urban creative networks that might be physically inaccessible for any number of reasons.

The Radical City

The rise of modern cities as concentrated networks of economic power has also been a story of resistance. As Stephen Tedeschi's recent study of *Urbanization and English Romantic Poetry* (2018) shows, poets have played a crucial role in offering 'alternative ways of thinking about urbanization' from more or less the moment urbanisation emerges as a seemingly self-evident ideology.²³ Against prevailing narratives which posit the industrial city as a 'natural' or 'necessary' symptom of human progress, poets living through the urban upheaval of the eighteenth and nineteenth centuries were loosely united by their sense that these developments were both 'historical and subject to reform'. By various means and modes, writers took up the task of showing that, as Tedeschi puts it: 'Other kinds of urbanization and other kinds of cities were possible.'²⁴ While specific historical moments have occasioned poetic expressions of resistance ever since – from Baudelaire's reaction to Haussmann's remaking of Paris to the modernist concerns with infrastructure noted above – the later twentieth century saw increasing attempts to reclaim urban spaces, retaining poetry as an important tool for those occupations. In contemporary writing, the proliferation of mostly Marxist, mostly European thinking about urban experience persists in a more general, oddly marketable idea of the city as an inherently radical space.

Twentieth-century continental theorists regarded as crucial to these alternative discourses looked to earlier writers, and poets especially, for re-visions of the city, building upon their emphasis on urban development's historical and material contingencies. Walter Benjamin in the 1920s and 1930s, followed by Guy Debord and the Situationist group from the 1950s, for instance, drew heavily on Baudelaire's conception of the *flaneur* (first articulated in essays from the 1840s and 1850s) as an explicitly 'heroic' figure of the modern metropolis. Baudelaire's descriptions of the flaneur align this heroism with the artistic sensibility of someone who wanders the city with no purpose but to observe 'the river of life flow[ing] past him in all its splendour and majesty'.²⁵ For Benjamin and others after, such anonymous wandering or 'flanerie' became increasingly politicised in its potential for reconceptualising urban spaces and resisting their economic expectations. Debord's re-framing of these impulses in 'Theory of the *Dérive*' (1956) promoted urban walking as a central, subversive strategy for the psychogeography movement originating in 1950s France.²⁶ Since the mid-1970s, psychogeographical practices have had their chief anglophone exponent in Iain Sinclair, although the poetic dimensions of urban life have also been widened in the same period by Henri Lefebvre's notion of meaningful 'habitation' (drawn from Friedrich Hölderlin's sense of poetic 'dwelling') and the importance of walking in Michel de Certeau's *Practice of Everyday Life* (1974). For Certeau, the city itself is rendered textual in so far as 'the act of walking is to the urban system what the speech act is to language'.²⁷ In this 'rhetoric' of movement, 'the long poem of walking manipulates spatial organizations', rewriting the city with each step.²⁸

Particularly in the United Kingdom, these approaches have sustained several generations of poets working in various formal traditions – from those in dialogue with Sinclair or other older avant-garde writers like Allen Fisher,

Bill Griffiths, and J. H. Prynne, to a generation of more lyrically oriented urbanists like Paul Farley, Deryn Rees-Jones, and Michael Symmons Roberts. Poets first published in the past 10 years, however, have been just as likely to seek out alternative models for their own alternative urbanisms. For many young writers, this means first extricating useful ideas and practices from a self-perpetuating chain of mostly white male thinkers.[29] Implicitly male conceptions of the flaneur, for instance, have by now been thoroughly called into question by scholars like Janet Wolff (1985), Elizabeth Wilson (1992), Deborah Parsons (2000), and, most recently, Lauren Elkin's cultural history of the *flâneuse* (2016).[30] Writers like Rebecca Solnit and Teju Cole have opened up urban geography more generally, while critic-editors like Zoë Skoulding have mapped an alternative network of female poets of the city.[31] Innovative presses like Test Centre and Penned in the Margins have bolstered a continued engagement with London's material layers and changing spaces. The awarding of the Ted Hughes prize to poets like Kate Tempest and Jay Bernard has brought urban explorations to new audiences, combining performance and social consciousness in ways that Blake or Baudelaire could never have dreamed of.

The Creative City

For the past two decades, approaches to urban development and artistic practice have both been dominated by new rhetoric of the so-called creative industries. As detailed in my introduction, successive governments since the late 1990s have used policy and reconfigured funding regimes to encourage a more holistic view of artistic production, bringing independent artists, musicians, and writers along with large film or video game studios, architecture and IT, all under the creative industries umbrella, in order to emphasise their collective economic potential. Although many theorists have noted the importance of cultural activity as a driver of urban economies, no writer looms as largely over twenty-first century 'creative city' agendas as Richard Florida. Florida's *The Rise of the Creative Class*, first published in 2002, 'has become a handbook for government officials' worldwide (in Sarah Brouillette's words), along with other policymakers, funding bodies, planners, and anyone figuratively or financially invested in the shaping of urban spaces.[32] As with creative industries rhetoric, an expanded definition of creative activity is central for Florida's statistical models. As he asserts in the revised 2012 edition of *The Rise of the Creative Class: Revisited*, 'The only way forward is to make all jobs creative jobs, infusing service work, manufacturing work, factory work, farming, and every other form of human endeavour with creativity and human potential.'[33] Florida repeatedly cites William Blake, and elsewhere looks to Charles

Baudelaire as a poetic model for the individualistic 'bohemianism' he absorbs into his vision for creative cities.

In Florida's analysis, the overall 'creative index' of a city's development prospects can be broken down into specific metrics for a 'Bohemian Factor', along with a 'Foreign-Born Index', 'Gay Index', and 'Composite Diversity Index'.[34] As Florida reports: 'Our work finds a strong correlation between, on the one hand, places that are welcoming to immigrants, artists, gays, bohemians, and socioeconomic and racial integration, and, on the other, places that experience high-quality economic growth.'[35] More specifically, he notes, 'urbanists have long recognized that gentrification (and the higher housing prices that follow) is set in motion by artists, creatives, and gays.'[36] As he explains the correlation, 'it's not that gays and bohemians drive up housing simply by paying more', but that 'their presence signals that a location has the very characteristics that drive innovation and growth'.[37] Florida admits he isn't the first person to draw a link between the presence of artists and gentrification, but he is particularly adamant (and influential) regarding this wider treatment of diversity and creative activity as economic 'advantages'. Beyond mere correlation, the narratives of this 'creative city script', as Oli Mould describes it in *Against Creativity* (2018), have succeeded in making *creativity* itself 'a byword for the economization of culture' and 'a flimsy pseudonym for real estate-led gentrification and "place-making" on a large scale'.[38]

The difficulty for artists (and poets among them) isn't simply that this script is fundamentally opposed to the anti-capitalist premises of urban psychogeography or other alternative networks and communities imagined above, but that creative city ideology is so effective at co-opting any and all discourses of resistance towards its ends – in a process described by the Situationists as 'recuperation'. In some instances, this recuperation functions as a rhetorical whitewashing, as in Florida's redefinition of bohemianism as essential 'apolitical' or his suggestion that Beat poets and others in the San Francisco counterculture movements of the 1950s and 1960s 'included a wide spectrum of views on work and economics'.[39] In other cases, resistance itself helps to establish what Florida calls the 'authenticity' of a place. As Mould explains:

> The 'new' creative city needs to have a veneer of 'edginess', appeal to hipsters and maintain a radical, progressive and perhaps even anti-capitalist aesthetic, all the while mobilizing these (not stabilized) aesthetics for the same traditional purpose: wealth generation for the elite.[40]

Beyond mere rhetoric, the recuperative gestures involved in corporate sponsorship, residencies, or advertising often help to legitimise 'urban renewal' projects, through a process often now described as *artwashing*. As Feargus O'Sullivan defines it in a 2014 essay for *CityLab*, artwashing is 'essentially a cleansing process in which the artist moving into a burgeoning area [are] treated by developers as a form of regenerative detergent'.[41] While BP's sponsorship of London's Tate Gallery has been a conspicuous focal point for UK activists, the more local and insidious effects of what Neil Smith describes as 'soft capitalism' mean that individual artists and writers are also at risk of being seen as the 'shock troops of neighbourhood reinvestment'.[42] This is the fine line that contemporary urban poets are made to tread, among institutions funded by an array of sometimes hidden partners, in the context of irresistible 'city of culture' schemes, or simply by living and writing in a place that exploits the image of their progressive, creative 'authenticity'.

In March 2019, London's National Portrait Gallery and the Tate group of British art galleries announced that they would no longer accept financial gifts from the Sackler family, who own the pharmaceutical company that manufactures the addictive painkiller OxyContin. The decision followed a series of protests organised by photographer Nan Goldin at New York museums, including the Metropolitan and Guggenheim, criticising the Sacklers' role in the US opioid crisis. Such protests have been rarer or less visible regarding poetry's infrastructure. This stems partly from the invisibility of the infrastructure itself within public discourse intent on promoting poetry's accessibility. As with fantasies of a global playing field made level by new technologies, the concentration of resources and publishers in urban hubs belies the extent to which poetry is not only an art form frequently concerned with 'place', but one whose business is geographically contingent. If anything, the rise of online commercial and social networks puts a higher premium on the face-to-face networks taken for granted by writers in cities. Within cities, poetry networks and institutions are also increasingly implicated by the degree to which, in Mould's words, 'creative city policies have come to be completely normalized in urban development.'[43]

After the Poetry Foundation, which publishes *Poetry* magazine, received a $200 million bequest from pharmaceutical heiress Ruth Lilly in 2001, the *New Yorker* suggested the gift 'was greeted with a measure of ambivalence'.[44] By the time the foundation opened its new $21.5-million home in Chicago's trendy Near North Side in 2011, Michael Hanson, co-editor of the crosstown *Chicago Review*, suggested the Poetry Foundation seemed 'disconnected' from the city, 'almost a commercial enterprise, walled off from the scene'.[45] The same divide was even more striking when the Poets House library and poetry centre moved to the heart of lower Manhattan's financial district in 2009. Poets House's $11.2-million new building – made possible by grants, private donations, and city incentives (including a rent-free lease until 2069) – sits around the corner from the Brookfield Place World Financial Center and the world headquarters of Goldman Sachs, which remains a regular donor and event sponsor, in an area that has seen near constant 'renewal' since the 1970s. Inspired by Florida's mentor Jane Jacobs's views on urban planning, the regeneration of derelict docklands and former landfill that became Battery Park has been accompanied throughout that time by 'creative' activity – from Agnes Denes's two-acre wheat field, planted and harvested in the shadow of the World Trade towers in 1982, to the prominent location of Poets House today.

At the very least, the expansion of city-centric poetry infrastructure over the past decade demands more discussion of the role these networks and organisations play in the inequalities exacerbated by urbanisation. As Scott Herring argues, metronormative assumptions are deeply entangled with the distribution of social capital, in which 'urbanity functions primarily as a psychic, material, and affective mesh of stylistics'. This includes a presumed '*knowingness* that polices and validates' cultural production, 'a *sophistication* that demarcates worldliness, refinement, and whatever may count as "the latest"' and, 'a *cosmopolitanism* that discriminates anybody or any cultural object that does not take urbanity as its point of origin, its point of departure, or its point of arrival'.[46] Redressing these narratives need not go as far as Plato banishing poets from his ideal city, nor William Morris's Victorian dream of a rural utopia with no cities in *News from Nowhere* (1890). Herring cites Leo Marx's vision of 'a far more inclusive if indirect and often equivocal attitude toward the transformation of society and of culture, of which the emerging industrial city is but one manifestation'.[47] In a critically equivocal stance, we should be able to consider poetry's deep and long dependence on cities in relation to the means by which urban development increasingly instrumentalises poetry and other arts to other ends. Organisations will have to go beyond virtual access or empty claims of inclusivity (e.g. Poets House's aim to 'make everyone feel that poetry belongs to them'[48]) in order to extend the benefits and responsibilities of poetic 'citizenship' – a term literally restricted to city dwellers for much of history. As the history of poetry's relationship with the city shows, poets have always been good at envisioning radical alternatives for their urban habitat, but urban interests have also gotten much better at co-opting them.

Notes

1   William Wordsworth, 'Preface to *Lyrical Ballads* [1802]', in *Prose Works of Williams Wordsworth*, ed. W. J. B. Owen and Jane Worthington Smyser, vol. 1 (Oxford: Oxford University Press, 1974), 128.
2   Manuel Castells, *The Rise of Network Society*, 2nd edition (London: Wiley-Blackwell, 2011), 406.

3   Frances Cairncross, *The Death of Distance: How the Communications Revolution Will Change Our Lives* (Cambridge, MA: Harvard Business School Press, [1997] 2001), 2.
4   Friedman, *The World Is Flat: A Brief History of the Twenty-first Century* (New York: Farrar, Strauss, Giroux, 2005), 8.
5   Marshall McLuhan, *Gutenberg Galaxy: The Making of Typographic Man* (Toronto: University of Toronto Press, 1962), 219.
6   Aristotle, *Poetics*, Part IX (*c*. 335 BC); Shelley, *The Defence of Poetry* (1840). Both are available online at the Poetry Foundation.
7   Joe Fassler, 'Write to Transcend Space and Time', *The Atlantic* (4 November 2014); Helen Vendler, *Soul Says: On Recent Poetry* (Cambridge, MA: Harvard University Press, 1995), 5.
8   Castells, *The Rise of Network Society*, 406. Emphasis in original.
9   'Poetry for Anyone and Everyone', Trade School Indianapolis website, no author.
10   Rachel Galvin, 'Conversing with the World: The Poet in Society,' *Poets.org* (16 January 2005).
11   Margot Atwell, 'Poetry, in the Wilds of the Internet,' *Kickstarter* (Medium, 29 April 2016).
12   Virgil, *Eclogues, Georgics, Aeneid*, trans. H. R. Fairclough, Loeb Classical Library (Cambridge, MA: Harvard University Press, 1916). Available online at the Theoi Classical Texts Library.
13   Terry Gifford, *Pastoral* (London: Routledge, 1999), 73.
14   E. P. Thompson, 'Time, Work-Discipline, and Industrial Capitalism', *Past & Present*, no. 38 (December 1967), 56–97 (97).
15   Jack Halberstam, *In a Queer Time and Place: Transgender Bodies, Subcultural Lives* (New York: New York University Press, 2005), 35–36.
16   Oliver Coutard and Jonathan Rutherford, *Beyond the Networked City: Infrastructure Reconfigurations and Urban Change in the North and South* (London: Routledge, 2015), 3.
17   It is worth acknowledging that Arts Council England has made a specific effort to distribute their National Portfolio funding more evenly across the country in recent years, with London organisations' share of funding down from 46.2 per cent to 39.7 per cent since 2012.
18   Jefferey M. Sellers, *Governing from Below: Urban Regions and the Global Economy* (2002), 37.
19   Stephanie Burt, 'Transatlantic Disconnections, or, the Poetry of the Hypotenuse', *PN Review 190* vol. 36, no. 2 (November-December 2009), 21. In the context of the rural–urban divide, Burt – without ever using the word 'pastoral' – emphasises the cultural specificity of British poets' relation to 'non-human nature', suggesting 'the rest of the Anglophone world might read more British poetry in order to think more clearly about poetry and ecology'.
20   It's worth remembering that SimCity 2000 was released alongside *SimFarm*, advertised as its 'country cousin'. Though this one-off version was far less successful than the city series, its own legacy of fantasy pastoral is clear enough in games like *Farmville, Farming Simulator, Stardew Valley*, or even *Goat Simulator*.
21   Leanne Townsend, Claire Wallace, Gorry Fairhurst, and Alistair Anderson, 'Broadband and the Creative Industries in Rural Scotland', *Journal of Rural Studies* vol. 54 (August 2017), 451–58.
22   Ibid., 455.
23   Stephen Tedeschi, *Urbanization and English Romantic Poetry* (Cambridge: Cambridge University Press, 2018), 2.

24 Ibid.
25 Baudelaire, 'The Painter of Modern Life', in *The Painter of Modern Life and Other Essays*, trans. and ed. Jonathan Mayne (Oxford: Phaidon, 1964), 11.
26 Debord, 'Theory of the *Dérive*', first published in *Les Lèvres Nues*, no. 9 (November 1956), and available in the *Situationist International Online* archive, trans. Ken Knabb.
27 Michel de Certeau, *The Practice of Everyday Life*, trans. Steven Randall (Berkeley: University of California Press, 1984), 97.
28 Ibid., 101.
29 Some scholars are at least aware of their gender biases, although John Kerrigan, as recently as the 2017 edition of *The Oxford Handbook of Contemporary British and Irish Poetry* (ed. Peter Robinson, Oxford: Oxford University Press) is content to repeat essentialist stereotypes from Peter Barry's *Contemporary British Poetry and the City* (Manchester: Manchester University Press, 2000), blaming the relative lack of women from their respective accounts on female poets' tendency towards 'internalisation of geography so that it represents and embodies such things as states of mind, and structures of feeling' (Barry, 16; qtd Kerridan, 361). Any number of examples, including those mentioned elsewhere, challenge Kerrigan's insistence that 'London is *still* an inwardly contingent, somatic space for women poets, not a mapped-out place' (361, emphasis added).
30 Wolff, 'The Invisible Flâneuse: Women and the Literature of Modernity', *Theory, Culture & Society* vol. 2, no. 3 (November 1985), 37–46; Wilson, 'The Invisible Flaneur', *New Left Review* vol. 1, no. 191 (January-Feburary 1992), 1–16; Parsons, *Streetwalking the Metropolis: Women, the City and Modernity* (Oxford: Oxford University Press, 2000); and Elkin, *Flâneuse: Women Walk the City in Paris, New York, Tokyo, Venice and London* (London: Chatto & Windus, 2016).
31 See especially Solnit's *A Field Guide to Getting Lost* (Edinburgh: Canongate, 2006) and *Wanderlust: A History of Walking* (London: Granta, 2014), Cole's *Open City* (London: Faber & Faber, 2012), and Skoulding's *Contemporary Women's Poetry & Urban Space: Experimental Cities* (London: Palgrave Macmillan, 2013) and *Metropoetica* anthology (Brigend: Seren, 2013).
32 Brouillette, *Literature and the Creative Economy* (Stanford, CA: Stanford University Press, 2014), 5.
33 Florida, *The Rise of the Creative Class: Revisited* (New York: Basic Books, 2012), xiv.
34 Oli Mould, *Against Creativity* (London: Verso, 2018), 152.
35 Florida, *Rise of the Creative Class*, 233.
36 Ibid., 243.
37 Ibid., 245.
38 Mould, *Against Creativity*, 151–52.
39 Florida, *Rise of the Creative Class*, 171.
40 Mould, *Against Creativity*, 159.
41 Feargus O'Sullivan, 'The Pernicious Realities of "Artwashing"', *CityLab* (24 June 2014).
42 Neil Smith, *The New Urban Frontier: Gentrification and the Revanchist City* (London: Routledge, 1996), 198.
43 Mould, *Against Creativity*, 156.
44 Dana Goodyear, 'The Moneyed Muse', *New Yorker* (19 February 2007).
45 Qtd in Christopher Borrelli, 'Poetry Magazine Well-Versed in Criticism', *Chicago Tribune* (20 June 2011).

46 Scott Herring, *Another Country: Queer Anti-Urbanism* (New York: New York University Press, 2010), 16. Emphasis in original.
47 Qtd in Herring, 12n33.
48 Executive Director Lee Briccetti, quoted in Robin Pogrebin, 'Transparent New Home for Poetry', *New York Times* (24 September 2009).

Chapter 8

FAKE MUSE: PLAGIARISM, CONCEPTUAL WRITING, AND OTHER SINS OF AUTHENTICITY

Historically speaking, the ideal of authenticity hasn't exactly stayed true to itself. In his canonical 1969 essay, 'What Is an Author?', the French theorist Michel Foucault locates an historical shift 'at the end of the eighteenth and beginning of the nineteenth century', in which the introduction of copyright laws helped to establish our modern sense of authorship in relation to the idea of texts as property.[1] But if copyright links the author to their text in legal terms, Foucault suggests it also invokes an older notion of the authority a text derives from its named creator. Scientific texts or historical accounts had long depended on naming authors for claims to empirical truth – both for their own authorship and by citing others (e.g. 'Pliny tells us that [...]'). While literary texts have often circulated anonymously, in folk tales and other oral forms, there is an analogous sense by which the moral or creative 'truth' of these narratives stems similarly from the naming of an author. Crediting the *Iliad* and *Odyssey* to a single poet, for instance – despite the poems' own evidence of collaborative composition and the lack of evidence that 'Homer' ever existed – shows the need to invent a figure to fill that authoritative role, licensing these texts as products of a single creative mind, partly to account to for their enormous influence on ancient Greek culture and Western culture since. In Foucault's terms, the author's existence is less important than the idea of an author as 'a function of discourse'. From the Greeks onwards, our way of experiencing and discussing texts has, in most cases, been structured by their ascription to a particular and original creator.

As Foucault suggests at the end of his essay, however, there may be something larger at stake. Rather than see this authorising effect as a peculiarity of writing or other artistic practices, the tendency to regard texts as the work of a single mind becomes an acutely existential matter in the degree to which it reflects our tendency to regard ourselves as the manifestation of a single and original consciousness. The author's individuality is tied to our own. This broader notion of the authentic self has its most forceful expression in the famous *cogito ergo sum* of seventeenth-century philosopher René Descartes, informing the rational conviction in our own subjectivity ever since. But other thinkers, at least since Immanuel Kant in the late eighteenth century, have also challenged this conviction, questioning both the moral and logical bases of our presumed self-authority. Literary critics in the early twentieth century, still defining the scope of a relatively new academic discipline, came to understand, in Foucault's words, 'that the task of criticism is not to re-establish the ties between an author and his work or to reconstitute an author's thought and experience through his works', but instead should 'analyze the work through its structure, its architecture, its intrinsic form, and the play of its internal relationships'.[2] Foucault himself is writing partly in response to Roland Barthes's equally influential 'Death of the Author', published the year before, but also in the wider wake of other formalist or structuralist analysis which sought ways of reading without recourse to an authorial presence. In the context of these and other cultural developments – not least Freud's work on the unconscious forces complicating any sense of our rational selves – writers and artists throughout the twentieth century challenged the relationship between art and its named creator as part of a more general questioning of authority, authenticity, agency, and other philosophical, political, legal, economic, and often biological means by which subjects are situated by those convictions within discourse and wider social structures. In this way, questioning our faith in authorship had become a means for grappling with an increasingly complex, but still compelling faith in ourselves.

The 'fake muse' in this chapter's title is only partly meant as a bad pun. It also frames the discussion of recent debates around authorship, both in relation to a wider contemporary crisis of 'post-truth' politics and in relation to a much older faith in an authorising force behind all texts, still often expressed in relation to moral convictions regarding originality and creative ownership. If, in everyday discourse, creative texts are still regarded by most readers as the products (and property) of original thought – with a source attributed to a 'muse' in some contexts and 'inspiration' in others – then the sense of scandal shared by the three very different case studies below stems from writers having broken that pact of authenticity. Without implying an ethical equivalence between these examples of plagiarism, conceptual writing, and poetry hoaxes, public reactions to each of them point repeatedly to feelings of transgression that go beyond legal rights over intellectual property. As Foucault points out, new copyright laws had their roots in blasphemy laws of earlier periods, where the need for a named author is the need for someone to be held to account. The three poetry 'scandals' below are ostensibly unrelated, but all came to a head in the spring of 2015. In that contemporary moment, they each show the degree to which notions of original authorship (and authority) are complicated by the history of thought above and, on the other hand, by political, cultural, and technological contexts which have added further layers to traditional ideas of creativity or to more recent theoretical presumptions of post-subjective positions. In either direction, these dilemmas are only exacerbated by their extension well beyond contemporary poetry culture.

Plagiarism

Accusations of plagiarism are nothing new in poetry, though methods of detection grow more sophisticated. Two months after Samuel Taylor Coleridge's death in July 1834, Thomas De Quincey published the first instalment of a long essay in *Tait's Edinburgh Magazine*. Amid reflections on Coleridge's life – his failed marriage, the breakdown of his relationship with Wordsworth, and a drug addiction with which De Quincey sympathised – the stubbornest legacy of this essay is its charge of plagiarism towards the late poet. It wasn't the first great literary heist in English – several high-profile trials had tested the limits of new copyright laws throughout the latter half of the eighteenth century. Yet, De Quincey's accusations and the public reaction to it have had a strange recent echo.

In January 2013, nearly 180 years after De Quincey's exposé, the *Western Daily Press*, in southwest England, broke the first of what would be a series of plagiarism stories over the next few years. As that small paper reported, the British poet Christian Ward had recently won the Exmoor Society's Hope Bourne prize for his poem, 'The Deer at Exmoor'. Ward's poem, however, had since been found to bear a 'striking resemblance' to Helen Mort's poem, 'The Deer', winner of another competition a few years prior.[3] That same day, following a flurry of online discussion, the poet Ira Lightman says he 'rang all the libraries in Exmoor for an hour and tracked down one that held the local magazine that had published Ward's winning poem'.[4] Once he posted the two poems in comments on the newspaper's website and elsewhere, anyone could see for themselves that Mort's poem not only bore a resemblance, but had been copied verbatim, save a handful of individual word changes. In an interview that spring, Lightman recounted the investigation that followed, in which he 'meticulously hunted for online poems by Ward and then checked each one line by line'. Lightman posted further calls to Facebook, he says, asking fellow poets: 'Everyone consult your magazines with him in, send me his poem; if he won't confess, I will.'[5]

Four months after the Ward revelations – which were also covered by the *Telegraph*, *New York Times*, and *Guardian* – the latter ran the headline, 'Another plagiarism scandal hits the poetry community.' A familiar story followed, regarding the poet David R. Morgan. Again, one striking resemblance drew attention to a pattern throughout his work. This time, the article credited the discovery to 'assiduous digging by the online poetry community, led by the poet and academic Ira Lightman', who is quoted on his methods:

> When an American poet spotted his own poem under David R Morgan's name on a website that blogs new work, he contacted its editor, and its editor contacted me. Within around one hour, I'd found a dozen more. Everything online by David R Morgan that I could find since Jan 2011 I could trace 90% of to another person's poem.[6]

The interview with *Write Out Loud*, published the following week, begins: 'He has been dubbed the poetry sleuth, tracking down plagiarism online and establishing the scale of misdeeds of serial offenders.'[7] Poet and critic Katy Evans-Bush called Lightman 'the Sherlock Holmes of poetry' in an article for *Little Atoms*; and Lightman himself embraced the image of consulting plagiarism detective: 'I'm glad that someone knew to bring the Morgan case to me. I cracked it quickly and through friends presented him with what we knew. I helped him to confess and get it all over with.'[8]

De Quincey begins his essay recalling a mutual friend's suggestion that Coleridge 'sometimes steals from other people'.[9] As with Lightman, the tip-off prompts further investigation and frames the investigator as someone not alone in the suspicions, yet singular in their determination to follow them through. There is similar hint of pride in the discovery 'first published to the world by me', in De Quincey's words, and in their respective methods. Where Lightman explains, 'I have to play Google quite assiduously to find plagiarism,' De Quincey says borrowings were 'noticed by myself in a very wide course of reading'.[10] For others as well, Lightman's methods are a point of fascination. Evans-Bush sensationalises his approach:

> The art form's recent plagiarism cases have been meticulously investigated by Ira Lightman, the UK's prodigiously gifted 'poetry sleuth', who has worked tirelessly to set the record straight, to find the copied poems and restore them, as it were, to their rightful owners.[11]

The *Write Out Loud* interviewer pries into Lightman's 'general technique', acknowledging he 'may not want to give away too many trade secrets'.[12] De Quincey and Lightman encourage interest in the plagiarists' motives as well. As Tillar Mazzeo notes: 'The psychological analysis of Coleridge's plagiarisms [...] began almost from the moment the obligations were publicly noted,' partly because De Quincey had 'characterized Coleridge's most culpable intellectual debts as a personal neurosis'.[13] De Quincey describes plagiarism as 'a trait of Coleridge's mind', or a kind of textual kleptomania, at other points linking compulsive borrowing to difficult periods in the poet's life.

In recent cases, the urge to psychologise the culprits is as strong as ever. The interviewer prods Lightman: 'How do you feel about the plagiarists themselves? What do you think their motivation is for such blatant theft?'[14] Amid the later 2013 case, *The Quietus* published an interview with Morgan himself under the headline 'Addicted to Plagiarism', in which the interviewer, Bobby Parker, admits to feeling 'like Jodie Foster in *The Silence of the Lambs*, interviewing Hannibal Lector'. Morgan echoes the defence prepared for Coleridge: 'It comes in cycles,' he says of the plagiarism, 'during profound stress [...] the past few years have been so awful, with marriage breakdown, house loss and splitting up of my children; ultimately, a breakdown'.[15] In another interview from late 2013, Lightman discusses the psychologising impulse with some sympathy: 'I won't just say "I can't understand this, it's a foreign mentality to me," because that's untrue.'[16] The focus on establishing patterns of behaviour are borne by a belief, like De Quincey's, that this must be a habit of mind.

The technological gap in detection methods parallels another important difference between publishing in a print magazine in 1834 and posting online in 2013 – namely, the speed and openness of feedback. It was only in private, for instance, that Robert Southey told Thomas Carlyle 'with extraordinary animosity' that he had said to Coleridge's son, Hartley:

> He ought to take a strong cudgel, proceed to Edinburgh, and give De Quincey, publicly in the streets, a strong beating – as a calumniator, cowardly spy, traitor, base betrayer of the hospitable social hearth, for one thing![17]

It's hard to imagine how Southey might have reacted on Twitter, and just as difficult to quantify the social media verbiage generated by Lightman's investigations, both by critics and supporters. Prompted by the former and encouraged by the latter, Lightman's motivations echo De Quincey's, to a point: 'If nobody was every going to publish him [Ward] again, well, why keep investigating? One answer is because I'm thorough. [...] I wanted facts, not speculation.'[18] This chimes with De Quincey's later defence: 'To *him* [Coleridge] I owed nothing at all; but to the public, to the body of his own readers, every writer owes the truth.'[19] Again, in the interview from May 2013, Lightman forges on: 'I'm not stopping. More is coming out. It takes someone who will stand up as a spokesperson for stopping poetry plagiarism for more witnesses to come forward.'[20]

These noble sentiments come in response to vehement and personal attacks on 'the self-appointed poetry police', as well as a wave of support that went as far as half-joking calls for Lightman's knighthood for services to poetry.[21] When the *Guardian* reported the Morgan story, an online comment from user 'hungryhungryho' (complete with cowboy hat in his thumbnail image) called on poets to 'ride him [Morgan] out of town on a rail! Tar and feather the fraudster!!'[22] Evans-Bush takes a more measured position between what she calls 'the "pitchforks at dawn" set' and 'those who feel sorry for the thief'. But even this middle ground rests on notions of poetic justice, in which plagiarism is equated with deeper moral or artistic weakness:

> It seems to me self-evident that this is self-harming activity; surely, every time a plagiarist publishes a poem and all their friends compliment them on it, it just confirms them in their own conviction that a poem is the very thing they can't write.[23]

Similarly, for the poet Helen Ivory, quoted in the *Guardian* coverage:

> As a writer who has spent years finding her voice and honing her craft, it is anathema that anybody should choose to replace this search for truth and meaning by stealing from the products of other peoples' searching.[24]

Such language has a regulatory function for the community it addresses, separating plagiarists who 'can't write' from real writers who do the work. For all the joking about Lightman's detective persona, the sense of justice is explicit in an October 2015 feature for Channel 4 News, which began: 'If poetry had a police force, it would be one man strong.'[25] In line with his 'forensic' methods, Lightman consistently refers to these episodes as 'cases' and 'investigations'. 'Morgan is undoubtedly the far worse offender', he offers, noting three further poems 'are still held under suspicion'.[26] If we accept the call for tar and feathering is in jest, other language of incrimination differs only by degrees from its extreme expression in a comment on the *Quietus* interview with Morgan, from user Aaron Poehler, who is grateful for the public hearing: 'So that similar scumbags are aware they too will inevitably be ferreted out and destroyed.'[27]

While Lightman worked to distance himself from accusations of bullying, another case in early 2015 suggested the pitchfork set would have their wish. In May, the publisher Andy Croft posted a message (since deleted) on Smokestack Books' Facebook page, summing up the situation:

> I recently received an e-mail from a Mr Ira Lightman, making allegations of plagiarism regarding Sheree Mack's collection *Laventille*. These have since been made public on his Facebook page (among a

great many photographs of Mr Lightman), kick-starting a long and mostly unpleasant 'thread' of abuse directed at Sheree.[28]

The outcome this time was the immediate cancellation of several reading events, Mack's withdrawal from all interaction with the poetry community, suspicions over her Creative Writing PhD, related accusations regarding her lecturing position with the Open University, and finally the pulping of the book itself. In Poehler's terms, another 'scumbag' had been thoroughly 'ferreted out and destroyed'.

Sustaining public interest might be more important than making an example, however. De Quincey's sense of Coleridge's plagiarism as a 'matter of literary curiosity' was somewhat overestimated. David Higgins points out that the final instalment in *Tait*'s ends with an unfulfilled editor's note – 'to be concluded in our next' – and suggests that 'what De Quincey could never admit publicly' about the essays 'was that they were gossip'.[29] While some critics have attempted to make critical substance of it – with Norman Fruman's *Coleridge, the Damaged Archangel* (1971), the most contentious example – others argue that these investigations have ultimately benefitted Coleridge scholarship, challenging critics to more rigorous reading. Perhaps the most telling discrepancy in these approaches lies in the fact that neither Coleridge's case nor any other history of literary borrowing has been brought to bear on the contemporary examples. While Lightman and others finger 'postmodernism' as the source of seemingly new ideas about the fluidity of intellectual property, De Quincey's essays attest to more complex notions of plagiarism in a period we might wrongly associate with the enshrinement of individual authorship. In that sense, even earlier discussions of copyright, such as Edward Young's 'Conjectures on Original Composition' (1759), are more accommodating of literature's long history of borrowing and collaboration than modern forensics and trial by social media seem willing to admit.

Conceptualism

If these instances of plagiarism are depicted as straightforward sins against individual creativity and the 'search for truth and meaning', the so-called conceptual writing has a more complex relationship with this poetic dogma. Whatever its many self-definitions, conceptual writing emerged in the early 2000s as a label for poetry that knowingly reuses or reconfigures material from other sources, often in ways that destabilise intended meanings. As with the conceptual art of the 1960s and 1970s, 'the idea or concept is the most important aspect of the work'.[30] Kenneth Goldsmith's *Day* (2003), transcribing an entire issue of the *New York Times*, or Vanessa Place's *Statement of Facts* (2010), reproducing legal testimony from sex offenders, are two defining examples of what the latter calls 'pure conceptualism' – in other words, placing language in new contexts with minimal intervention, in a linguistic equivalent to Marcel Duchamp's urinal.[31] Conceptual writing, in its most forceful formulations, takes aim at notions of originality and creativity itself, with Goldsmith heralding a revolution in 'uncreative writing' and the critic Marjorie Perloff championing 'unoriginal genius'. Thus, the dynamic between guilty plagiarists and readers is reversed. Conceptual poets are mostly upfront about their borrowings, since the act of appropriation is intended as an aesthetic or intellectual feature.

The distinction between plagiarism's secrecy and conceptualism's openness becomes a matter of culpability. Sandra Beasley, on the Christian Ward case for the *New York Times*, writes: 'I can admit conceptual poets like Kenneth Goldsmith, whose pieces are often a transparent pastiche of borrowed texts. This is none of that.'[32] And Lightman himself insists, 'I like postmodernism. I like found poetry. They just have to document their sources.'[33] However, the problem with conceptualism also lies in that reversal, in the assumption of neutrality behind its open provocations. By overcompensating for the persistence of the lyrical self and ideology of individual authorship, 'appropriation' relies on a denial of material conditions that still render different poetic subjects unequal. In its supposedly radical erasure of self, conceptual or experimental poetry's rally cry 'against expression' (in the title slogan of Goldsmith and Craig Dworkin's 2011 anthology) is often itself an expression of racial privilege, for instance. As Cathy Park Hong argues:

> The avant-garde's 'delusion of whiteness' is the specious belief that renouncing subject and voice is anti-authoritarian, when in fact such wholesale pronouncements are clueless that the disenfranchised need such bourgeois niceties like voice to alter conditions forged in history. The avant-garde's 'delusion of whiteness' is the luxurious opinion that anyone can be 'post-identity' and can casually slip in and out of identities like a video game avatar, when there are those who are consistently harassed, surveilled, profiled, or deported for whom they are.[34]

Writing in late 2014, Hong's comments couldn't have been more prescient of debates the following spring, when works by Goldsmith and Place provided focal points for growing criticism. At a conference in March 2015, Goldsmith performed what he called 'The Body of Michael Brown', reciting a 30-minute edit of the autopsy report for the unarmed teenager murdered the previous summer by a white police officer in Ferguson, Missouri. The online backlash was immediate, then exacerbated by Goldsmith's defensive apologies, his re-tweeting of criticism, and insistence that footage of the performance be withheld by Brown University. The long-term consequences were less clear, for a poet who had performed at the White House in 2011, and whose reach had extended far beyond typical poetry audiences by 2013, following his appointment as the Museum of Modern Art's first poet laureate and an appearance on *The Colbert Show*. Fawning media profiles continued: a *New Yorker* interview in September 2015 portrayed Goldsmith as 'beleaguered' victim, while a playful feature in *Slate* just a month after the Brown University performance focused on his 'Wasting Time on the Internet' course at the University of Pennsylvania, where he continues to teach.[35]

Goldsmith's crass provocation may have given impetus to Hong's wider critique, however, and helped precipitate conceptualism's brand decline. As Michael Leong points out, the death of conceptualism had been a theme almost since its inception, noting 'significant poets and critics have declared poetry dead or dying in 2012, 2014, and 2015'.[36] These include its practitioners, among whom Vanessa Place claimed defiantly in 2012: 'If conceptualism is dead, it is because poetry is dead.'[37] But it was Place herself who bore at least some of the more immediate consequences of Goldsmith's offense in 2015, when debates following his Brown performance drew attention to a project she had been developing since 2009, re-purposing racist language from the novel *Gone with the Wind*. Two longer excerpts were published in *Poetry* and *Drunken Boat* in 2009, followed from 2011 by a period of tweeting the novel in its entirety from her own Twitter account, the profile photo of which she had changed to Hattie McDaniel's character 'Mammy' from the film adaptation, with a background image of another Mammy figure from the sheet music of an 1890s song.[38] An online petition led to Place's removal from the selection committee for the upcoming AWP (Association of Writers and Writing Programs) conference, along with other cancelled events – as outlined, nevertheless, by a similarly defensive *Guardian* interview in June 2015, bemoaning the 'political correctness' that has 'sanitised' art, and 'made her persona non grata in American cultural institutions.'[39]

For some, the long-term viability of conceptual techniques should be disentangled from recent controversies. Leong, for instance, argues against conflating the entirety of what he describes as 'late conceptualist practice – which is diverse in aesthetic philosophy and socio-political positioning' with the specific work and theorization of conceptualism by writers like Kenneth Goldsmith or Vanessa Place.[40] For others, the racist trajectories of Goldsmith and Place's recent work stem from a 'colonial aesthetics' at the root of all conceptual practice, inherent to the very idea of appropriation as a creative act.[41] In contrast with debates around plagiarism, the very white and Euro-centric history of authorship and subjectivity described above is overinvested in conceptualism as a foil for privileged notions of fluidity. With further hindsight, it is hard not to see Goldsmith and Place's work portending open expressions of white supremacy and bad-faith attacks on 'freedom of speech' in the age of Trump.

An Irish Hoax

At the same time these controversies were playing out in England and the United States, a playful episode in Ireland showed authorship and accountability being reassessed in online spaces. While online commentary and social media provided essential platforms for debating plagiarism and conceptualism, the substance of those debates concerned publications, prizes, and performances in the offline world. Much of the humour of and eventual hostility towards the #IrishPoets2015 campaign, on the other hand, centred on its digital provenance. The context of meme culture and the inherently unreliable (or at least unverifiable) nature of online identities meant that what began as a fun, but pointed spoof encountered criticism that again demonstrated the inadequacy of simplistically rigid or simplistically fluid notions of authorship.

It's difficult to summarise what I refer to as the #IrishPoets2015 campaign (although its reach continues to extend beyond that introductory joke) without going too deeply into the history and politics of Northern Irish poetry, which is partly why the joke itself found such a limited, but receptive audience. The shortest version of the story might begin by explaining that in 2014, the Verbal Arts Centre – an organisation based in Derry, publicly funded in part by the Arts Council of Northern Ireland – announced it would revive the poetry magazine, the *Honest Ulsterman*, following its original and influential run from 1968 to 2003. Soon after the announcement, a WordPress site was set up for 'The Hanest Ulsterman', with the tagline: 'Born: 1968. Died: 2003. Exhumed: 2014. Died Again: 2014.' The site's first post, from the 28th of October, 'Hanesty is the best Palicy', announced an alternative initiative, under a deadpan media-speak introduction:

> Northern Irish Poetry is an industry waiting to boom. With more arts festivals per capita than any other European nation, it is important that we maintain a healthy relationship between the tourism sector and that most evocative of media: poetry.[42]

It included three aims, offering 'advice on making your poem/s more Irish, or Northern Irish (as you prefer)', 'advice on how your poems can attract tourism', and 'advice on how to increase your poem's ownership'. If the joke wasn't clear enough, the post asked that poems be sent to the email address 'rankformsby@gmail.com' (a spoonerism of Frank Ormsby, who edited the

Honest Ulsterman for more than twenty years) with the subject line 'SHYSTER' or 'GOMBEEN' (Irish slang for a self-serving wheeler-dealer). In November, a Twitter account with the username @hanestulsterman and handle 'Rank Formsby' began directing tongue-in-check questions to the Verbal Arts Centre and new *Honest Ulsterman* about details of the relaunch. A number of further spoof accounts appeared, including @HonestUlsterMEN, @hunestulstermin, and @HonestUIsterman (with a capital 'I' in place of the 'l'). A more concerted effort began, however, with the post 'FIVE NEW IRISH POETS TO LOOK OUT FOR IN 2015' on the 6th of January, partly sending up '5 British Poets to Watch in 2015', on the *Huffington Post* the day before. The post was eventually expanded to include poems alongside the five invented poets' bios and photos, in a pitch-perfect pastiche of cultural stereotypes and poetry blurb-speak. (It really is impossible to do justice to the subtle satire without losing myself in examples.) Each of the five poets also now had their own Twitter accounts.

Similar gags continued, including a hashtag séance for Yeats's birthday on January 25, and the announcement of the Formsby Prize for Poetry 2015 in early February, for 'poems on the theme of Honesty or Tourism, Culture and Leisure or Ireland or Northern Ireland'.[43] Although these various enterprises had been announced with just enough ambiguity, so that some readers or tweeters (victims of the earnestness being spoofed, perhaps) may have been taken in by the prizes or publication opportunities on offer, it was only in later February that the project spilled into real hoax territory. On 27 February, Formsby tweeted: 'I have been planting PO-EMS in magazines. I will award prizes if you find any of them.'[44] The following week, a statement from the real *Honest Ulsterman* explained 'with great disappointment' that they had been duped in publishing 'The Wren' by Ainé Callan (one of the #IrishPoets2015), which contained the acrostic 'this is a poem by rank formsby'.[45] Although the Twitter account for Callan extended the game – tweeting her excitement about the publication, then insisting that Formsby had introduced the secret message through his edits – the *Honest Ulsterman* described it as 'the latest episode of an anonymous troll with an unspecified problem against the magazine', citing the attempt 'to fake one of the magazine's social media accounts as well as establish multiple online personalities'.[46] In return, the *Hanest Ulsterman* issued their own 'statement and apology' copying the language of the *Honest Ulsterman*'s statement about 'the whole sordid, difficult debacle'.[47]

It wasn't the first time the anonymous group/individual had been criticised. Amid generally supportive interactions with other Irish and British poets, especially around the wider satirising of poetry's professionalisation and co-option by cultural agendas, the *Honest Ulsterman* had suggested in December that Formsby 'start your own [magazine] if you aren't happy. You sound like a sad childish troll.'⁴⁸ To another Twitter account, 'Totally Not The HU' (@HinastUlstorman), they repeatedly insisted in January that 'what you were doing is illegal.'⁴⁹ Others had tried to puncture the joke as well, with Dave Lordan commenting on the #IrishPoets2015 list: 'And to think they all came alive in persons [*sic*] head. Surely you must tell us which archetypes they correspond to?' To which Formsby replied in couplets, asking him

> to suspend your chronic disbelief
> and save us all from petty grief
> by accepting in your heart as truth
> that these folk are real (Sean is living in Maynooth).⁵⁰

The fact that Callan's poem had made it past the *Honest Ulsterman* editors after such exchanges was as cutting as the publication of a poem by 'Phil O'Connor' by Lordan's own semi-satirical journal, the *Bogman's Cannon* on 12 April, in which an acrostic was found this time for 'Eustace McNally', another of the #IrishPoets2015. The following day, Formsby tweeted that Eustace had left for a new life in New Zealand and a heartfelt farewell to her from Malachy Curren (another #IrishPoets2015 name) was read out on Northern Irish radio station U105, which had also aired Curren's announcement about the list in January.⁵¹ In the following days, however, the saga took a weirder turn. *Bogman's Cannon*, rather than issuing a victimising statement like the *Honest Ulsterman*, published a post (since removed) entitled 'Eustace Unmasked'. In it, the poet Kevin Higgins (to whom the 'Phil O'Connor' poem had been dedicated) took credit for the entire hoax, with help from Lordan and his journal. While it wasn't the end of the project – and many of the spoof accounts remain active – this bizarre reversal certainly shifted the tone of things, with Higgins not only taking credit for what was clearly someone else's satire, but, with Lordan and others, harassing anyone showing support for Eustace and Formsby, and threatening to expose the original hoaxers.

Conclusion: Fake Future

Again, none of this is to imply that these episodes are in any way equivalent. Where those associated with #IrishPoets2015 continue to raise very reasonable questions about the business of contemporary poetry with a measure of good fun, the work of Kenneth Goldsmith and Vanessa Place is rightly criticised for racial insensitivity bound up in the self-serving extremes of that industry. Emphatic policing of plagiarism, on the other hand, may have deflected consideration of the degree to which these 'crimes' might be related to or even symptomatic of those same industry pressures.[52] Rather than deliver verdicts on cases that have had plenty of judgement elsewhere, the juxtaposition of these accounts shows just how ethically complex the question of authenticity has become. The overlap of these authorial dilemmas on either side of the Atlantic, building up to those same few months in early 2015, foreshadows debates around 'fake news' that would dominate the US election in 2016. Much like the use and abuse of that phrase in political contexts, with Donald Trump and his supporters adopting it as a label for any unfavourable news items, there is a danger that some of the dogmatic claims made on behalf of poetic authenticity have the effect of obscuring real issues around representation and accountability. It wasn't very long ago that poets belied their amateurishness by including a copyright notice on each poem submitted to a magazine. There is still something quaint and reasonable about cries for 'truth and meaning', and something equally naïve, though more insidious, in the distortion of these sentiments as justification for certain 'conceptual' approaches. Neither position seems well equipped to consider the radical effect new political realities and new technologies are having on the 'author function' as Foucault described it half a century ago.

Notes

1 Michel Foucault, 'What Is an Author?', in *The Foucault Reader*, ed. Paul Rabinow (New York: Pantheon Books, 1984), 108.
2 Ibid., 103.
3 'From bad to verse' [no author], *Western Daily Press* (5 January 2013).
4 Greg Freeman, 'The Write Out Loud Interview: Ira Lightman', *Write Out Loud* (28 May 2013).
5 Ibid.
6 Alison Flood, 'Another plagiarism scandal hits poetry community', *Guardian* (22 May 2013).
7 Freeman, 'The Write Out Loud' (2013).
8 Katy Evans-Bush, 'Poetry Has a Plagiarism Problem', *Little Atoms* (6 July 2013); Freeman, 'The Write Out Loud' (2013).
9 Thomas De Quincey, *De Quincey's Works: Volume II – Recollections of the Lakes and the Lake Poets: Coleridge, Wordsworth, and Southey* (Edinburgh: Adam and Charles Black, 1842), 42.
10 Lightman, qtd in Freeman; De Quincey, *De Quincey's Works*, 43. In a note added to the end of the volume where De Quincey's essay was republished in 1842, he insists: '*I* certainly was the first person first (I believe, by some years) to point out the plagiarisms of Coleridge' (242).
11 Evans-Bush, 'Poetry Has a Plagiarism Problem' (2013).
12 Freeman, 'The Write Out Loud Interview' (2013).
13 Tilar Mazzeo, 'Coleridge, Plagiarism, and the Psychology of the Romantic Habit', *European Romantic Review* vol. 15, no. 2 (June 2004), 335–41 (335).
14 Freeman, 'The Write Out Loud Interview' (2013).
15 Bobby Parker, 'David R Morgan: Addicted to Plagiarism', *The Quietus* (16 June 2013).

16 Claire Trévien, 'In Conversation with Ira Lightman', *Sabotage Reviews* (17 December 2013).
17 Thomas Carlyle, *Reminiscences* (New York: Harper, 1881), 324.
18 Freeman, 'The Write Out Loud Interview' (2013).
19 De Quincey, *De Quincey's Works*, 243.
20 Freeman, 'The Write Out Loud Interview' (2013).
21 Noted by Kei Miller, 'Plagiarism in Poetry; Looting in Laventille; Carelessness in the Caribbean', Under the Saltire Flag [personal website] (15 May 2015).
22 Comment on Flood, 'Another Plagiarism Scandal'.
23 Evans-Bush, 'Poetry Has a Plagiarism Problem' (2013).
24 Qtd in Flood, 'Another plagiarism scandal'.
25 'Plagiarism in poetry: the man tracking down the cheats', *Channel 4 News* (25 October 2015).
26 Freeman, 'The Write Out Loud Interview' (2013).
27 Comment on Parker (June 2013).
28 Andy Croft, post on Smokestack Books page, Facebook (7 May 2015).
29 David Higgins, *Romantic Genius and the Literary Magazine: Biography, Celebrity and Politics* (London: Routledge, 2005), 88.
30 Sol Lewitt, 'Paragraphs on Conceptual Art', *Artforum* (1967), rewritten as Kenneth Goldsmith, 'Paragraphs on Conceptual Writing', Poetry Foundation (posted 10 May 2007).
31 See Vanessa Place and Robert Fitterman, *Notes on Conceptualisms* (New York: Ugly Duckling Press, 2009).
32 Beasley, 'Nice Poem; I'll Take It', *New York Times* (26 April 2013).
33 Freeman, 'The Write Out Loud Interview' (2013).
34 Cathy Park Hong, 'Delusions of Whiteness in the Avant-Garde', *Lana Turner* (3 November 2014).
35 As Hong described the *New Yorker* piece, in response to a request for her contribution: 'Wilkinson's profile conforms to all the lazy templates: the mea culpa story of the contrite racist, the aging enfant terrible, the comeback kid who is resurfacing just in time to publicize his book (or the con artist who pulls a fast one by using racial shock tactics to win himself a *New Yorker* profile). Goldsmith has risen and fallen and by the end of the profile, we are to forget his shrill critics and feel compassion for the pitiable man.' (Cathy Park Hong, 'There's a New Movement in American Poetry and It's Not Kenneth Goldsmith', *New Republic* (1 October 2015)).
36 Michael Leong, 'Conceptualisms in Crisis: The Fate of Late Conceptual Poetry', *Journal of Modern Literature* vol. 41, no. 3 (Spring 2018), 109–31 (109).
37 Place, 'Poetry Is Dead, I Killed It', *Harriet* blog (Poetry Foundation, 5 April, 2012). Introducing Place's essay, Goldsmith writes: 'Even if conceptualism is facing crisis and decline, it is also being constantly (and artificially) reinvented, reinterpreted, refashioned, reborn, rechannelled, and repackaged. [...] After our production has become limitless in size and scope, after it has been quantified, analysed, and left for dead, conceptualism will still find another vehicle by which to survive and expand.'
38 John Keene's essay 'On Vanessa Place, Gone with the Wind, and the Limit Point of Certain Conceptual Aesthetics' on his J's Theater website (18 May 2015) provides an especially comprehensive account of Place's project and its fallout as it occurred. Also see Ken Chen's 'Authenticity Obsession, or Conceptualism as Minstrel Show', *The Margins* (Asian American Writers' Workshop, 11 June 2015).

39 Edward Helmore, 'Gone with the Wind tweeter says she is being shunned by US arts institutions', *Guardian* (25 June 2015).
40 Leong, 'Conceptualisms in Crisis', 111.
41 Anonymous, 'The Mongrel Coalition against Gringpo Responds to the Links between Conceptual Art and Conceptual Poetry', *Montevidayo* (22 January 2015).
42 'Hanesty is the best Palicy' (no author), *Hanest Ulsterman* (28 October 2014).
43 'The Formsby Prize for Poetry 2015' (no author), *Hanest Ulsterman* (1 February 2014).
44 Rank Formsby (@hanestulsterman), Twitter (2:16 p.m., 27 February 2015).
45 Anonymous, 'Open Submission' (February 2015 Edition), *Honest Ulsterman* (no date or author specified).
46 Ibid.
47 Rank Formsby, 'A Statement on "The Wren"', *Hanest Ulsterman* (7 March 2015).
48 The HU (@HonestUlsterman), Twitter (3:48 p.m., 12 December 2014).
49 The HU (@HonestUlsterman), Twitter (2:16 p.m., 27 February 2015).
50 Comments by 'davelordan' (6 January 2015) and 'rankforsmby' (7 January 2015) on 'FIVE IRISH POETS TO LOOK OUT FOR IN 2015', *Hanest Ulsterman*.
51 Rank Formsby (@hanestulsterman), Twitter (13 April 2015). Recordings of the radio mentions were posted and can be heard under 'Air Time for the #IrishPoets2015' (11 January) and 'The Radio Talks to Malachy and Eustace' (17 April) on the *Hanest Ulsterman* site.
52 And indeed, in July 2015, the #IrishPoets2015 took aim at Lightman himself, with Formsby tweeting: 'My least favourite bit-part player in UK poetry is that guy who goes around being the Dr Who of plagiarism', adding, 'I might have a go at plagiarism', before repeating the *Guardian* headline 'POETRY HAS A PLAGIARISM PROBLEM' with a rewrite of Seamus Heaney's poem 'Digging' as 'Boring', for which Formsby and Curren then both took credit (all tweets 7 July 2015).

Chapter 9

ALL OUR EXPLORING: POETRY'S CRITICAL TURN

The idea of a creative-critical divide is nothing new to poetry. Already in 380 BCE, Plato describes 'an ancient quarrel between philosophy and poetry' in Book X of the *Republic*, before banishing the latter from his utopia.[1] The origins of this 'disconnection', as Kim Lasky calls it, are less clear. Yet its persistence is manifest in the perceived division between theory and craft, market distinctions between poetry and nonfiction, and academic structures separating research from practice. As Lasky writes, 'Somehow, conceptually, the creative and critical processes have become falsely separated.'[2] In this, she echoes T. S. Eliot nearly a century ago, lamenting a 'dissociation of sensibility' in the seventeenth century, which severed thought from feeling in the poetry of Milton, Dryden, and others.[3] In Eliot's timeline, this 'dissociation' loosely coincides with the historical influence of René Descartes, whose mind-body dualism also persists in popular notions of divisions *within* the mind: between the rational and emotional or analytic and creative thinking, often envisioned in relation to a physical division between the brain's right and left hemispheres. These are often invoked to justify a practical separation of 'creative' writing from other modes of research, critique, or commentary. But they have also begun breaking down in recent years. In this chapter, I consider poetry's status within a growing overlap of creative and critical modes in contemporary literature. In terms of wider book culture, that means assessing poetry's relation to a more widely acknowledged 'critical turn' or 'theoretical turn' in fiction since the 1990s, before considering the surge of non-fiction sales in the past decade as a backdrop for the spread of non-fiction-like tropes in mainstream poetry discourse. I conclude by examining a parallel shift in disciplinary language around 'creative-critical' writing, and in research policy and funding guidelines especially, pointing to where these discursive layers both recognise and help define the twenty-first-century (re-)emergence of what Eliot elsewhere called 'critical poetry'.[4]

The Long Turn

My characterisation of literature's 'critical turn' – in reference to the increasing use of whatever we might understand as 'critical' practices by whatever we might understand as 'creative' modes of writing – risks oversimplification, admittedly. It should not be taken to imply a precise historical moment, for instance, nor a prescriptive or narrow set of practices. Literature which deals with facts and draws on extensive research, or which offers reasoned arguments or social commentary, perhaps by way of allegory, satire, or historical or speculative settings, literature which dabbles in didacticism, discursiveness, philosophy, sciences, theology, or politics, in so-called novels of ideas, or metanarratives, true crime, autobiography, or other engagements with 'real-world' concerns – none of these are new to fiction or literature as a whole. What is relatively new are the ways in which the publishing industry and the academic discipline of creative writing have responded to and fortified creative literature's explicit engagement with 'wider issues' and, in some cases, specific critical discourses. In this sense, we might think of creative writing's critical turn as having three distinct, though sometimes overlapping phases (or faces, perhaps). First, the literature itself leads the way, experimenting and further developing all the possibilities listed above and more. The publishing industry follows, chasing and attempting to sustain successes and trends, while helping to define them through marketing language and review culture. Finally, however belatedly, academia catches up through the generally slower publication of literary criticism on the one hand and through the teaching of creative writing on the other.

There's a strange and layered circularity to this long feedback loop, which is dramatised in the specific influence of critical theory on literature over the past fifty years. Judith Ryan's broad claim might seem self-evident, in *The Novel After Theory* (2012), that 'in the last third of the twentieth century [...] an entire array of novels appears that might be said to "know about" literature and cultural theory'.[5] In this evolutionary model, the rise of 'theory' from the late 1960s onwards – concentrated around the now-canonical work of Derrida, Foucault, Lacan, Barthes, Adorno, and other French or European thinkers – exerted its influence on writers either studying or teaching at universities in the 1970s and 1980s, naturally finding its way into their work. Again, in that third phase, it is only in recent years that scholars, such as Ryan, have begun to account for the various manifestations of this influence. In some cases, the presence of theory is obvious, embodied in the positive or negative caricatures of campus novels by David Lodge, Malcolm Bradbury, or A. S. Byatt. With writers who move between critical work and fiction, like Umberto Eco or Julia Kristeva, the connections are even more direct. More broadly, 'postmodern' fiction of the 1980s and 1990s, by writers as different as Don Delillo, David Foster Wallace, J. M. Coetzee, Angela Carter, Jeannette Winterson, John Banville, and Thomas Pynchon, is often characterised by its implicit or sometimes very explicit engagement with concepts from literary or cultural theory.

The aim of this chapter is not to rehash these developments, nor to transpose critical assessments onto poetry from the same period. Rather, my focus is on the latter phases of that turn, in which public literary discourse, book marketing, sales, and other forms of recognition increasingly display thinking and working that may have developed in academic contexts. That doesn't imply that writing has retreated to any ivory tower, to be clear. As Ryan writes, 'the success of these novels is testimony to the skill with which their authors engage with theory while still speaking to a wide range of readers.'[6] The same can be said of critical gestures more generally, I would argue. The past decade has seen unprecedented success for poetry that adopts many of the critical modes listed above, engaging not only with self-reflective theory regarding the nature or language or authorship, but also with more specific concepts from feminist and queer theory, postcolonial theory, animal studies, and countless other areas that inform poetry's approach to historical and contemporary social issues, including climate change, migration, issues of race, gender, and sexuality, or economic inequalities, drawing on rigorous research and experimenting with forms more conducive to argument, testimony, allegory, satire, protest, polemic, or commentary more typically associated with prose. As with scholars still interpreting contemporary fiction's critical turn, a comprehensive account of this shift in the poetry is beginning to emerge across a spectrum of public and academic criticism.[7] My small contribution might be simply to attest to such a turn taking or having taken place, marked by changes in industry and institutional rhetoric.

The Genre Problem

To some extent, the idea of a critical turn in fiction might be better understood as one side of a mutual movement between fiction and nonfiction. In the same period that fiction increasingly experimented with non-fictionality, following successes like Truman Capote's 'non-fiction novel' *In Cold Blood* (1965), non-fiction also increasingly adopted narrative forms and techniques previously associated with fiction. The so-called new journalism of the 1960s and 1970s, emerged from US writers like Joan Didion, Norman Mailer, and Tom Wolfe (with Wolfe's co-edited anthology using the term in 1973), followed in the later 1970s and 1980s by the broader category of 'creative nonfiction'. Following the cycle described above, the first creative non-fiction MFA programme was launched at the University of Pittsburgh in the 1990s by Lee Gutkind, who also launched the journal *Creative Nonfiction* in 1993. Although genre labels often first emerge as marketing tools – as Neil Gaiman suggests, 'genres only start existing when there's enough of them to form a sort of critical mass in a bookshop'[8] – the turns of fiction towards critical approaches and non-fiction towards fiction-like narrativity shows a reciprocal evolution that begins in the work itself, before being recognised by new labels, and finally accommodated by institutional structures. Broad definitions of 'creative nonfiction' are now part of most creative writing master's and PhD programmes.

The trouble with poetry is its natural resistance to genre categories, where a fiction–non-fiction binary or spectrum seems generally unsuitable. It was a surprise to many, for instance, that Robert McCrum's recent list of 'the 100 best nonfiction books of all time' for the *Observer* newspaper included poetry collections by Ted Hughes, Seamus Heaney, Sylvia Plath, and Edward Lear, as well as *The Waste Land* as an individual poem.[9] McCrum explained their inclusion in fairly vague terms, with his entry on Hughes's *Birthday Letters*: 'Poetry will be braided into this series like a golden thread, because in every generation it is the poets who replenish and tantalise the collective consciousness.'[10] Rather than seeing poetry's non-fictional tendencies as a timeless effect of 'every generation' feeding the 'collective consciousness', it may be that different communities have differently recognised a more specific turn in the past 10 years. Jack Miles's short essay, 'Poetry as Nonfiction', published in *Poetry* magazine in 2007, still looks backward more than forward, taking Alexander Pope's poem, *An Essay on Criticism* ('truly an essay and truly a great poem') as its main example.[11] A more recent essay on *The Ploughshares Blog* by Emilia Phillips, on the other hand, finds 'Poets Turning to Nonfiction' in the movement between verse and prose by writers like Maggie Nelson.[12] Poets in Australia and New Zealand have been especially proactive in addressing poetry's non-fiction potential in recent years. *RABBIT*, 'a journal for non-fiction poetry', was founded by Jessica L. Wilkinson at Melbourne's RMIT University in 2011, 'encourag[ing] poets to openly engage with auto/biography, history, politics, economics, mathematics, cultural analysis, science, the environment, and all other aspects of real world experience, recollection and interpretation'.[13] Wilkinson and Ali Alizadeh's 'Realpoetik Manifesto' followed in *Cordite* magazine in 2012, calling for 'an end to the segregation of poetry from and by the authoritative discourse of prose', 'celebrat[ing] the power of the poetic form to realise and enact factual content', and 'advocat[ing] rigorous research as poetic process'.[14] A symposium in 2013 was recorded in a 2014 special issue of *Axon*, edited by Wilkinson and Alizadeh, which 'aimed to investigate the rapport between the genres of poetry and nonfiction'. In 2014 and 2017, a pair of conferences and edited collections at Wellington's Victoria University also considered the specific relationships between poetry and biography and poetry and the essay.[15]

Across the publishing industry, there is also a sense of these questions and developments coinciding with changing readerships. Tom Tivnan, from the UK trade magazine *The Bookseller*, recently summarised a dramatic shift in sales: 'narrative long-form reading habits are switching, in part, from fiction to nonfiction'.[16] In the United States, non-fiction sales overtook fiction in 2013, and the gap has only widened since, with fiction seeing an overall drop of 16 per cent between 2013 and 2017.[17] In the United Kingdom, non-fiction sales have risen almost 30 per cent in the past five years, while fiction sales have dropped by 4 per cent.[18] Various explanations have been offered, including online buying being less conducive to the bookshop browsing required for fiction sales or the narrative needs associated with fiction being delivered by TV. As Stephen Lotinga, chief executive of the UK's Publishing Association, suggests, 'fiction is most exposed to people's leisure time. Whether it's Netflix or playing computer games or going on social media, they are in competition.'[19] But fiction also has to contend with non-fiction's perceived 'relevance'. For example, as Jim Milliot and Rachel Deahl explain under the headline 'What's the Matter with Fiction Sales?,' 'the Trump presidency has made political books *the* hot category in recent years.'[20] As Tivnan puts it: 'Non-fiction is where it's at.'[21] Poetry's ambiguous position on the fiction–non-fiction spectrum means that these conversations have focused on prose. Yet, prose non-fiction and critically minded memoirs by authors who also publish poetry have been a driving force for these sales, with major successes in Helen MacDonald's *H is for Hawk* (2014), Maggie Nelson's *The Argonauts* (2015), and Patricia Lockwood's *Priestdaddy* (2017).

The New Explorers

It might be a coincidence that the growth of non-fiction sales since 2013 maps so neatly onto rising poetry sales in every year of that same period.[22] But whether or not more non-fiction-like poetry is being written or published, it's clear that the same industry chasing 'hot' non-fiction sales has increasingly found ways to frame poetry titles in line with those trends. Perhaps no single verb has been more overused in recent poetry blurbs than 'explores', followed by the unifying subject or list of subjects explored. The word implies a conscientious, even methodical approach – perhaps less academic than 'investigates' or 'examines' would suggest, though these crop up as well. Thus, in all this exploring, a gradient of critical commitment emerges. On the one hand, it retains a more abstract sense in blurbs like that for Sinéad Morrissey's TS Eliot-winning *Parallax* (Carcanet, 2013) suggesting: 'Morrissey's poems explore the paradoxes in what is seen, read and misread in the surfaces of the presented world.' More concretely, Sarah Howe's *Loop of Jade* (Chatto, 2015) and Hannah Sullivan's *Three Poems* (Faber, 2018) foreground their autobiographical focus, as Howe 'explores a dual heritage, journeying back to Hong Kong in search of her roots' and Sullivan 'explores the birth of a child and the loss of a father with exacting clarity' in their Eliot-winning collections. Bridging poetry's abstraction with its practical relevance, Jorie Graham's *Place* (a US poet, but also Eliot-winning collection published by Carcanet, 2012), 'explores the ways in which the imagination, intuition and experience help us to navigate a life we will have no choice but to live'.

The versatility of 'exploring' as a premise for poetry can also be seen giving way to more explicitly critical or non-fiction-like synonyms in recent years. In addition to its exploration, for instance, Morrissey's *Parallax* 'documents what is caught, and what is lost', while Heaney's final collection, *Human Chain* (Faber, 2010) 'broaches larger questions of transmission, as lifelines to the inherited past'. But with these near synonyms, there remains a clear distinction between the sense in which John Burnside's *Black Cat Bone* (Cape, 2011) 'examines varieties of love, faith, hope and illusion' and Claudia Rankine's *Citizen* (Penguin UK, 2015) 'examines the experience of race and racism in Western society'. Beyond the verbs, we can follow a marked shift across the decade's blurbspeak. From the more traditional platitudes for Don Paterson's 'assembly of masterful lyrics and monologues' (*Rain*, Faber, 2009), Burnside's 'love, faith, hope and illusion', or Michael Symmons Roberts's 'hymns of praise and lamentation, songs of wonder and despair, journeying effortlessly through physical and metaphysical landscapes' (*Drysalter*, Cape, 2013), we have the much more effortful invocations of Rankine's 'powerful testament to the individual and collective effects of racism', Vahni Capildeo's 'address[ing of] wider issues around identity in contemporary Western society' (*Measures of Expatriation*, Carcanet, 2016), or the 'urgent subjects, and performative power' of Danez Smith's *Don't Call Us Dead* (Penguin UK, 2018).

Rankine provides a particularly illustrative case study for this rhetorical shift, and subtle distinctions between the US and UK markets. Both *Don't Let Me Be Lonely* and *Citizen* were subtitled 'An American Lyric', with blurbs acknowledging the fusion of 'the lyric, the essay, and the visual' (*Lonely*) or 'essay, image, and poetry' (*Citizen*). When first published in the United States in 2004, however, Graywolf described Rankine's *Don't Let Me Be Lonely*, as a

> politically and morally fierce examination of solitude in the rapacious and media-driven assault on selfhood that is contemporary America [and] an important new confrontation with our culture right now, with a voice at its heart bewildered by the anxieties of race riots, terrorist attacks, medicated depression, and the antagonism of the television that won't leave us alone.[23]

Ten years later, the US blurb for *Citizen* (Graywolf, 2014) extends this critically charged language and sense of social urgency, explaining that the

> bold new book recounts mounting racial aggressions in ongoing encounters in twenty-first-century daily life and in the media. [...] Our addressability is tied to the state of our belonging, Rankine argues, as are our assumptions and expectations of citizenship.[24]

Between these two, the need to spell out the earlier volume's 'political' and 'moral' investments, or the slippage between *Lonely*'s 'confrontation' and *Citizen*'s 'argument', reflects the heightened seriousness of these extra-poetical contexts as well as the audience's growing acceptance of poetry's critical premise, as *Don't Let Me Be Lonely*'s more diffuse list of bewildering 'anxieties' gives way to a 'bold' focus on racism and citizenship.

Blurbs for the Penguin UK editions are even more different, despite remixing some of Graywolf's language. *Citizen* was re-published first, in 2015, as a 'moving, critical and fiercely intelligent collection of prose poems'. As noted above with other UK prize-winners, it 'examines the experience of race and racism in Western society', but does so

> through sharp vignettes of everyday discrimination and prejudice, and longer meditations on the violence – whether linguistic or physical – which has impacted the lives of Serena Williams, Zinedine Zidane, Mark Duggan and others. *Citizen* weaves essay, images and poetry together to form a powerful testament to the individual and collective effects of racism in an ostensibly 'post-race' society.[25]

The need to quickly clarify the genre of 'prose poems' is followed here by a careful balance of specific contents with a greater emphasis on craft – the 'moving' and 'fiercely intelligent' qualities of its 'sharp vignettes' and 'longer meditations' all expertly 'woven' together. *Don't Let Me Be Lonely* was re-published by Penguin UK in 2017, after *Citizen* had won the Forward Prize for best collection (when much of the commentary focused on its prose-hybridity and, in some cases, its eligibility for a poetry prize). Its UK blurb extends this emphasis on 'meditation', as opposed to 'argument', repeating the word in reference to 'Rankine's meditation on the self bewildered by race riots, terrorism, medicated depression and television's ubiquitous influence' and the book's 'unflinching and deeply felt meditation on life and death in a nation in flux'.[26] The more lyrical abstractions of either book's content also diverge from the use of first-person plural. Although moving away from the 'our' echoing throughout the US blurbs might seem practical enough for re-publication in another country, combined with the deflected emphasis on craft, this distancing gesture towards some other 'nation in flux' directly undermines the 'addressability' of a book that foregrounds the critical power of interpellation.

The Institutional Phase

In the remainder of this chapter, I want to turn from industry language to that of higher educational institutions, with a sense of critical poetry now spread between those two latter phases of its 'critical turn', in which academia begins to account for changes that began in the literature itself, before being recognised by the market. In the language of creative writing as an academic discipline, this is visible in relation to the slow, ongoing shift from creative non-fiction's codification in the 1990s and early 2000s to a more recent interest in 'creative and critical' or 'creative-critical', hyphenated, hybrid practices. In that regard, it might be a bit unfair to suggest the discipline is only beginning to recognise these forms, especially in the United Kingdom. The University of East Anglia's (UEA's) PhD in Creative and Critical Writing was launched in 1990, and has since been followed by 'Creative and Critical' MA, MPhil, or PhD programmes at a number of universities, including Sussex, Cardiff, Bangor, and Birkbeck, along with similarly named programmes in 'Creative Critical Writing' (University College London and even 'Creative Writing and Critical Life' (Leeds). At my own institution, the University of York, we recently introduced a new PhD in 'English with Creative Writing', to emphasise the composite approach. In parallel with Australian and New Zealand conferences pairing poetry with non-fiction, UEA has done more than most institutions to propagate creative-critical modes, with conferences on 'hybrid writing' in 2016, 'critical reinventions' in 2018, and a 'summit' on the 'the creative-critical' and contribution to a 'workshop on creative-critical teaching' at London's Institute of English Studies in 2019. The anthology *Creative Criticism* (2014) edited by UEA colleagues Stephen Benson and Claire Connors also provides an important foundation for this emerging area.

Nevertheless, it's worth acknowledging that many of these discussions favour the hybrid capacity of prose, under the influence of continental theorist-writers like Kristeva, Derrida, Hélène Cixous, or former UEA professor W. G. Sebald. Although Benson and Connors' anthology includes a number of poets, for example, almost all of their contributions take the form of prose, and none of them connects specifically with the forms of criticality described above. In these contexts, it is obvious that poetry's more experimental or avant-garde strands have long been engaged with any mode of critical practice now emerging from its more mainstream lyrical branches. Even so, the latter has different implications for poetry's changing public role. Responding to current events, social issues, or political situations with critically engaged verse might be old hat in some circles, but the interest of the commercial market – in publishing rhetoric, prize culture, and public commentary – has encouraged more writers, publishers, and readers to 'explore' these possibilities.

Universities are also uniquely entrenched in debates about audience and the aims of criticism. Discussing or legislating for new forms of dissemination cannot be separated from wider debates around accessibility – or open access publication, in most practical terms – or from buzzwords like 'impact' and 'knowledge exchange', emphasising the responsibility of academic criticism towards non-academic communities. In this context (again, especially in UK higher education, where changing regulations are the only constant), research definitions, funding guidelines, and academic subject benchmarks have not only accommodated more fluid creative-critical crossover, but proved in some cases more open to that fluidity than the discipline of creative writing. As distant as policy and guidelines might seem from the writing of poetry, their language directly affects the language available for defining and supporting (financially or otherwise) creative practices. Understanding this regulatory language, I suggest, in terms of its potential impact on student expectations, public expectations, and writers' own ability to think beyond such guidelines can help poets see the limits and potential of their work more clearly, in order to push back more effectively where necessary. (I would have included a disclaimer that anyone unconcerned with writing in academic contexts might skip to the conclusion, if the aim of this entire chapter wasn't to demonstrate the circularity between academic and 'non-academic' trends.)

The most unavoidable source of policy for UK academics, including poets employed to teach creative writing, is the Research Excellence Framework (or REF). Those outside the United Kingdom often find it difficult to understand why so much time and resources is spent on a national assessment exercise every five or six years, ranking research 'outputs' for the sake of league tables and a shrinking portion of shrinking research funding. For creative writers within the United Kingdom, it has sometimes been difficult to find their place within the REF, with their differently shaped outputs. But regardless of different institutions or departments' approaches, the official guidelines have been clear enough since at least the 2008 cycle, when the Research Assessment Exercise (the REF's former incarnation) introduced the guiding principle of 'equity', with an explicit openness towards forms we might recognise as 'hybrid':

> Panels [i.e. central assessment panels] have been instructed to adopt assessment processes and criteria that enable them to recognise and treat on an equal footing excellence in research across the spectrum

of applied, practice-based and basic/strategic research, wherever that research is conducted.[27]

This wording has remained more or less identical in the guidance for REF2014 and the current REF2021. 'Equity' remains the first listed principle, for 'the fair and equal assessment of all types of research and forms of research output'.[28] Like much government policy on education, the language comes from and speaks primarily to the sciences, but the adaptability of terms like 'applied' or 'practice-based' research to the humanities proves essential for justifying support in many cases.

When it comes to more direct funding, we find a similar openness in the 'definition of research' provided by the UK's Arts and Humanities Research Council (AHRC), which states unequivocally that 'creative output can be produced, or practice undertaken, as an integral part of a research process'.[29] In literary subjects, we partly have other arts disciplines to thank for this concession, since academic research in the visual arts, design, and performance-based subjects like music, theatre, and dance has recognised the role of creative practice for more than forty years. These subjects have also provided models for more recently established Creative Writing PhDs. Nevertheless, the AHRC's guidance includes a caveat, which makes all the difference when considering possibilities for creative-critical fluidity within these schemes:

> The Council would expect [...] practice to be accompanied by some form of documentation of the research process, as well as some form of textual analysis or explanation to support its position and as a record of your critical reflection. Equally, creativity or practice may involve no such process at all, in which case it would be ineligible for funding from the Council.[30]

Again, those of us engaged in research involving literary practice can see the precedent set by other arts disciplines, where the need for accompanying 'documentation' might be self-evident in the case of an exhibition or performance. For writers, however, importing this binary model (creative practice, critical documentation) into a discipline where the medium of documentation is the same as that of the practice reflects a dilemma felt at every level of teaching and research.

In most cases, creative writing as a discipline has accepted the model wholesale. For teaching, Michelene Wandor notes, the most common strategy for assessing the critical dimensions of creative practice

> has been to develop, for both undergraduate and postgraduate students, what is variously called commentary, self-reflective writing, a critical

essay, a writing journal, an exegesis, ficto-criticism, or the supplementary discourse.[31]

Wandor herself is deeply critical of this 'solution, which might appear to hybridize the relationship between the creative and the critical, or even transcend their differences', but ultimately 'raises more questions and problems', precisely because of its 'accompanying' status.[32] Kim Lasky describes the practical challenge:

> Faced with the task of producing a preface, introduction, commentary, or some other critical discourse related to their work, writers often forget that they have, actually, been engaged in a wealth of critical activity during the process of composition.[33]

This is where I begin to feel like a traitor to my discipline, where I confess my sneaking suspicion that creative writing, with its celebrated rise as a distinct academic field might also, by virtue of that distinction, be the greatest institutional barrier to poetry and other writing's 'critical turn'. For all sorts of administrative reasons – along with a kind of academic identity politics – the publication of the first QAA (Quality Assurance Agency) benchmarks for UK creative writing was an important moment in February 2016. And yet, binary creative-critical logic is implicit or very explicit throughout the document, with its default emphasis on 'critical reflection' or 'critical awareness', but nowhere considering critical practice as such, nor the critical potential of creative practice. Again, when laying out principles of assessment that will define the subject for years to come, the QAA benchmark suggests 'a critical commentary, critical reflection or preface to the creative work discussing creative context, influence, and process', but never acknowledges forms of practice-based research in which the relationship between research and practice is more fluid.[34] For PhDs, the guidance is perfectly clear:

> A doctoral thesis in Creative Writing consists of a complete creative work that constitutes an original contribution to its field and written to its natural length, *accompanied* [my emphasis] by a critical thesis or exegesis relating to the genesis and execution of the creative work or to a related field of knowledge that is contiguous with or illuminates their creative work.[35]

As with the AHRC definition, the notion of criticality as 'accompaniment' is enshrined here in policy that effectively forecloses on the possibility of true hybridity or criticality in the creative work itself. Regardless of how open-ended and 'equitable' the REF and other research guidelines are in principle, these are the official benchmarks against which, in practice, every UK university writing programme must be validated.

Finally, alongside the REF, the United Kingdom now has the Teaching Excellence Framework, with its own definitions and assessment of university teaching. It's worth acknowledging the direct challenge to fluidity and creativity posed by the proliferation of these metrics as well, alongside their instrumentalisation of education more generally. At the research level, the language around improving support for 'interdisciplinarity' across the subject-specific 'sub-panels' of REF2021 and 'incentivising' diversity in practice might prove either helpful or a ruse in the results. Approaching the language of the TEF pragmatically, one of the biggest challenges to creative-critical experimentation in the classroom rests in the fact that its metrics include feedback from the National Student Survey. This questionnaire, completed by final year undergraduates, includes a particular set of questions around 'Assessment and Feedback', which has proven notoriously difficult for many departments, based on students' perceptions of whether, 'the criteria used in marking have been clear in advance'. Even with all the support and invaluable examples provided by Benson and Connors's anthology, these now financially loaded survey questions tap into an understandable, but circular logic which transcends all ideas of creative writing as a speculative foray into the unknown, with all the vulnerability and productive failure that comes with it. In short, new modes of creative-critical practice will have to be more circumscribed in their language and expectations.

Wayward terms like 'paraliterary' (from Rosalind Krauss, 1980) or 'confessional criticism' (Elaine Showalter, 1985) were coined with the same aim of clarity, at a time when trans-genre writers like Roland Barthes and Jacques Derrida were still finding their place in academic syllabi. 'Ficto-criticism', first used in an article by Australian academics in 1991, has been joined more recently by notions of fluidity and hybridity or metaphors like 'veering', from Nicholas Royle's 2011 book. These labels add to the further tangle of practice-led, practice-based, practice-as-research, research-informed practice, or other permutations of what some of these documents call 'applied' research. Any confusion is understandable. Whether seeking clarity in the form of precision or in the possibilities within meaningful gaps, poetry especially might benefit from renewed attention to discourses of its criticality. If the desire for new categories also reflects the need to communicate research to wider audiences, it also means developing a language that students and administrators will understand, without sacrificing scholars and writers' own understanding. As much as this might be a tale of two disciplines – Literature and Creative Writing – which have had their own good reasons for needing to establish separate identities, the collapse of creative and critical practice *in practice* demands a reassessment of their mutual resources.

Work by Rankine and many others shows the enormous range of critical strategies employed by contemporary poetry. As with fiction's critical turn, we might think of recent poetry moving freely among three broad modes: marking their engagement with critical discourses or theory in a *citational* mode; adopting gestures of critique, argument, or polemic ('exploring', 'investigating', or 'examining', in blurb terms) in what might be thought of a *rhetorical* mode; or adapting forms more typically associated with criticality (e.g. the essay, prose generally, longer forms, or other schematic structures) in a *formal* mode of critical poetry. Recent work has also drawn upon and exceeded critical or non-fictional traditions within poetry. Verse autobiography and memoir has thoroughly reimagined what were once called 'confessional' approaches; uses of archival material have grown far more nuanced and complex than those branded 'conceptualism'; and more broadly, in the more performative sense of political engagement, work like Rankine's has combined formal, rhetorical, and citational strategies to go well beyond mere social commentary, becoming a form of literary activism in its own right. Though much work remains to account for the variety of critical modes in contemporary poetry, the examples above show the degree to which publishing rhetoric has adapted to their ubiquity. Although Eliot was referring to a broader sense of self-reflexivity in his notion of 'critical poetry', the term is useful for understanding the circularity of its phases – from the academic theory already indebted to the literature it studies, into actual poetic practice, into marketing language, and back again for critical reflection. It seems clear at least, in those much-abused lines of Eliot's later poem:

> We shall not cease from exploration
> And the end of all our exploring
> Will be to arrive where we started
> And know the place for the first time.[36]

Notes

1. Plato, *The Republic*, Book X, trans. Benjamin Jowett (New York: Vintage Classics, 1991), 378.
2. Lasky, 'Poetics and Creative Writing Research', in *Research Methods in Creative Writing*, ed. Jeri Kroll and Graeme Harper (London: Palgrave, 2013), 16.
3. Eliot, 'The Metaphysical Poets', in *Selected Prose* (New York: Penguin, 1958), 111–20.
4. Eliot, 'Introduction', *The Use of Poetry and the Use of Criticism* (London: Faber, 1933), 29.
5. Ryan, *The Novel After Theory* (New York: Columbia University Press, 2012), 1.

6   Ibid., 17.
7   See the discussion of 'project' books in Chapter 4, for example.
8   Neil Gaiman and Kazuo Ishiguro, '"Let's talk about genre": Neil Gaiman and Kazuo Ishiguro in conversation', *New Statesman* (4 June 2015).
9   McCrum, 'The 100 best nonfiction books of all time: the full list', *Guardian/Observer* (31 December 2017).
10 McCrum, 'The 100 best nonfiction books: No 4 – Birthday Letters by Ted Hughes (1998)', *Guardian* (22 February 2016).
11 Jack Miles, 'Poetry as Nonfiction', *Poetry* vol. 191, no. 2 (November 2007), 138–40.
12 Emilia Phillips, 'Poets Turning to Nonfiction', *Ploughshares* blog (11 July 2018).
13 *RABBIT* website main page.
14 Wilkinson and Alizadeh, 'The Realpoetik Manifesto', *Cordite* (14 November 2012).
15 Wilkinson and Alizadeh, 'Introduction', Nonfiction Poetry issue, *Axon: Creative Explorations* vol. 4, no. 2 (December 2014). NB: Chapter 3 from this book originated as a contribution to Victoria University's 'Poetry and the Essay' conference and edited volume.
16 Qtd in Flood, 'Death of the novel is greatly exaggerated, say UK booksellers', *Guardian* (28 June 2019).
17 Adam Rowe, 'Traditional Publishers Are Selling Way More Non-Fiction Than Fiction', *Forbes* (30 August 2018), citing data from the Association of American Publishers, the US Bureau of Economic Analysis, and Neilsen BookScan.
18 Flood, 'Death of the novel' (June 2019).
19 Qtd in Flood, 'Death of the novel' (June 2019).
20 Milliot and Deahl, 'What's the Matter with Fiction Sales?', *Publishers Weekly* (26 October 2018).
21 Qtd in Flood, 'Death of the novel' (June 2019).
22 Donna Ferguson, 'Poetry sales soar as political millennials search for clarity', *Guardian* (21 January 2019), citing figures from Neilsen BookScan.
23 Graywolf website (2004), no author.
24 Graywolf website (2014), no author.
25 Penguin UK website (2015), no author.
26 Penguin UK website (2017), no author.
27 'Guidance on Submissions', Research Assessment Exercise 2008 (June 2005), 5.
28 Repeated in various documents, including the HEFCE (Higher Education Funding Council for England, now the Office of Students) REF Consultation document (2017), 4, and the current 'FAQ' section on the main REF site.
29 Arts and Humanities Research Council (now part of UK Research and Innovation) website.
30 Ibid., 'Definition of Research'.
31 Wandor, *The Author Is Not Dead, Merely Somewhere Else* (London: Palgrave, 2008), 145.
32 Ibid.
33 Lasky, 'Poetics and Creative Writing Research' (2013), 16.
34 'Subject Benchmark Statement: Creative Writing', *Quality Assurance Agency* (Feburary 2016), 16.
35 Ibid., 19.
36 Eliot, 'Little Gidding', in *The Poems of T.S. Eliot Volume I: Collected and Uncollected Poems*, ed. Christopher Ricks (London: Faber, 2015).

PART IV

NEW PRODUCERS

Chapter 10

POETRY AND WORK: SOME THOUGHTS ON *PATERSON*

1

I used to give a pep talk to new undergraduates at the start of their creative writing degrees, showing stills from films about writers. They were mostly recent films I hoped they might know – *Adaptation, Wonder Boys, Stranger Than Fiction, Miss Potter, Becoming Jane, The Hours* – with images of authors staring into the distance, chain-smoking at manual typewriters, unshaven or in dressing gowns, all awaiting the muse. The point was to get the students thinking realistically about the work of writing, beyond its cultural baggage. I would end by showing the scene in *Breakfast in Tiffany's* when Audrey Hepburn's Holly Golightly asks George Peppard's Paul Varjak whether he writes every day. When he says, 'Sure', she points out that his typewriter has no ribbon. 'Don't be like Paul Varjak,' I'd say. 'You have to do the work.'

Poetry's status as 'work' has been up for debate since at least the eighth century BCE, when Hesiod spent 828 lines of it extolling the virtues of an honest day's graft to his good-for-nothing brother in *Works and Days*. 'Between us and goodness, the Gods have placed the sweat of our brows,' he writes. 'Work is no disgrace: it is idleness which is a disgrace.'[1] Though Hesiod is dogmatic about work's value, he seems less interested in what qualifies as work or not. We're left to infer that the making of verse seemed worthwhile labour for the poet, alongside managing the family farm. Twenty-seven centuries later, Philip Levine's best-known book is just as slippery with its definitions, despite being called *What Work Is* (1991). 'You know what work is,' the speaker says twice, almost accusingly, near the start of the title poem. 'If you're / old enough to read this you know what / work is, although you may not do it.' By the end of the poem, we ('you') are waiting in a queue for daily work outside an automotive plant. Yet any assumption of work's hard, physical nature is reconfigured towards what we might now call the 'emotional labour' of loving one another (or someone who looks a bit like our brother, in this case). The reason we have failed in that is 'because you don't know what work is' after all.[2]

With Hesiod and Levine's lost brothers, we're left with the same question: is poetry *work* because it attempts to restore some human connection? Or conversely, do we understand *work* more generally as, like poetry, an activity that necessarily extends beyond ourselves?

By the standards of self-discipline I hoped to instil in those students, Adam Driver's character 'Paterson' in the Jim Jarmusch's 2016 film *Paterson* does the work. The film's repetitive structure outlines the regimen of a presumably typical week: Monday through Friday, the protagonist wakes just after 6:00 a.m., walks to the bus depot, drives a city bus all day, walks home, checks the mail, and walks the dog after dinner. Writing fills the gaps: in voice-over as he walks to work, in lines jotted in a notebook while waiting for his route to begin, then in lunch breaks, and early evenings again, at a makeshift desk in his garage. In all, we see him finish seven new poems. Not bad for one week.

Yet, the question of whether this creative productivity is being depicted as 'work' is posed in several, occasionally conflicting ways. Like other fictional artists at work, the writing routine in *Paterson* first invites us to gauge the apparent effort involved. By this most basic high school physics definition, 'work' is an action involving a certain amount of force. We see this in defences of poetry like T. S. Eliot's 'Tradition and the Individual Talent' (1919), where the misconception of poets' 'necessary laziness' is rebuffed by a sense of the poet's training as 'a great labour,' which one 'must sweat for'.[3] *Paterson*'s presiding spirit, William Carlos Williams, also takes effort as a mark of value in *Spring and All* (1923), where he writes: 'The better work men do is always done under stress and at great personal cost.'[4] Beyond these two modernist figureheads, early twentieth-century poets (and American poets, especially) embraced this conception of poet's labour, recoiling perhaps from older notions of Romantic inspiration or art for art's sake. Louis Zukofsky, in his introduction to a 1932 'Objectivist' anthology (which included Williams), writes repeatedly of 'poetry defined as a job, as a piece of work'.[5]

On the basis that work equals effort, and compared to other toiling cinema caricatures, the writing in *Paterson* come suspiciously easily. Even when revisiting one poem in another free moment, not a single word is crossed out or reconsidered. Many are written straight through, titles included, with Driver's voice-over mimicking the pace of transcription, rather than compositional hesitation. We might compare this to the labour on display in a 2017 issue of the *New York Times Book Review*, for instance, which included heavily annotated drafts of 'poetry in action'.[6] From interviews around the release of *Paterson*, we might suspect the character's writing process is a reflection of the writer-director's own. 'I don't rewrite,' Jarmusch has insisted. 'I don't do multiple drafts.'[7] In a thoughtful comparison of *Paterson* with Terence Davies's Dickinson biopic, *A Quiet Passion* (also 2016), Lucy Scholes argues that this apparent effortlessness, as much as 'frustrated genius' clichés, points to formal limitations when depicting creative labour. Perhaps, her headline suggests, 'the lives of the poets aren't all that cinematic'.[8] After all, no one wants to watch someone question a tiny decision for hours or days, eventually reverting to the initial choice, then rethinking the entire poem in a way that makes the reworked bit irrelevant. Real-world creativity is hopelessly non-linear, full of false starts and trial and error. Too much happens invisibly, unconsciously. Cigarettes and crumbled pages around the bin are easy visual shorthand. If a story requires actual progress at some point, a montage will suffice. I've stopped assuming writers on film hold sway over students.

2

If poetry's status as work is worth asserting, it needs to go beyond semantics and subjective difficulty into more practical considerations of how the making of poems is valued alongside other kinds of labour. To this end, *Paterson* nudges the question of whether poetry *is* work towards a more interesting one about what *kind of* work it might be. In subtle and less subtle ways, Jarmusch's film gives us a chance to weigh poem-making against, on the one hand, more material types of 'creative' work, and on the other, the waged work of Paterson's bus driving job. The structure and editing foreground a sustained comparison of the former. While Paterson writes 'at work', his wife Laura makes things at home: sewing or painting curtains, making or refashioning clothes, redecorating their house, learning to play the guitar, or baking cupcakes for the local farmers market. Immediately, we're confronted with the historically lopsided status and gendered division of work in the public or private sphere.

For the philosopher Hannah Arendt, this apparently ancient division of public and private is linked to the elevation of intellectual labour over manual labour (or what we now call white- over blue-collar work) in classical Greek society.[9] In *The Human Condition* (1958), Arendt singles out 'poetry, whose material is language' as 'perhaps the most human and least worldly of the arts, the one in which the end product remains closest to the thought that inspired it'.[10] In other words, poetry is nearest to purely intellectual labour. Beyond questions of effort, this gives us the option of evaluating the nature of poetry-work in terms of its material (or immaterial) context. In *The Craftsman* (2008), however, Richard Sennett diverges from Arendt (his former teacher), insisting on the blend of mental and manual labour in the type of work he venerates as 'craft'. 'Every good craftsman conducts a dialogue between concrete practices and thinking,' Sennett argues. In this way, *craft* and its products represent 'the intimate connection between the hand and head'.[11] But Sennett also acknowledges the unequal status of different crafts, recalling Arendt's distinction between public and private labour in his defence for the male focus of *The Craftsman*. 'Most domestic crafts and craftsmen seem different in character than labor now outside the home,' he writes. 'We do not think of parenting, for instance, as a craft in the same sense that we think of plumbing or programming, even though becoming a good parent requires a high degree of learned skill.'[12] In Sennett's account, this is simply the way it is. The preface of Matthew Crawford's *Shop Class as Soulcraft* – published the year after Sennett's book (and in the United Kingdom as *The Case for Working with Your Hands*) – defends is male focus likewise: 'It so happens that most of the characters who appear in this book are men, but I am sure that women, no less than men, will recognize the appeal of tangible work that is straightforwardly useful.'[13]

When *Paterson* premiered at the Cannes festival in May 2016, Jarmusch recalls some 'feminist French journalist' accusing him of making 'a throwback to '50s domesticity, et cetera, with this character of Laura'. He finds this 'a little shallow', however, and is ready with a long rebuttal, which ends with him exclaiming, 'I'm a feminist!'[14] Elsewhere, he tempers it to 'I consider myself a feminist, in a way.'[15] To the French journalist and anyone questioning the film's undeniably regressive gender roles, Jarmusch explains:

> Laura lives how she wants; she does what she wants. She's entrepreneurial, even if it's in a domestic set-up like selling cupcakes. She wants to maybe be musical – she's very artistic in décor – so to say that she is not liberated, if one were to say that, then I wonder how these people think of all the working-class women in the world that are washing their families' clothes or making food.[16]

Jarmusch telling a female interviewer that 'domesticity is a fact of how social structure works' isn't far from Sennett's matter-of-factness regarding the difference in character of gendered work. Yet, his defence of Laura's 'entrepreneurial' set-up also points to an essential difference in the two main characters' approach to their respective crafts.

Jarmusch comments and his film's characterisation of Laura situate her creative labour within what is often enthusiastically described as a new craft economy. As Judy Hong, an analyst at Goldman Sachs, puts it in a video guide to market trends from May 2016: 'We are in the midst of a craft revolution.'[17] Although corporations might focus on the economic impact (or threat) of craft beer and other locally sourced or handmade 'artisanal products', books like Mark Hatch's *The Maker Movement Manifesto* (2013), Chris Anderson's *Makers: The New Industrial Revolution* (2013), Peter Korn's *Why We Make Things & Why It Matters* (2017), Richard Ocejo's *Masters of Craft: Old Jobs in the New Urban Economy* (2017), and many more, promote ways in which individual 'makers' can thrive within a growing creative marketplace. Sales of sewing machines have boomed in recent years, the fibre arts forum Ravelry boasts 8 million users, and the UK chain Hobbycraft reported a record annual sales up 63 per cent in 2016, the same year that Etsy, the central online marketplace for handmade and vintage items, oversaw more than US$2.84 billion in purchases.[18] In the United Kingdom, television phenomena like the *Great British Bake Off* or *Great British Sewing Bee*, often credited as drivers of the 'craft revolution', are also symptomatic.

In *Paterson,* Laura's work reflects this cultural sense of creative activity being increasingly bound up in commercial ambition or viability. Although we're not told whether she has an Etsy account or sells her work anywhere besides the local farmers market, the lure of the so-called creative industries is explicit in other ways. Making a plea for a new guitar and DVD lessons, she parrots its YouTube advert: 'In no time at all, I could be playing away and realising my dream!' On another day, it's her baking that will fulfil 'my dream – to have my own cupcake business, of course.' With a child-like, manic pixie enthusiasm, which Driver's character seems to find amusing at best, she swears her music could make her 'a big star, like one of the greats' or that 'we could be rich from cupcakes.' Despite the writer-director's claim that this makes her 'liberated,' the film is fairly consistent in the humour it derives from her capricious and unrealistic dreams.[19]

Shown alongside the treatment of Paterson's writing, the film's spoofing or outright sneering towards the craft economy returns us to the question of poetry's work status. Is poetry a 'craft', if that category implies (for Sennett, Crawford, and the film) commercial potential? Or is its economic autonomy preserved in Arendt's sense of its relative immateriality? Although some debate the definition of craft as the making of things for sale,[20] Jarmusch's praise for Laura's entrepreneurialism also contradicts his own film's persistent portrayal of her partner's poetry as a special mode of activity, removed from the economic contingencies associated with other creative work – to the point that it ceases to be work at all. This is demonstrated by the apparent ease with which Paterson composes, his invisible intellectual labour taking precedent over the sort of material labour with which we see Laura dirtying her hands. But Arendt herself, clarifying her suggestion that 'of all things of thought, poetry is closest to thought, and a poem is less a thing than any other work of art,' is quick to add that even a poem 'will eventually be "made," that is, written down and transformed into a tangible thing among things'.[21] ('Poetry', after all, means 'making'.) Although she is critical of Marx's theory of labour in other ways, Arendt follows his emphasis here on its essential material context. 'Labour is, first of all, a process between man and nature,' Marx writes in *Capital* (1867), or the means by which a person 'confronts the materials of nature as a force of nature'.²² It is, by definition, an activity that affects and manipulates the world beyond our thoughts.

In *Paterson*, resistance to seeing poetry as 'a tangible thing among things' is crucial to the narrative, to the extent that – avoiding a predictable spoiler – the notebook in which the protagonist records his poems becomes literally immaterial. Of course, to Laura's craft mentality, Paterson's reluctance to share his writing seems unimaginable. 'You know, darling,' she says as an afterthought to the cupcake conversation, 'I really think you should do something about those beautiful poems. They should belong to the world.' Though he laughs off her phrase 'the world,' he also opts to recite other people's poems whenever she asks to hear any of his work. On another day, softening him up for the guitar conversation, Laura makes Paterson promise he will photocopy what she calls his 'secret notebook' – 'Baby, I've been asking for a year, at least.' In this sense, the pure action of poetry is under pressure to 'do something' with it. But ultimately, these worldly considerations are superseded by Paterson's stoic and solitary dedication to his art. If *work* is necessarily social – in any economic, ethical, or otherwise interpersonal sense – this must be something else.

3

An economic definition of *work* is one with which poetry remains distinctly uneasy, perhaps because it is used so often to disqualify it from that category. Basil Bunting (another occasional Objectivist) satirises an all-too-typical attack in his poem 'What the Chairman Told Tom', in the voice of an arts council committee chair, denying support for Tom Pickard's writing. It starts:

> Poetry? It's a hobby.
> I run model trains.
> Mr. Shaw there breeds pigeons.
>
> It's not work. You don't sweat.
> Nobody pays for it.²³

While some contemporary poets might argue that the fact 'nobody pays for it' affords poetry a freedom or degree of autonomy from market values, others, like Kate Fox, are increasingly vocal in defending the role of 'professional poet' as 'a job like any other', as grounds for fair compensation.²⁴

Compared to the film's interest in poetry's relation to other creative practices, *Paterson* is resolute in its separation from the protagonist's waged work. The decision to make Paterson a bus driver simply facilitates his writing habit, within the film's broader fantasy of working-class life and the place for creative practice within it. Rather than a means of survival, Jarmusch describes the character's job as what allows him 'to drift, allows him to create things'.[25] Elsewhere, he explains: 'Because he doesn't have to think about what clothes does he wear each day, what time does he go to work [...] everything is laid out for him, and that lets him be a poet.'[26] (It is unclear where this leaves Laura, with her lack of routine or uniform.) Reviewing the film for the *Times Literary Supplement*, the poet Alan Brownjohn agrees that the film 'sensibly implies that writing poetry is helped by a stable, ordered, even unromantic life'.[27]

In *Shop Class as Soulcraft*, Crawford sets out his case against the romanticisation of seemingly 'unromantic' life. He writes, 'I want to avoid the precious images of manual work that intellectuals sometimes traffic in. I also have little interest in wistful notions of a "simpler" life that is somehow more authentic, or more democratically valorous for being "working class."'[28] In *Paterson*, by contrast, a child poet who the protagonist encounters on his way home from work doesn't hide her amusement at 'a bus driver who likes Emily Dickinson'. In the film's closing scenes, Paterson himself is dubious of a poet visiting from Japan, who sagely assures him, 'a bus driver – this is very poetic'. For the sake of realism, Adam Driver apparently spent three months taking lessons to get his bus licence before filming began. The poems his character writes, however, are all by the veteran New York poet Ron Padgett.[29] This is suggestive in itself – the assumption that one might learn to drive a bus convincingly in three months, but that the poetry needs a ringer. Alas, rather than explore the comparison between the work of writing and the work of driving a bus, the latter remains at best a useful routine or quirky visual backdrop. One of Padgett's new poems written for the film extends this wholesome distancing of waged labour:

I knock off work
Have a beer at the bar
I look down at the glass and feel glad.[30]

Again, William Carlos Williams is a curious point of reference. As the film's last scene briefly acknowledges, Williams was another writer with a day job, working as a general practitioner and paediatrician, delivering over 2,000 babies in his long medical career. 'I love that poets have other jobs,' says Jarmusch, namechecking Frank O'Hara and Wallace Stevens. 'You've got to have another job to do this stuff. No poet ever did it for the money.'[31] The sense of a work routine facilitating creative practice, like Paterson's bus route, is recorded by Williams as well. 'Only medicine, a job I enjoyed, would make it possible for me to live and write as I wanted to,' he says in his *Autobiography*

(1955).³² In 'times of stress,' he explains in the same book, 'it would be comforting to be carrying a poem in my head, searching for an aberrant structure – and unable for the whole day to get it down.'³³ We can imagine Jarmusch's Paterson agreeing.

However, Williams's wider thoughts on work suggest a deeper correspondence than the film allows. An insistence on work's inherent virtue connects Williams not only to Sennett's elevation of 'an enduring, basic impulse, the desire to a job well for its own sake', but to strand running back through American pragmatist philosophy, a Protestant work ethic, probably all the way to Hesiod.³⁴ 'One must work, hard at times, to no purpose other than the bare mechanics of the work itself,' Williams writes in one letter, before a long account of recent patients. In another, to his adult son, he explains:

> I don't want a vacation and couldn't enjoy it if I had one. I want to work and to keep working, it soothes my mind. I feel then that I am doing my part as I want to. For wherever we are, every stitch of work we do all helps the general cause.³⁵

In *A Novelette*, from the 1920s, he puts it most bluntly: 'I cannot not work.'³⁶ These excerpts blend the compulsion and inherent value of work in a way that splits the difference between Marx's emphasis on alienation – the idea that all work 'is *external* to the worker, i.e., it does not belong to his essential being'³⁷ – and the sense of reconnecting through work, which Sennett or others inherit from William Morris and Arts and Craft notions of 'creative labour'. What Williams (like his friend Zukofsky) resists, importantly, is the drawing of hard and fast distinctions between the writing of poetry and other waged work. Unlike Jarmusch's *Paterson*, he frequently compares or slides between them, using the word 'work' in reference to both types of activity throughout his writing.

Another quirk of Williams's writing career is illustrative alongside the anticlimactic loss of Paterson's notebook. While the film takes its name and premise from Williams's five-volume 'long poem upon the resemblance between the mind of modern man and a city', Jarmusch admits that '*Paterson*, by the way, is not one of my favorite poems – in fact, it goes over my head. I don't understand a lot of it.'³⁸ Instead, he compares the film's interest in 'anti-significance' to Williams's more famous poem, 'The Red Wheelbarrow'.³⁹ Although the book that poem comes from, *Spring and All* (1923), is now safely regarded as Williams's most important contribution to twentieth-century poetry, there were 47 years after its publication, when it was not only lost to readers in its complete form, but disregarded by its author even more emphatically than Paterson lets go of his 'secret notebook'. In 1923, after a friend in Paris agreed to print *Spring and All*, most of the 300 copies were destroyed by customs officials when they reached the United States. As Williams's biographer Paul Mariani tells the story, they were simply confiscated 'as foreign stuff and therefore probably salacious and destructive of American morals'.[40] It might also have had something to do with the fact that Williams's little blue book had come from the same printer as James Joyce's banned *Ulysses* the year before.

While *Spring and All*'s lost history is a curiosity of publishing, the more pertinent aspect may be that Williams himself made no effort to reprint the volume in his lifetime. Not only that, he later dismisses the book – which Ron Silliman would dub 'the apotheosis of modernist writing' – as a mere 'travesty', which he 'had a lot of fun with [...] a mixture of philosophy and nonsense'.[41] Williams makes no mention of it in his otherwise comprehensive *Autobiography*, and his determination to carry on with new work offers a parallel, not only after the fact, but in the opening lines of *Spring and All* itself:

> If anything of moment results – so much the better. And so much the more likely will it be that no one will want to see it.[42]

In my experience of teaching *Spring and All*, students sometimes find those first sentences hard to take at their word. How can anyone – especially students self-funding a return to education in hopes of improving their writing to a publishable standard – not care if no one sees their work? When Williams answers himself in a later interview, admitting that indeed, 'Nobody ever saw it – it had no circulation at all,' it seems too easy to read this as retrospective bitterness regarding a book written in relative obscurity, partly in response to T. S. Eliot's *The Waste Land* (1922).[43] Yet, Williams's enormous output – more than 40 volumes of poetry, novels, plays, and criticism, without retiring early from his medical practice – reflects his understanding of poetry as worthwhile work. Like the notebook tucked in Paterson's jacket or behind the driver's seat of his bus, Williams scribbled lines onto prescription slips in any spare moment between patients. Although no one would accuse Williams of lacking publishing ambitions, the work ethic in his day job carries into the 'hard battle', as he describes it in *Spring and All*, confessing: 'I myself seek to enter the lists with these few notes jotted down in the midst of the action, under distracting circumstances – to remind myself of the truth.'[44]

Along with the book's material loss and Williams's later dismissal, *Spring and All*'s opening is as bracing as ever in its rejection of the sort of professionalism Andy Merrifield takes to task in his provocative study, *The Amateur* (2017). Rather than accept a rigid distinction between 'professional' and 'amateur' based on pay, Merrifield advocates amateurism as 'an alternative sensibility,' which might be as readily adopted by 'underground amateurs', working to 'de-professionalise' themselves and the hyper-professionalised world around them.[45] Outsider writers and thinkers like Franz Kafka, Jane Jacobs, Rachel Carson, and Arendt are Merrifield's examples – among whom Williams and his fictional acolyte would sit well. For both, it is continuing the work that matters.

4

In the months or years I've been searching for a line through notions of poetry as work – before Jarmusch's *Paterson* offered so many obvious points to push against – or in the couple of weeks I've spent writing and rewriting this essay, I've had plenty of time to wonder: 'Is this work?' And worse: Is my struggle to articulate these issues partly rooted in anxieties about the enforced valuation of my own writing practices, as someone paid an academic salary in expectation of critical and creative 'outputs'? Maybe this explains my wariness about leaping to comparisons between poetic and academic labour.

I stopped by campus this morning to pick up some marking, one part of my job that I am certain is work. This was despite having taken annual leave for the week, hoping to finish this essay before the new term starts. I feel bad about working on leave, for the sake of employment rights and my own wellbeing, though trying to cram leave into term breaks makes the days I put up an away message feel arbitrary. And where does the work end anyway, I reassure myself. Am I allowed to read the news, if I promise not to write about it or ever reference it in teaching? Coming from the post room with my stack of marking, I bumped into our departmental manager in the stairwell, where so many unscheduled meetings take place.

The whole summer in 2017, we have had the politician Andrew Adonis gunning for higher education on Twitter, taking crowd-pleasing potshots at our '3-month summer holiday'. Colleagues quickly filled social media with photos and other proof of work with the hashtag #academicsummer. Mary Beard explained 'what do academics do on their summer "vacation"'' in the *TLS*.[46] Of course, I'm in complete solidarity against Adonis's ruse. But I still feel guilty bumping into anyone on campus when I've been working from home. I tell myself that having worked as a university administrator for a year and a half after my PhD makes me more empathetic regarding our industry's unique divide between 'faculty' and 'staff', not to mention those on permanent and precarious contracts. But all of these questions about the nature of 'work' have practical repercussions in a workplace where some employees are paid to be there nine to five and others insist our flexibility just means we're always working.

I ask about the holiday our manager mentioned when we spoke last month. I hadn't realised it was a diving trip, with real shipwrecks. I tell her the idea fills me with dread, but admit it sounds amazing. (Automatically, I also make a mental note to check if the library was able to get the new edition of Adrienne Rich for my teaching next term.) She is a certified instructor, it turns out. 'It's my other life,' she laughs, and explains: 'I know all of you have your personal lives and interests bound up in your jobs, but I have to get away to be myself.'

The idea of poetry as 'work' is only worth defending if it leads to better questions about its material contexts. These might be questions around material resources for this supposedly 'least worldly of the arts' and ways in which unequal access to them works to exclude or privilege. Or they might be questions about how poetic labour is regulated, subsumed, or exploited in relation to other, interconnected labour markets. In any event, the naming of poetry as 'work' might play a part in wider efforts to dispel the myth of poetry's economic autonomy – the primary myth behind which it hides its own labour, alongside other myths of its inherent virtues or radicality. Poetry can't be both 'work' and unquestionably edifying. But reconsidering poetry's status as 'work' or 'creative labour' or 'a job like any other' can be more than a claim to value or a demand for respect, if it avoids glib comparisons that overlook the alienating effect of most waged labour. It can be more than a means for gatekeeping between 'professional' poets and the so-called hobbyists. Finally, it can be less a kneejerk defence of poetry's cultural value and more of a means for acknowledging its complex, relatively privileged status. Not all work, not even all craft or creative work, has a place in school curriculum or as many different periodicals or prizes discussed in mainstream press, for instance. Not all work has access to public funding or to so many institutions that support its training and propagation. Not all work was included in the list of trades that Boris Johnson suggested will sustain the UK economy after Brexit.[47] Not all work is admired by strangers in ways that might come across as patronising. Not all work has films made about it. Most importantly, not all work allows for the self-actualisation presumed of poetic labour. Most work is 'external' to our 'essential being'.

None of this has any implication for the privilege or struggle of individual poets, of course. Nor it is to suggest poets ought to shy away from claims to work or labour. Rather, it is in hopes of shifting the emphasis of that claim towards the material circumstances of poetry's production and the material impact of its products. This means being less enamoured of poetry's presumed virtues than of its social potential – less the fantasy of solitary toil than its debt to human and worldly connections. As Philip Levine doesn't quite say, that's what work is.

Notes

1. Hesiod, *Works and Days* (ll. 285 and 311) in *The Homeric Hymns and Homerica*, trans. Hugh G. Evelyn-White (London: William Heinemann, 1914).
2. Philip Levin, *What Work Is* (New York: Knopf, 1991).
3. Eliot, 'Tradition and the Individual Talent', *Selected Essays: 1917–1932* (London: Faber, 1932), 14.
4. Williams, *Spring and All*, in *Imaginations*, ed. Webster Schott (New York: New Directions, 1971), 101.
5. Zukofsky, '"Recencies" in Poetry', from *An "Objectivists" Anthology* (1932), reprinted in *Prepositions: The Collected Critical Essays*, ed. Mark Scroggins (Hanover, NH: Wesleyan University Press, 2000), 207.
6. Gregory Cowles, 'Poetry in Action', *New York Times Review of Books* (1 August 2017).
7. Amy Taubin, 'Common Sense', *Film Comment* (November-December 2016 Issue, online).
8. Lucy Scholes, 'The Lives of the Poets Aren't All That Cinematic', *LitHub* (13 April 2017).
9. Among other examples, Arendt offers lines from Aristotle's *Metaphysics*: 'We consider that the architects in every profession are more estimable and know more and are wiser than the artisans, because they know the reasons of the things which are done' (qtd Arendt, *The Human Condition* (Chicago, IL: University of Chicago Press, 1998), 23).
10. Arendt, *The Human Condition*, 169.
11. Sennett, *The Craftsman*, reprint edn (London: Penguin, 2009), 9.
12. Ibid., 23.
13. Robert Crawford, *The Case for Working with Your Hands: Or Why Office Works Is Bad for Us and Fixing Things Feels Good* (London: Viking, 2010), 5.
14. Taubin, 'Common Sense'.
15. Colleen Kelsey, 'Jim Jarmusch's Poetic Verse', *Interview* magazine (19 December 2016).
16. Ibid.
17. Judy Hong, 'Artisanal Appeal: The Rise of Craft', Goldman Sachs website (10 May 2016).
18. Sarah Butler, 'Hobbycraft sales and profits rise amid art and craft boom', *Guardian* (23 June 2016).
19. Although the couple in the film have no children, many of these stereotypes align with the 'desperate success' described by Jo Littler (*Against Meritocracy: Culture, Power and Myths of Mobility*, London: Routledge, 2018) in relation to 'mumpreneurs', which I return to in Chapter 11.
20. Among many examples, the anonymous *Yahoo Makers* article, 'Never Say This to a Knitter. Really, Just Don't Do It' (26 January 2015), sparked an online debate by suggesting someone should sell their work was 'one of the worst things possible to tell a knitter'.
21. Arendt, *The Human Condition*, 170.
22. Marx, *Capital*, vol. I, trans. Ben Fowkes (New York: Vintage, 1976), 283.
23. Bunting, *Complete Poems*, ed. Richard Caddel (Newcastle: Bloodaxe Books, 2000), 138.
24. Fox, 'Where There's Poems There's Brass?', personal website (23 February 2015).
25. Interview with Adam Driver and Jim Jarmusch, 'Exclusive: What Is "Paterson"?' *IMDb* (18 April 2016).
26. Taubin, 'Common Sense'.

27 Alan Brownjohn, 'Poetry in Paterson', *TLS Online* (16 January 2017).
28 Crawford, *The Case for Working with Your Hands*, 6.
29 In an interview for *Deadline* (with Anthony D'Alessandro, 22 November 2016), Driver explains: 'I think the biggest thing was learning how to drive a bus; I had an elementary knowledge of poetry. I knew of Allen Ginsberg's *Howl* and E.E. Cummings. I didn't know about Ron Padgett's poems that appear in *Paterson*, and the New York School. Jim also turned me on to Frank O'Hara.'
30 *Paterson* (dir. Jim Jarmusch, 2016).
31 Taubin, 'Common Sense'.
32 Williams, *Autobiography* (New York: New Directions, 1955), 51.
33 Ibid., 307.
34 Sennett, 9.
35 Williams, *Selected Letters*, ed. John C. Thirwall (New York: New Directions, 1985), 174, 198.
36 Williams, *Imaginations*, ed. Webster Schott (New York: New Directions, 1970), 291.
37 Marx, *Economic and Philosophical Manuscripts of 1844*, trans. Martin Milligan (New York: Dover, 2007), 72.
38 Williams, *Paterson*, ed. Christopher MacGowan (New York: New Directions, 1992), xiii; Stephanie Zacharek, 'Jim Jarmusch Talks About His New Movie, *Paterson*, and the Exuberance of Great Poetry', *Time* (21 December 2016).
39 Taubin 'Common Sense'.
40 Mariani, *William Carlos Williams: A New World Naked* (New York: McGraw-Hill, 1981), 209.
41 Silliman, untitled entry on personal website (30 June 2008); Williams, *I Wanted to Write a Poem: The Autobiography of the Works of a Poet* (Boston: Beacon Press, 1958), 37.
42 Williams, *Imaginations*, 88.
43 Williams, *I Wanted to Write a Poem*, 36. In his *Autobiography*, Williams describes the publication of *The Waste Land* in the years before *Spring and All* as 'the great catastrophe' (146) or 'an atom bomb', referencing Eliot's dedication '*il miglior fabbro*': 'being an accomplished craftsman, better skilled than I could ever hope to be, I had to watch him [Eliot] carry my world off with him' (174).
44 Williams, *Imaginations*, 98.
45 Merrifield, *The Amateur: The Pleasure of Doing What You Love* (London: Verso, 2017).
46 Mary Beard, 'What do academics do in the summer "vacation"', *Times Literary Supplement* (25 July 2017).
47 Boris Johnson, 'My vision for a bold, thriving Britain enabled by Brexit', *Daily Telegraph* (15 September 2017). Full context: 'Indeed, a recent estimate by the Henry Jackson Society just this month made a tally of the various nations' political, economic and cultural throw-weight, and concluded that, with the second biggest contribution to Nato; with our forces deployed around the world; with our bankers, our chefs, our scientists, our poets and, yes, our diplomats, Britain at the beginning of the twenty-first century was the second-greatest power on Earth after America.'

Chapter 11

THE POET AS ENTREPRENEUR

There is a literal sense in which the figures of the *poet* and *entrepreneur* are fundamentally opposed. The Greek root of the former is a verb that means 'to make' – as several previous chapters have already mentioned, in my broader attempt to draw attention to poetry's material contexts and material conceptions of its production, as distinct from its circulation as a commodity. The word 'entrepreneur' is a much more recent, mid-eighteenth-century coinage even in French, before it shortly thereafter entered English usage. The Irish-French writer Richard Cantillon, known as the 'Father of Political Economy', first described the 'entrepreneur' in his *Essay on the Nature of Trade in General* (1755) as a figure who 'carries' or 'bears' financial risk, while Jean-Baptiste Say, in his *Treatise on Political Economy* (1800), supplements this with an emphasis on 'undertaking' a new enterprise.[1] Whether we understand the French etymology with a focus on 'carrying between' or 'undertaking', there is a meaningful antipathy between a notion of *poetry* as 'making' and *entrepreneurship* as 'taking'. This becomes important when considering the applicability of the latter term to the work of poets (or the work of most creative practitioners, I would argue). In many cases, this conceptual gap signifies a real division in practice, between the actual 'making' of poems and all the other stuff required to 'take' these goods to market.

As part of the book's final section on poetry's 'new producers', this chapter considers the influence of entrepreneurial culture on contemporary poetry. In the mode of many preceding chapters, the discussion is grounded in its attention to the rhetoric of entrepreneurship. Building particularly on the last chapter's conceptions of poetic work and labour, my simple argument is that this changing language has real consequences. Moreover, given the strong business connotations of entrepreneurship, I want to stress from the start that these consequences for contemporary poetry culture do not depend on the adoption or rejection of that language by individual poets. To some extent, this book's emphasis on the wider influence of new creative industries discourse culminates in the degree to which entrepreneurial values have become normalised and internalised – not only for those involved with poetry, but for all of us. As Jo Littler argues, though a 'blend of government policy and cultural and media discourse, glossy media features, workplace subcontracting and incentivisation to those with limited possibilities, individuals are increasingly encouraged to become entrepreneurs'.[2] Whatever our response to this encouragement, as Pierre Dardot and Christian Laval put it, the marketisation of daily life under neoliberalism means that the label of entrepreneur might be applied to 'potentially, any and every economic subject'.[3] By reframing every activity through the lens of competition, inspiring a constant state of self-evaluation and cost-benefit analysis in relation to personal goals, the various cultural economies, attention economies, and real economies not only intersect on the entrepreneur as a legible trope for channelling cultural, social, and economic capital through the actions of the individual, but also ensure that participation in these economies requires the adoption, however unconsciously or unwillingly, of entrepreneurial values and ways of thinking.

Rather than accuse any particular poet or publisher of being more or less 'entrepreneurial', I'm looking for ways of understanding the more general influence of entrepreneurial ideology on contemporary poetry – ultimately, in hope of finding points of resistance. The task is complicated, I suggest here, by the degree of overlap between what those from business contexts might regard as entrepreneurial values and those in poetry might see as inherent to their art form, or inherent to creativity as such. As Oli Mould argues in *Against Creativity* (2018), this is partly the result of economic culture's appropriation of the language of creativity in recent years, in which 'creativity became *the* critical paradigm of economic growth'.[4] As I discussed in Chapter 7 (on cities), much of this rhetoric stems from writers like Richard Florida, whose conception of a new 'creative class' extends the value of creativity to nearly all sectors. Florida insists we 'need to put entrepreneurialism front and center on the economic agenda', due to the correlations between the 'Global Entrepreneurship Index' and 'Global Creativity Index' for countries positioned to foster either entrepreneurship or creativity, at least according to his formulae.[5] (In the context of anglophone poetry, it's worth noting that English-speaking countries make up four of the top five rankings in either case.[6]) The ubiquity of creative and entrepreneurial rhetoric makes it difficult to find a recent advertisement that doesn't aim to inspire personal innovation, some level of risk-taking, the seizing of opportunities or better management of resources, self-fulfilment, and, above all, creativity. If these are the core values of entrepreneurship, this chapter shows how difficult it has become to distinguish them from poetry's core values. In the endless recycling of generic slogans or 'inspo' quotations through social media memes or think pieces, the rhetoric of creative entrepreneurship has come full circle: economic theorists, policy makers, and marketers have fetishised creativity to the point of removing all meaning from the term, while creative workers have had little choice but to absorb an entrepreneurial spirit. To understand its mechanics, I start with examples from the first part of that turn, in which creative models are appropriated for entrepreneurial messages. From this, I consider the problems that result from this convergence of values or the fact that, as Mould puts it, 'being creative today means seeing the world around you as a resource to fuel your inner entrepreneur.'[7]

Creative Models

The following comes from an article published by Michelle Chaffee on her *LinkedIn* page on 22 April 2016, the day after the singer Prince died:

> There is something that fuels every entrepreneur or artist, a compelling desire to create, whether it's a song, a poem, a device or a solution, it's is a driving force and I think we all want that moment when what we imagine is realized. To touch a portion of humanity in some way is, I imagine, intoxicating and goes beyond monetary success or public accolades.[8]

Chaffee, the founder and CEO of the homewares brand Älska, suggests Prince's 'artistry had the ability to unite people of all races and bring a unique and beautiful clarity to the face that we really aren't so different from one another', but also admits that 'as news stories abound about his life and who he was there are things that ring true to me as an entrepreneur'. Among these, she highlights lessons from Prince's life and career, including the following: 'Connecting with your inner passion and purpose is extremely powerful', 'Success takes hard work and persistence', and 'You can come from nothing and be successful.'

Without any mention of specific business decisions or skills, it is clear that Chaffee's admiration of Prince as 'The Consummate Entrepreneur' (in her headline) depends on a conflation of what she sees as his creative achievements with generic advice for all entrepreneurs. The 'desire to create' is the same 'driving force' for both artist and entrepreneur, and clearly resonates – judging by the hundreds of comments, thousands of likes, and more than 100,000 views Chaffee's article received in the days after the singer's death. And it was hardly unique in its sentiments or promptness. *Entrepreneur* magazine published three online features on Prince the same day, followed by many more since, including: 'Remembering Prince: What the Purple One Can Teach You About Creativity', 'Prince's Unique Brand of Trustworthy Leadership', and 'Model Yourself after Prince for the Best in Business and Life'. However ambivalent we might feel about the appropriation of a beloved artist – whose 'passion for producing what he believed in and pushing boundaries rivals that of Steve Jobs or Bill Gates', according to Chaffee – the celebration of the so-called creative entrepreneurship has become a dominant trope in economic discourse.

As outlined in my introduction, the arts agenda for the United Kingdom, as set out by New Labour after the 1997 general election, has been essential to developments reinforced by the party's 'Creative Britain' manifesto in 2010. The historian Robert Hewison explains the logic behind the UK government's great cultural intervention:

> Creative Britain needed a creative economy in order to ensure the continuous innovation on which growth depended. This would be served by a 'creative class' whose occupation was the production of signs and symbols that could be consumed in commodified form. Creative Britain would be populated by young and eager people, who, in spite of their techno-savvy, clung to the romantic image of the struggling artist, whose individualism would make the breakthrough that justified their insecurities and self-exploration.[9]

Despite funding cuts by successive coalition and conservative governments, the legacy of Creative Britain persists in celebrations of culture linked to the 2012 London Olympics, with its Cultural Olympiad and Poetry Parnassus, or the British Council's 'Creativity is Great' campaign, launched in 2014. In January 2016, the Department for Culture, Media and Sport valued the newly defined creative industries at almost £10 million (US$12 million) an hour, or more than £84 billion ($102 billion) per year.[10] By 2018, the creative industries were growing annually by an average of 11 per cent, twice as fast as the UK economy as a whole.[11] Amid such quantifiable success, Hewison and others have begun asking more difficult questions about the legacy of what former prime minister Tony Blair once sold as 'a golden age for the arts'.[12]

Among these questions, we might ask about poetry's particular susceptibility to entrepreneurial rhetoric. On the one hand, lowly, struggling poets might seem less likely to be mistaken for models of business acumen, at least not to the same extent as an artist with Prince's commercial power. 'Can Artists Be Entrepreneurs?' a *Forbes* headline asked in 2015, then confidently answered, 'Absolutely':

> Contrary to the stereotype of 'starving artists' who've given up hope of life's comforts, a burgeoning category of creative entrepreneurs are building wealth, creating jobs and becoming a major force in national and global economies.[13]

Again, for poets or readers of poetry, one response might be that wealth-building, sustainable job creation, and the idea of being 'major forces' in the global economy sounds far more applicable to the digital media, music, and film industries celebrated in the UK government's £10 million-an-hour press release. Helpfully, in 2016, *Forbes* published another article, on 'The Millennial Entrepreneur Capturing the Spirit of Her Generation with Poetry'. Twenty-six-year-old Samantha Jayne, it tells us, had been working in advertising when she began posting poems and illustrations inspired by 'things that people can relate to' on her Instagram and Tumblr accounts, accumulating over a hundred thousand followers even before the *Forbes* feature.[14] She had recently published her debut collection, *Quarter Life Poetry: Poems for the Young, Broke and Hangry*. So, there are certain poets at least who, like Samantha Jayne, 'see making money as a way to make what I really want'. Beyond social media and print, a TV pilot adapted from the book premiered at Sundance in January 2019, to be followed by a series on FX later this year.

Rather than see poetry's relative precarity – in terms of audience or financial resources, but also in its emphasis on solitary labour and risk – as a condition that protects the art form from co-option into these narratives, it is precisely the 'romantic image of the struggling artist', in Hewison's terms, that makes poetry so vulnerable to entrepreneurial thinking. If precarity is a wider symptom of neoliberalism, entrepreneurial ideology is its primary tool for placing the burden of risk on individuals. The normalisation of entrepreneurial culture in this century coincides with some of the highest-ever rates of self-employment in the United States and the United Kingdom, with the latest figures showing more than 15 per cent of the UK labour force self-employed, and more than a third of the US workers. While entrepreneurial rhetoric emphasises the positive aspects of self-employment, being 'your own boss', or flexible working hours, the overall rise in self-employment is also driven by a significant rise in part-time employment, and a much greater rise in self-employment for those below 25 or above 65.[15] (Uber's ongoing UK legal battle to retain its drivers' classification as 'self-employed', for instance, shows whose interests are served by this rise.) Self-employment is therefore a direct measure of precarity, regardless of celebrations of entrepreneurship that reframe it as a matter of meritocratic creativity. As Jo Littler argues in *Against Meritocracy* (2018), such myths are perpetuated in figures like the 'mumpreneur', whose success in setting up home businesses is balanced against domestic challenges, or the goal of 'having it all'.[16] As bestselling family cookbook author Annabel Karmel writes in her guide, *Mumpreneur* (2015):

> Whatever background you come from, however little money you start off with, there is no getting away from the value of talent, hard work and

vision. If you have passion for something and plenty of entrepreneurial spirit, you can do it.[17]

Only slightly rephrasing the exact language of Chaffee's lessons from Prince, the values of 'passion' and 'hard work' combine with a sense of everyone's potential – 'whatever background you come from, however little money you start off with', in Karmel's terms, or in Chaffee's promise that 'you can come from nothing and be successful'. Much of this language might be weirdly familiar to anyone who has either studied creative writing, attended the Q&A of a successful writer, or read any advice on success in writing. Poetry prides itself on the same meritocratic self-image. Anyone can succeed with a bit of 'talent, hard work and vision'. As the 'punk poet' John Cooper Clarke puts it: 'It's got to be the most accessible art form in the world, poetry. I've never had anything from the arts council. What could I ask for? All they could say to me is, "Ere, ave a quid and get yersen a biro." '[18] In the context of growing precarity, we can see how neatly such claims align with those of entrepreneurialism, and how readily such rhetoric targets what Samantha Jayne jokingly refers to as the 'young, broke, and hangry'.

Poetic Models

Given these affinities or descriptions of multimillion-selling Rupi Kaur as 'the ultimate poet-entrepreneur', we shouldn't be surprised to find other business writers applying the Prince treatment to poets more generally.[19] In an essay on 'The Poetry of Business' for his promotional website, *The Startup Garden: Ideas and Resources for Entrepreneurs*, Tom Ehrenfield offers direct comparisons:

> Essentially, entrepreneurs are people who are creating value by inventing or discovering new ways to connect people, ideas and organizations to one another – in much the same way that poets surprise and inspire us with their ability to make the world new through language. [...] The art of trusting the intuitive leap and of creating meaning in a place where it didn't exist before – and then communicating that to an audience – are fundamental to both.[20]

Here, the importance of passion and hard work gives way to specific ideas about how the very process of poem-making might be entrepreneurial, in its 'intuitive leaps' and production of new language and meaning. Abstracted from its material contexts, the shared work of poets and entrepreneurs is focused on the making of connections, between words and people. Again, it's hard to disagree. Ehrenfield cites tech executive and former poetry MFA David Levine's veneration for Arthur Rimbaud, who the latter describes as 'the ultimate "poetic entrepreneur" '. In Ehrenfield's summary, 'Interestingly, Rimbaud dropped poetry to become an entrepreneur, dealing guns in North Africa.' This makes sense, Levine explains, since 'there is a violence in [Rimbaud's] poetry, as there is a violence inherent in entrepreneurialism.. At the very least, the strained example draws out that violence.

Robert Smith, of the Aberdeen Business School, makes a similar case in 'Entrepreneurship and Poetry', a 2015 article for the *Journal of Small Business and Enterprise Development*: 'Entrepreneurship with all its eulogizing and hero worship should be the perfect subject matter for the poet because poetry is ultimately about articulating power and passion in a memorable way.'[21] The example of Rimbaud also raises a question of historical specificity. As noted above, modern usage of the word 'entrepreneur' – in reference to 'one who undertakes an enterprise; one who owns and manages a business; a person who takes the risk of profit or loss' (*OED*) – enters English from French in the course of the nineteenth century. If that century gave rise to the recognisably modern figures of the self-made poet and self-made businessperson, their histories of 'power and passion' intermingled with the rise of the modern publishing industry and industrial capitalism, it also throws up other candidates for the role of archetypical poet-entrepreneur.

A 2014 article for *Techcrunch* advises start-ups to 'channel your inner Walt Whitman'; and Whitman becomes a recurring prop in such contexts, especially in American business journals.[22] In March 2016, shortly before the headline re-discovery of Whitman's guide to 'Manly Health', the *Investor's Business Daily* published a substantial feature on the poet's life and work. Like Chaffee's tribute to Prince, the most striking aspect is how little effort is required to translate Whitman's independent spirit, his 'breaking every rule', and his dismissal of criticism into business principles.[23] At this point, such analogies are apparently self-evident. A trickier question might be to what extent Whitman's non-conformity – or Emersonian self-reliance, or Wordsworthian egoism – informs poetry's shared inheritance of these ideals. In other words, rather than dismiss these business inspo-pieces as cases of misappropriation, to what extent are the ideals of contemporary poetic practice bound up in those admired by contemporary business practice? As Mould writes, it is the nineteenth century in which:

> The artist producing the work became increasingly important, a development that, over time, wrenched artistic production out of the collective social arena, individualized the creative process and gave birth to the modern conception of the 'creative genius'.[24]

Along with the exploitable value of poetry's romanticised precarity, poetry's fixation on individual achievement and innate talent or 'genius' aligns it seamlessly with the rhetoric of entrepreneurship. The mirror held up by these bits of business clickbait shows the extent of poetry's investment in entrepreneurial notions of self-making and individualism. Whatever stigma remains (if any) in the 'careerist' activities of brazenly entrepreneurial contemporary poets, it falls away in this context and in the debt to savvy writers like Whitman, who self-published and self-promoted expanding editions of *Leaves of Grass*, flogging it door to door, even writing pseudonymous reviews of it himself. Poetry's entrepreneurialism runs deeper than twenty-first century creative industries discourse.

The Split Self

As discussed throughout this book, there remains an even bigger question regarding poetry's economic autonomy, or the extent to which poetic labour connects with the wider production and circulation of goods and capital. Like poetry's valorisation of precarity and individualism, the notion of its market autonomy stems from wider cultural assumptions about the relationship between art and commerce, in which the figure of the 'creative entrepreneur' is often conjured as an unnatural hybrid. In a much-debated article from the *Atlantic* in early 2015, for example, William Deresiewicz makes a broad, historical case for 'the death of the artist and the birth of the creative entrepreneur'. Like Mould, he argues that the rise of modern capitalism in the eighteenth and nineteenth centuries effected a shift from 'craft' to 'art', or from a more collective notion of artisanal labour to ideas of solitary genius, followed by the professionalisation of creative practice in the twentieth century, and finally the rise of creative entrepreneurship in the twenty-first century. After recounting this history fairly matter-of-factly, Deresiewicz offers a sobering punchline:

> When works of art become commodities and nothing else, when every endeavor becomes 'creative' and everybody 'a creative,' then art sinks back to craft and artists back to artisans – a word that, in its adjectival form, at least, is newly popular again. Artisanal pickles, artisanal poems: what's the difference, after all? So 'art' itself may disappear: art as Art, that old high thing. Which – unless, like me, you think we need a vessel for our inner life – is nothing much to mourn.[25]

Many cultural theorists suggest this is precisely our situation, rendering the question of whether a particular writer relates their poetic production to the production of pickles or any other commercial goods either moot or a matter of self-delusion. Theodor Adorno and Max Horkheimer's classic conception of the 'culture industry' defined mass cultural products by their relationship to mass consumption. Leaving aside the question of whether poetry sales or readership have ever qualified as 'mass' (though note Kaur, earlier), Adorno's distinction between a 'mainstream' culture industry and what might be thought of as a more 'authentic' avant-garde is less a matter of commercial value, than it corresponds to a distinction between art-commodities that serve primarily to reassure consumers in perceptions of their own autonomy and, on the other hand, art which challenges such positions. As in the discussion in Chapter 8 of 'fakes', the narrative of artistic autonomy and originality connects with and helps fortify a general sense of human subjectivity. In the 75 years since Adorno and Horkheimer's formulation, the process of commodification has been reassessed as having advanced to the point at which, in Frederic Jameson's words, 'aesthetic production [...] has become integrated into commodity production generally'.[26] Or, as Nicholas Brown has argued, 'What differentiates Adorno's culture industry from the self-representation of our contemporary moment is that the art-commodity now has no other.'[27] As Deresiewicz fears, the possibility of un-commodified 'art as Art, that high old thing' is gone. But paradoxically, the belief in art's autonomy persists precisely because of its market value, in the same way that belief in our autonomous rationality makes us such compliant consumers.

A difficult question for poetry is whether awareness of this paradox helps resolve it. Introducing first-year undergraduates to Adorno some years ago, I remember a particular student's vocal resistance to what others in the room also took to be a kind of snobbery inherent in Adorno's critique. At one point, this student began quoting Radiohead lyrics to the group, from the song 'My Iron Lung': 'This is our new song / Just like the last one / A total waste of time.'[28] This showed the band's self-awareness of their market complicity, according to the student (who is now a fairly well-known and prize-winning poet, I feel obliged to add). As with Prince, discussions of economic and creative autonomy around a band like Radiohead offer a handy comparison for poetry's market relations. The emphasis on this sort of Iron Lung's irony or Radiohead's general meta-knowingness is a common theme in media praise, seen again in the hype around their 2016 album, *A Moon Shaped Pool*. A *Guardian* survey of the band's 'unconventional' approach to album releases points predictably to *Kid A* (2000), as the first of their studio albums to be 'made in reaction to the music industry rather than in conjunction with it'.[29] Another *Guardian* article admiring 'Radiohead's corporate empire' points out the playful names of the band's registered businesses, including Random Rubbish LTD, Unreliable LTD, and even LLLP LLP.[30] Again, such wry self-awareness is offered in support of claims to artistic integrity. Although Radiohead has 'the sort of financial structure you would expect to be more associated with Silicon Valley entrepreneurs', Ian Mack, a music business tutor at the British and Irish Modern Music Institute weighs in: 'I look at their business structure and it doesn't make me say, "Oh my gosh"':

> Does it remove the romance from their music? Of course not. I don't think financial structures come into any musician's head when they sit down at a piano, let's put it that way. They can split the business side from the creative side.[31]

It is in this split-logic that the contemporary creative-entrepreneur thrives, and through which they appear able to reconcile the integrity of creative work with the practicalities of the 'business side'. Or for poetry, come to terms with the division between 'making' and 'taking'. As discussed in my introduction, it's worth remembering that Marx acknowledged this split with an example from poetry. In a chapter drafted for the first volume of *Capital*, he writes:

> Milton, who did *Paradise Lost*, was an unproductive worker. In contrast to this, the writer who delivers hackwork for his publisher is a productive worker. Milton produced *Paradise Lost* in the way that a silkworm produces silk, as the expression of his own nature. Later on he sold the product for £5 and to that extent became a dealer in a commodity.[32]

Milton was initially 'unproductive', in Marx's terms, in so far as the labour involved in writing *Paradise Lost* had direct value, compared with the professional writer whose labour is already contracted. It was only when Milton sold the finished product that it became a commodity and he became something like an entrepreneur, exploiting his own labour for profit, as it were. In this regard, the creative entrepreneur maintains a delicate division within themselves and in the conception of their work, between the presumption of autonomy for the 'creative side', head down at the piano or writing desk, making things freely of their 'own nature', and the intervention of their entrepreneurial 'business side', when the time comes to deliver that product to market. In a contemporary context, the split is experienced most acutely in relation to what Alison Hearn calls the 'branded self' or the self-image curation demanded by social media and other visible promotion. 'The "branded self" is a commodity sign,' Hearn writes, 'it is a body that works and, at the same time, points to itself working, striving to embody the values of its corporate working environment.'[33]

Although poets might see themselves striving towards a different set of values, the sense of needing to 'point to' themselves working is clear in the claims to work status discussed in Chapter 10, as well as the frequent self-references to that labour in social media contexts – with the hashtag #amwriting, for instance. Cory Arcangel's *Working on My Novel* (2014) is another silly, but clear example, collecting the self-conscious tweets of people who claim to be 'working on my novel'. A further manifestation of the doublethink and doublespeak required to preserve this split branded/branding self recurs in discussions around self-promotion, and especially the 'rules' of online self-promotion, framed in terms of etiquette or effectiveness. On 13 April 2015, for example, the American sci-fi novelist Delilah Dawson published a widely shared blog post entitled, 'Please shut up: Why self-promotion as an author doesn't work.' The very next day, responding to a flurry of comments and pushback on social media, Dawson published, 'Wait, Keep Talking: Author Self-Promo That Actually Works.'[34] Later that week, the British poet and editor Josephine Corcoran followed with 'Poetry and Self-Promotion' on her own blog, writing: 'I agree that there is something extremely distasteful about the idea of self-promotion.' Nevertheless, she continues: 'Of course, there is a difference between blatant self-promotion and establishing an online presence.'[35] These fine distinctions between what 'works' and what is 'distasteful' or what is 'blatant' and essential appear almost every time the topic arises, or in self-conscious tweets and mass emails apologising for 'shameless' self-promotion. In interviews with writers, the most typical refrain for those negotiating the creative-business divide might be variations on the advice: 'These days, you have to [...]' whether followed by a list of things necessary to increase exposure and opportunities ('These days, you have to build up a mailing list, keep your website up-to-date, ask readers directly to write reviews [...]') or a list of more general values ('These days, you have to make sacrifices, be pushy, have a clear sense of your brand [...]'), the entrepreneurial imperative is clear. Poetry has changed *these days*, and these are things we simply *have* to do.[36]

Satirical Splits

As with Radiohead, the split-self of the creative entrepreneur is often expressed ironically. In the introduction to *The Program Era* (2009), Mark McGurl interprets the proliferation of satirical campus novels as a response to the institutionalisation of creative writing.[37] For poets and beyond universities, Michael Lewis's 'How to Make a Killing from Poetry' in *Poetry* magazine (2005) offers a joking 'six point plan of attack' advising poets to 'think positive', 'think about your core message', and 'strive to be relevant'.[38] A few years later, Jim Behrle's '24/7 Relentless Careerism' was the most viewed article on the Poetry Foundation's website in 2010, suggesting aspiring poets be more 'devious, sinister, and craven' in order to 'destroy' others. In both cases, the earnestness of below-the-line comments – despite Lewis's piece being included in 'The Humor Issue' with a bio saying 'his interest in saving poets from themselves is insincere' – shows the difficulty or, at worst, tone-deafness of satirising the very real pressures felt by many poets.

A more sustained performance of ironic double-consciousness is Sam Riviere's collection, *81 Austerities*. The poems were first posted on Riviere's Tumblr page in 2011, alongside text fragments, screen captures, photo collages, and other material curated around the theme of austerity. The project described itself as follows:

> The brief was to publish a passive/aggressive response to the 'austerity measures' implemented by the UK government in the wake of the late-2000s financial crisis.' The collection aims to apply such 'cuts' preemptively to poetry itself, experiencing this deprivation primarily on the levels of sentiment, structure, and subject matter.[39]

Published in book-form by Faber the following year, the blurb was adapted with an emphasis on self-reflexivity:

> Initially conceived as a response to the 'austerity measures' implemented by the coalition government in 2011, the poems quickly began taking on a life in kind: 'cutting' themselves on levels of sentiment, structure and even subject matter. Not content to merely build a series of freethinking poems, these remarkable pieces seem eagerly and mischievously to analyse their moment of creation, then weight their worth, then consign their excess to the recycling bin thereafter.[40]

Not unlike Radiohead, the book is recommended here for its 'mischievous' self-awareness regarding its own production and value, ironising the conditions of its making through the 'cuts' re-enacted in its forms and content. 'The effect,' the blurb concludes, 'is as funny as it is startling, beguiling as it is surprising, and makes *Austerities* a vivid reminder that deprivation, as Leonard Cohen puts it, can be the mother of poetry.' The book itself dramatises that split-self in its collage of corporate and policy language, or a sense of its complicity in the careerism spoofed by Lewis and Behrle above. Defying Cooper Clarke's pride in having never received arts council money, the first poem begins:

> In 3 years I have been awarded
> £48,000 by various funding bodies
> councils and publishing houses
> for my contributions to the art .[41]

From there to its extensive and self-critical endnotes, or in the very notion of having written to an un-attributed 'brief', the book dramatises the double-consciousness of the entrepreneurial imperative. By rephrasing this 'passive/aggressive response' as something much more insular, however, the published blurb offsets whatever might be 'startling' or 'surprising' in the poems' political critique with their 'beguiling' humour. In Leonard Cohen's line, Faber's repackaging underlines the degree to which 'deprivation' – as 'the mother of poetry', rather than being 'experienced' (in the original description) – may be exploited for content, valorising the precarity to which the poems might otherwise bear critical witness. By the time the book won the 2012 Forward Prize for Best First Collection, its political content had been reduced by a *Guardian* summary (quoting the judges' comments) to 'an "effortless, wide ranging and confident" look at everyday life in the digital world'.[42]

Conclusion: Against Redemption

This chapter's self-determined brief was to show ways in which poetry's valorisation of creativity, meritocracy, precarity, autonomy, and individual achievement are precisely what make it vulnerable to the contemporary entrepreneurial imperative. I use the word 'valorisation' here in the very literal sense of imbuing these ideals with *value* within a cultural field – even or especially where the ideals themselves might be aligned with resistance. What I call an entrepreneurial imperative is established in turn as the quintessentially neoliberal force by which individual poet-producers are made to feel the necessity of certain traits, values, and practices – all the things you simply *have to do* these days. These imperatives are often rationalised, either pragmatically or ironically, through the reification of a split-consciousness between the creative-self and business-self, the maker and the taker, the poet and the entrepreneur. Much of this appears to be the result of overlapping and increasingly indistinguishable rhetoric around the arts and commerce. While countless examples show creativity being fetishised by business culture, it is also clear that many aspects of contemporary poetry culture, through a process of re-appropriating that 'tainted' language, have had no choice but to become more entrepreneurial.

One of the most striking, but least remarked symbols of contemporary poetry's accommodation of entrepreneurial forces might be the sponsorship, since 2003, of the Forward Prize for best first collection by Felix Dennis. Dennis came to public attention in the late 1960s and 1970s, initially for being the first person to use the c-word on British television, then for a prison sentence on obscenity charges, after the infamous 'Schoolkids' issue of *Oz* magazine. From the 1970s onwards, he built up one of the largest magazine publishing companies in the United Kingdom, finding his greatest success in the 1990s with the so-called lads mags *Maxim* and *Stuff*, before selling these and other US titles for $240 million in 2007. Throughout his career, Dennis held the media spotlight with tales of drug benders, sex workers, and, at one point, the claim he had killed a man. In later years, he supplemented his more-than £500-million net worth by publishing business self-help guides, including *How to Get Rich* (2006) and *How to Make Money* (2010) – the latter of which includes a chart describing those with merely £1–£2 million in liquid assets, not counting property, as 'the comfortable poor'.

While recovering from an illness in 2001 at age 52, Dennis also became a poet, publishing ten volumes of poetry before his death in 2014. Media coverage of the period consistently indulges a narrative of poetic recovery. 'I am absolutely convinced,' he tells an interviewer in 2008, 'that my life was redeemed by poetry.'[43] Poetry 'transformed my somewhat reprehensible life', he tells another in 2013.[44] Another interview in that final year before his death paints a similar picture: 'I am a total prick, but I hope my poetry isn't a reflection of that.'[45] Amid self-funded volumes of light verse and sold-out reading tours that tempted listeners with the promise of expensive wine from his own cellars, his sponsorship of the Forward First Collection prize from 2003 suited this narrative perfectly. Even if no one reads his poetry, his financial legacy has bound him to the future of British poetry with annual prize coverage, ensuring that the worst excesses of Dennis's particular brand of entrepreneurship are concealed beneath the artwashed sheen of fairly meagre philanthropy, at £5,000 each year.

I mention him only to suggest how vividly Felix Dennis embodies the divided self of the creative entrepreneur. In a reverse image of the writer who resents careerist imperatives, the poet in Dennis appears to interrupt his entrepreneur, insisting in *How to Get Rich*:

> In and of itself, great wealth very rarely, if ever, breeds contentment. Believe me, I know. I'm both an entrepreneur and a poet. Perhaps it is the poet typing these words now and not the entrepreneur.[46]

His follow-up, *How to Make Money*, opens by disavowing the first volume with its 'deliberately crass title whose irony escaped all but a few reviewers' and concludes by suggesting the successful reader now give their money away, since 'it was all just a silly game, wasn't it?'[47] Again, tropes of belated redemption echo through his self-satire, through those crass titles or the way he spells his surname with a dollar-sign on the cover of these volumes, but not his poetry books. What might be an embarrassing association for the Forward organisation or winners of the Dennis prize sits comfortably with an abiding belief that the game of entrepreneurship – a world in which, according to Dennis, 'Western capitalism is only made bearable by competition' – will be perpetually redeemed by poetry.[48]

Notes

1 See Andrew C. Corbett and Jerome A. Katz, *Entrepreneurial Action* (Bingley: Emerald Books, 2012), ix.
2 Jo Littler, *Against Meritocracy: Culture, Power, and Myths of Mobility* (London: Routledge, 2018), 185–86.
3 Pierre Dardot and Christian Lavel, *The New Way of the World: On Neoliberal Society* (London: Verso, 2014), 102.
4 Oli Mould, *Against Creativity* (London: Verso, 2018), 11.
5 Florida, *The Rise of the Creative Class*, 389.
6 The most recent Global Entrepreneurship Index rankings were produced by the Global Entrepreneurship and Development Institute in 2018, and the most recent Global Creative Index by Martin Prosperity using figures from 2015, with Florida's guidance, in both cases.
7 Mould, *Against Creativity*, 12.
8 Chaffee, 'Prince; The Consummate Entrepreneur', *LinkedIn* personal page (22 April 2016).
9 Hewison, *Cultural Capital: The Rise and Fall of Creative Britain* (London: Verso, 2014), 5–6.
10 DCMS press release, 'Creative industries worth almost £10 million an hour to economy', Gov.uk (26 January 2016).
11 Reported by many media outlets, but also a press release by NESTA (originally the National Endowment for Science, Technology, and the Arts), reporting their original research, 'Creative industries are driving economic growth across the UK, on track to creative one million new creative industries jobs between 2013 and 2030' (15 February 2018).
12 Blair, 'Blair's speech on the arts in full', *Guardian* (6 March 2007). See Introduction.
13 Cheryl Conner, 'Can Artists Be Entrepreneurs? Absolutely', *Forbes* (25 April 2015).
14 Natalie Sportelli, 'The Millennial Entrepreneur Capturing the Spirit of Her Generation with Poetry', *Forbes* (7 April 2016).
15 'Trends in self-employment', Office of National Statistics (7 February 2018).
16 See Littler's chapter, 'Desperate Success: Managing the Mumpreneur', in *Against Meritocracy*, 179–211.
17 Karmel, *Mumpreneur: The Complete Guide to Starting and Running a Successful Business* (London: Random House, 2015), 15. Also qtd in Littler, *Against Meritocracy*, 188.
18 Rosa Abbott, 'Sadistic Romantic: John Cooper Clarke Interview', *Totally Dublin* (20 May 2014).
19 Faith Hill and Karen Yuan, 'How Instagram Saved Poetry' (originally published online as 'Rupi Kaur and the Rise of the Instagram Poet-Entrepreneur'), *The Atlantic* (15 October 2018).
20 Tom Ehrenfeld, 'Just Managing: The Poetry of Business', *The Startup Garden* website (2002).
21 Robert Smith, 'Entrepreneurship and Poetry: Analysing an Aesthetic Dimension', *Journal of Small Business and Enterprise Development*, vol. 22, no. 3 (2015), 450–72 (454).

22   Zachary Hanson and Diogo Duarte, 'The Poet, Scientist, Journalist, Boxer Approach to Entrepreneurship', *Techcrunch* (9 August 2014). For other examples see Lisa Hix, 'Walt Whitman – Patriotic Poet, Gay Iconoclast, or Shrewd Marketing Ploy?', *Collectors Weekly* (3 May 2016), *Forbes*' 'Who Said It? Meg Whitman v Walt Whitman' (13 September 2013), or another video from John Lee Dumas's 'Entrepreneurs on Fire' YouTube series with 'daily inspiration from Walt Whitman' (19 August 2019). Duke University is also currently running a project, '"After 33 y'rs of hackling at it": The Echoes of Walt Whitman's Entrepreneurial Publishing in Digital Content Creation'.
23   Daniel Allnott, 'Walt Whitman Built Free Verse And Freedom Into His Poetry', *Investor's Business Daily* (21 March 2016).
24   Mould, *Against Creativity*, 7.
25   Deresiewicz, 'The Death of the Artist – and the Birth of the Creative Entrepreneur', *The Atlantic* (January-February 2015 Issue).
26   Jameson, *Postmodernism, or, the Cultural Logic of Late Capitalism* (Durham, NC: Duke University Press, 1991), 4.
27   Nicholas Brown, 'The Work of Art in the Age of its Real Subsumption under Capital', *Nonsite.org* (13 March 2012). Less convincingly, Brown also suggests the 'assertion of autonomy' retains its potential as a 'precondition for any politics at all other than the politics of acquiescence to the dictates of the market.'
28   Radiohead, 'My Iron Lung', *The Bends* (Capitol, 1995).
29   Michael Hann, 'All surprises: Radiohead and the art of the unconventional album release', *Guardian* (2 May 2016).
30   Alex Marshall, 'Radiohead's corporate empire: inside the band's dollars and cents', *Guardian* (29 April 2016).
31   Qtd in Marshall, *Guardian* (29 April 2016).
32   Marx and Frederick Engels, *Collected Works: 1861–1864*, vol. 34, trans. Ben Fowkes (New York: International Publishers, 1994), 448.
33   Hearn, 'Insecure: Narratives and Economies of the Branded Self in Transformation Television', *Continuum* vol. 22, no. 4 (2008), 495–504 (497).
34   Dawson's personal website, *whimsydark* (April 2015).
35   Corcoran, 'Poetry and Self-Promotion', personal website (19 April 2015).
36   Though it's worth remembering that 'these days' is an always sliding moment. In an article on 'Writing and Publishing' for the *London Review of Books* in 1982, the novelist Alan Sillitoe laments the fact that 'Grub Street, however, is there for every writer, though these days you have to be quick, and make sure you have a driving licence, because it has turned into a motorway' (*LRB* vol. 4, no. 6 (1 April 1982)).
37   McGurl, *The Program Era*, 47.
38   Michael Lewis, 'How to Make a Killing from Poetry', *Poetry* vol. 186, no. 4 (July/August 2005), 358–61.
39   Riviere, 'What It Is', *81 Austerities* Tumblr page (austerities.tumblr.com), since removed.
40   Faber website and jacket copy for Sam Riviere, *81 Austerities* (Faber, 2012).
41   Riviere, 'Crisis Poem', in *81 Austerities* (London: Faber, 2012), 3.
42   Alison Flood, 'Jorie Graham takes 2012 Forward prize', *Guardian* (1 October 2012). These varied responses to the self-division required of creative entrepreneurship might also be read along gendered or racial lines. That these ironic or satirical takes are offered predominantly by white, male artists corresponds to the unequal ways in which other artists are credited for balancing their creative and business sides. Arielle

Bernstein, for instance, notes the incongruity between praise for Radiohead's 'corporate empire' (above) and reviews accusing Beyoncé of an 'inauthentic' or 'calculated nature' when *Lemonade* was released the same month as Radiohead's album in 2016. (Bernstein, 'Burn the Witch: The Gender Politics of Being an Auteur', *Balder & Dash* (rogerebert.com) (6 May 2016). These dynamics might be read into Behrle's most sustained spoof of Maya Angelou in '24/7 Relentless Careerism' or Riviere's follow-up collection, *Kim Kardashian's Marriage* (Faber, 2015).

43 William Leith, 'Drunks talk trash, don't they?', *Guardian* (2 October 2008).
44 Una Mullally, 'Felix Dennis': "It's really about sensing trends and having the arrogance to think, 'I know I'm right.'"', *Irish Times* ((11 July 2013).
45 Sean O'Hagan, 'The nine lives of Felix Dennis: "I've lived an unbelievable life, even if I did do my best to kill myself"', *Observer* (2 June 2013).
46 Dennis, *How to Get Rich* (London: Ebury Press, 2007), 99.
47 Dennis, *How to Make Money: The 88 Steps to Get Rich and Find Success* (London: Ebury Press, 2011), xi, 250.
48 Ibid., 208.

Chapter 12

THE PROMISE OF PROFESSIONALISM

1

> Professionalism is a dull, ugly word: but it means dull, ugly things, a perversion of the higher activities of man, of art, literature, religion and philosophy.
>
> –Arthur Clutton-Brock (*Times Literary Supplement*, 1918)[1]

In March 2018, the Jerwood Foundation hosted an event at London's Free Word Centre asking, 'Are Poets the New Creative Entrepreneurs?' Anthony Anaxagorou, one of four poets on the panel, had tweeted: 'This will be really helpful for anyone interested in making a living as a poet, or thinking about poetry in more entrepreneurial ways.'[2] Waiting for the roundtable to start, two young writers in the row behind me were discussing Jack Canfield's business handbook, *The Success Principles: How to Get from Where You Are to Where You Want to Be*. I thought of the time my salesman father took me, aged 14 or so, to a conference room in a hotel, where someone explained how much money we could make peddling magazine subscriptions through their fail-proof system. I thought of people dismissing creative writing as a pyramid scheme, predicated on endless growth to sustain book sales and teacher-writers' salaries. I thought of Randall Jarrell, complaining to Elizabeth Bishop in 1956: 'Who'd have thought the era of the poet in the grey flannel suit was coming?'[3]

Anxieties around professionalisation are nothing new to poetry, but the Jerwood event felt different. Its title and mere existence suggested something had shifted in the way we approach the business of poetry – which is to say, the stuff necessary to writing that isn't writing itself. Watching the speakers enter, pose for official photos and perch with varying degrees of discomfort while microphones were clipped to lapels (no grey flannel in sight), it was hard to imagine the question about creative entrepreneurship being formulated in quite that way a few years ago. It's not that everyone now agrees on the answer – another panellist, Inua Ellams, was quick to say he 'resents' such labels – but it was clear that the terms of debate were changing. The eager, standing-room-only crowd for a frank discussion of something like 'professional development' clearly marked a growing need for practical career advice. This chapter attempts to balance those changing professional needs with the specific pressures around entrepreneurialism discussed in the previous one.

The Jerwood event felt symptomatic of a wider shift that Alison Gerber examines in *The Work of Art: Value in Creative Careers* (2017). 'In recent decades,' Gerber writes, 'artistic practice has undergone a sort of occupational turn, with artists today experiencing their practices as "serious" "work," a "job," a "profession" – this despite the minority of artists who make a living at art work.'[4] The phrasing of this definition is recognisable and refreshing. It's the way artists *experience* their practice that has altered, demonstrated in the language used when discussing these things. As Anaxagorou suggests, it depends as much on '*thinking* about poetry in more entrepreneurial ways.' Although the event's question was about poets in general, the discussion showed that what we think of (or fear) as the professionalisation of the field will always be a matter of individual experience. Auden wasn't wrong when he wrote in *The Dyer's Hand* (1962) that 'writers have no impersonal professional interests'.[5] Their professional interests are absolutely personal.

The changing language around professionalisation is both symptom and driver of changing realities, with real effects. The word 'professionalisation' (like most '-isations') is still mostly invoked in a negative sense, conjuring a top-down process or policing of behaviours. In a 2016 essay from *ArtNews*, for example, the critic and curator Daniel Palmer decries 'the hyperprofessionalization of the emerging artist', pitting 'conformity' against a notion of artistic 'freedom'.[6] Similar complaints are common in academia. Leonard Cassuto, in 'The Problem of Professionalization' (*Chronicle of Higher Education*, 2015), argues that 'professional conformity in graduate school stifles the creative soul'.[7] In these clichés, they parrot Arthur Clutton-Brock in the epigraph above, wringing his hands over 'Professionalism in Art' a century ago.

More positive views foreground an image of savvy individuals – 'poets who are successfully negotiating their creativity, artistry and integrity with commercial considerations', in the language of the Jerwood event flyer. Often, the emphasis is on a more straightforward definition of the professional poet as one who earns money in connection with their writing. Debris Stevenson began her comments on the Jerwood panel by saying her aim was always to make poetry a full-time career. Kate Fox, a leading campaigner for poets' fair pay, also reiterated sentiments that she has written about elsewhere, underlining the importance of viewing 'professional poet as a job like any other'.[8] But as Gerber makes clear, the wider 'occupational turn' is more experiential than financial. Those able to make a living from art will always be in a small minority. The difference between resisting the faceless threat of 'professionalisation' or identifying as a 'professional' poet in a more fluid sense might be whether one experiences it as an active or passive shift, as something either structurally imposed or conscientiously adopted. Whether the reflex is to bristle or brighten at the evolving language of these debates, a clearer focus on its practical effects will help us understand the new situation it creates. Alongside questions of pay, we might come to view poetry's occupational turn as less a threat to creative integrity than a reflection of the need to widen its opportunities.

2

> Professionally, the bird sings
> Through fight or love, the new leaved willow
> Bends, the children swing in blue
> And green, and the wet clouds extend.
> –Geoffrey Grigson, 'The Professionals' (1941)[9]

Jo Bell and Jane Commane's *How to Be a Poet: A Twenty-First Century Guide to Writing Well* (2017) was published a few months before the Jerwood event. Again, its mere existence marks a cultural and linguistic shift. Although many poetry guidebooks conclude with a few tips on publishing, *How to Be a Poet* is unique in its combination of writerly and professional concerns. As Jo Bell explains in the first chapter, the book's title reflects its dual purpose:

> This project isn't called *How to Write a Poem* or *How to Get Your Poetry Published*, though we'll talk at some length about both. It isn't called *Get Rich Writing Poetry* because nobody knows how to do that. We called our project *How to Be a Poet* because it's not just a writing manual.[10]

The first 15 of the book's 33 chapters make up the 'writing manual' part, dealing with standard craft topics, such as form and editing. With these issues out of the way, chapter 16, 'How to Explore the World of Poetry Magazines and Journals', encapsulates Gerber's occupational turn in its first sentence: 'While these powerful ideas on poetry-writing percolate, let us take a little step in another direction and start to think about the ways in which poetry starts its journey out into the world.'[11] Pointedly avoiding jargon we might associate with new creative economy-speak, the tone throughout *How to Be a Poet* finds a delicate balance between the personal and professional. 'Much of this book is also about granting yourself permission', we're told in the opening pages, 'equipping you with the ideas and knowledge that will help make your participation in poetry as an art form more fulfilling, life-enriching and creatively satisfying'.[12] In the book's second half, what could have been pitched as brass-tacks business advice is translated into self-help-like reassurances, regarding your work's 'journey' and 'participating' in a poetry community.

To gauge this tonal shift over the past decade or so, we might compare Chris Hamilton-Emery's *101 Ways to Make Poems Sell*, published by Salt in 2006. From its title and self-description as 'an insider's guide to the poetry business', Hamilton-Emery's book is an anomaly among poetry guides in its unwavering attention to professional matters, adopting a tone that those aspiring writers sat behind me might have recognised from Canfield's *Success Principles*. 'This book is about the business side of the poetry scene, about making sales and profits to fund literature in a sustainable way', we're told in the preface. 'The only way forward is to learn some basic business and marketing skills, and to hustle for all you are worth.'[13] The matters of craft that comprise the first half of *How to Be a Poet* are cordoned off in one line: 'Let's take all this as read.'[14]

Although *How to Be a Poet* has similar chapters on 'How to Build a Track Record' and 'On Money', the tone is in stark contrast. 'Your private success is the one that will sustain you,' Bell writes in 'On Success': 'Sharing your work with a wider community is a further step. It gives you a chance to hear praise or useful feedback, and to contribute the same to the creative ecology of which you are a part.'[15] Amidst these communal sentiments, the word *ecology* leaps out as a flash word of recent years, with creative work increasingly discussed in ways that attempt to reconcile art's social and commercial preoccupations. In Kate Fox and Tamar Yoseloff's 'Poetry and Spoken Word Artists Network Fees and Needs Survey' (2015), it crops up repeatedly. For example: 'For most poets/spoken word artists, their work consists of an ecology of readings/ performances and education work of some kind.'[16] In revived debates around authors' pay in 2018, the word was pivotal in Philip Pullman's rallying cry against publishers 'acting without conscience and with no thought for the future of the ecology of the trade as a whole'.[17]

As a euphemism for business-tainted words like 'economy' or 'market', *ecology* evokes a sense of social conscience, framing the arts as an organic system whose sustainability might be analogous to the natural environment's. References to cultural or poetry 'landscapes' have a similar effect. It also echoes the ethically branded language of state-sponsored arts policy. In February 2011, for example, Ed Vaizey, conservative minister for Culture, Communications and Creative Industries, delivered a speech at the Royal Society entitled 'The Creative Ecology'. 'I want to take the opportunity today to make the case for the importance of the creative ecology,' he began, defining it as 'an alliance between the subsidised and commercial arts; the professional and the voluntary arts; and the arts and the creative industries'.[18] In 2015, a

40-page report on 'The Ecology of Culture', commissioned by the Arts and Humanities Research Council, offered another fuzzy explanation:

> Culture is often discussed as an economy, but it is better to see it as an ecology, because this viewpoint offers a richer and more complete understanding of the subject. Seeing culture as an ecology is congruent with cultural value approaches that take into account a wide range of non-monetary values.[19]

Mirroring ways in which 'professionalisation' is used to connote a negative view of structural changes that impinge on individual freedom, these ecological metaphors seem to make such matters palatable, through connotations of natural order and social responsibility. A hopeful view would be that, despite its fashionable use in policy intended to obscure economic realities, poets are better equipped than anyone to apply such rhetoric meaningfully. In a relatively short period, we have gone from Hamilton-Emery's provocation that 'the world of poetry can be a bear pit' (and Salt's subsequent retreat from poetry hustling) to *How to Be a Poet*'s emphasis on 'sharing your work with a wider community'.[20] That doesn't necessarily mean poets have become nicer or more community-spirited in that time. These buzzwords can be superficial, but they can also be performative of changing attitudes. At the very least, they suggest ways in which professionalisation might be directed towards less individualistic ends.

3

> You that are sneering at my profession,
> Haven't you juggled a vast amount?
>
> —George Meredith, 'Juggling Jerry' (1859)[21]

Later in *The Work of Art*, Alison Gerber describes the mentality behind art's occupational turn as an 'occupationally committed pose' or 'the performance of occupational commitment'.[22] Understanding professionalism as primarily an attitude or performance helps to account for different reactions poets have to it. It also makes it easier to link the linguistic shifts described above with changing resources around professional development, in so far as new language (as all poets know) soon effects new ways of being.

Another relevant definition of 'professionalisation' is that of a process by which an occupation comes to require specialist training – in other words, becoming a profession, as opposed to a trade or vocation. The rise of university creative writing programmes has occasioned plenty of debate regarding the role of formal qualifications, especially for poets. However, the focus on whether a master's in Creative Writing is the only route to professional status overlooks the proliferation of other training schemes over the past 20 years. Many of these programmes and mentorships place a notable emphasis on professional development. The Complete Works project, for instance, founded by Bernardine Evaristo in 2005, promises 'professional development' and 'career support and advice' in its calls for applications.[23] The Jerwood Foundation's own mentoring programme, run jointly with the Arvon Foundation since 2010, also highlights 'professional development', along with 'specialist advice sessions with industry insiders'.[24] New Writing North's New North Poets mentorships, running since 2015, place a typical emphasis 'on both the craft of writing and the professional skills necessary to a working poet'. Since 2016, Nine Arches Press has also run its mentorship scheme, Primers, with the Poetry School, for which *How to Be a Poet* might be read as a self-guided supplement.[25]

The Poetry School has been the most prominent provider of poetry courses and mentorship outside higher education institutions since 1997. However, the launch of their own MA in Writing Poetry with Newcastle University in 2015 acknowledges the growing demand for a balance of creative and professional support, in whatever form. Across commercial and funding-supported offerings, the expansion and diversification of available training must be central to any narrative of poetry's professionalisation. Not only has it left other university writing programmes scrambling to incorporate more professional development, but collectively, these new schemes are also reconfiguring our sense of the skills involved in poetry-making – and showing why access to them is so important.

4

> I wrote my first poem, my first published poem, when I was eight and a half years old. [...] from then on, I suppose, I've been a bit of a professional.
>
> –Sylvia Plath, BBC interview (1962)[26]

The question of whether professionalisation has, on the whole, been good or bad for poetry might ultimately hinge less on our instinctive reactions to words like 'entrepreneurship' or 'professionalisation', than on the real opportunities such new language gives rise to. In the chapter 'On Money' from *How to Be a Poet*, Jo Bell takes an optimistic view, spelling out ways in which being professional (in the paid sense) might translate into a more inclusive poetry culture. 'Ignore those who sniff at the jobbing poet,' she writes:

If we subscribe to the idea that poets should be 'above' taking money for their art, then we perpetuate the idea that good writing should never be paid for. [...] This is a bigger issue than your pay packet or mine. Poets of all classes and backgrounds need to be represented in our schools, our institutions and our publications.[27]

Gerber makes a similar point in *The Work of Art*, linking diversity and professionalism in the visual arts, while highlighting an important paradox. 'The requirement of the occupationally committed pose', she argues, means 'a low bar for entry'. In turn, 'the "working artist" identity is available to a broader and more diverse group than ever before'.[28] We might think of Virginia Woolf's famous suggestion in 'Professions for Women' that 'The cheapness of writing paper is, of course, the reason why women have succeeded as writers before they have succeeded in other professions' – and extend it to other social inequalities.[29] Engaging with and re-shaping the language of professionalisation – through the events, training schemes, or books like *How to Be a Poet* – can help combat poetry's historical biases by improving access to industry knowledge and skills. The Complete Works project makes this explicit, in its commitment to creative and professional development for black and Asian poets. The Jerwood's Compton fellowships 'are looking to identify and encourage those who may not normally consider applying for development opportunities, awards or prizes'.[30] Nine Arches' new Dynamo scheme, co-run with Writing West Midlands, is also 'targeted at communities who are currently under-represented in poetry publishing and in contemporary poetry in general'.[31] It's worth noting that all of the programmes mentioned above are founded and/or run by women.

Notwithstanding points made in Chapter 11 about the specific pressures of entrepreneurialism, any attempt to separate the practical side of professionalisation from serious political or poetical concerns should seem increasingly dubious. Access to skills is a social issue, and we should welcome a further blurring of lines between 'professional' acumen and 'writing well', working against the split-consciousness discussed in Chapter 11. Teaching people to write a cover letter, book proposal, or event budget, for instance, needn't be entirely disconnected from writing poems. A retreat to aestheticism or other notions of poetry's social autonomy has always been a mark of privilege, and ignoring the importance of professional skills in the name of keeping the art sullied becomes a cover for false claims to meritocracy. As Mark Banks acknowledges in *Creative Justice: Cultural Industries, Work and Inequality* (2017):

> Perhaps now the best guarantee of success in creative arts education (and in the creative economy beyond) is not the possession of a 'raw' talent,

but the ownership of an inherited ease and the capacity to expend a dispositional currency available only to a privileged few.[32]

But new language and opportunities are changing the disposition of poetry more generally. More diverse support is leading to more diverse writing. In turn, the variety of routes by which underprivileged writers might acquire a 'dispositional currency' in the form of practical skills offers hope that the behaviours and markers of professionalism might be diversified. Rather than being opposed to political, ethical, or even aesthetic commitments, the widening of support for new poets is essentially progressive, even radical in its potential to challenge gendered, racialised, ageist, ableist, and other assumptions by which certain poses and performances are legitimised as 'professional'. Though the experience of professionalisation is individual, poets collectively will determine the character of their profession. If new language is needed to move beyond either 'entrepreneurship' or the 'bear pit', they can make it. The more they're able to acknowledge and discuss this shifting landscape, the better chance poets have in sustaining it.

Postscript

It feels unprofessional to admit I may have missed something crucial in my conception of professionalism. Conflicting definitions are part of the problem. As noted above, a common rejoinder to suggestions of poetry's professionalisation is that it pertains only to pay or qualifications. In either case, the scarcity of financial remuneration and prevalence of self-taught successes are taken as proof of poetry's non-professional status. If poetry is at risk of professionalisation, blame is often attributed to the spread of creative writing as a university discipline over the past century, in what Mark McGurl neatly dubbed 'the program era'. Along with the corresponding proliferation of literary prizes in that same period, this institutionalisation has promoted a culture of credentialism, leaving many poets' biographical notes indistinguishable from mini-CVs. Publishers have done their part as well, as noted above, expecting writers to demonstrate a 'track record' of publications and/or awards before submitting. All of this contributes to a credentialist view of what professionalisation entails. A long 2010 thread on *Magma*'s blog is a case in point, with poets responding passionately to the knowing provocation, 'Should We Restrict the Title of "Poet"?'[33] In such discussions, the title 'professional poet' (or here, even 'poet') implies an opposition from the 'amateur', with only the placement of the dividing line up for debate. The professional-amateur binary marks an attitude of what sociologists refer to as 'occupational closure'. In lieu of official qualifications or licensing bodies, individuals will have their own views or anxieties about how membership is 'restricted' in order to fortify the occupation's status. A more visual example is the lock and key on the cover of Chris Hamilton-Emery's *101 Ways to Make Poems Sell*, discussed above and designed by his own side business, The Cover Factory, with its implied promise of access to a restricted sphere.

What I liked about Gerber's idea of creative work as an 'occupationally committed pose' is the 'low bar' it sets for access to creative identities and communities. But it's worth noting that Gerber herself makes a distinction between the broader 'occupational turn' she describes and a specific process of professionalisation, which she also understands only in terms of formal credentials:

> If the professional project continues in the art world, we might expect to see the development of strong artists' associations with control over important resources, an increased emphasis on narrowly defined training and qualifications and theoretical knowledge, and occupational closure to keep 'amateurs' and other outsiders from practicing or being recognized for their efforts.[34]

Angela McRobbie's *Be Creative: Making a Living in the New Cultural Industries* (2016) offers various examples of ways in which professionalism has already been extended to creative practitioners and 'informal activities such as freelance and precarious work, where in the past it was associated only with occupations such as teaching, law, medicine, etc.' Like Gerber, she suggests that professionalism in creative fields 'has been synonymous with specialism, expertise, qualification, accreditation and possibility membership of an association'.[35] To some extent, McRobbie's slightly broader definition of professionalism, by acknowledging the importance of specialisation and expertise alongside formal accreditation, aligns with my sense above that the required skill set is being expanded in the training of poets, especially through new mentorship schemes, to include 'career' skills alongside creative ones. But the comparison to traditionally licenced professions like law and medicine is potentially misleading, if the only points of comparison are skills and qualifications. Alongside this broader sense of expertise demanded of creative professionals, I want to amend this chapter by considering the degree to which those historically professionalised fields conceive of their professionalism not only in relation to pay, expertise, or qualifications, but just as importantly in its *ethical* dimensions.

The preamble to 'Medical Professionalism in the New Millennium: A Physician Charter', produced in 2002 by the American College of Physicians, American Board of Internal Medicine, and the European Federation of

Internal Medicine, begins with this statement in bold text: 'Professionalism is the basis of medicine's contract with society.' From there, the charter comprises a set of 'Fundamental Principles' and 'Professional Responsibilities', repeatedly emphasising medical practitioners' 'individual and collective obligations' to 'patient welfare' and 'quality of care', but also to 'social justice', in terms of 'the fair distribution of health care resources' and 'access to care'.[36] As the charter acknowledges in its 'roots extending back to Hippocrates', the social role and responsibilities of 'healer' have a much longer history than the 'complicated political, legal, and market forces' with which the profession now contends. Like that of lawyers, the oath taken by physicians might vary in its wording for different countries or institutions, but the notional 'contract with society' remains a central part of the profession's self-conception, with that sense of duty or service every bit as important as skills and qualifications. As Roger P. Worthington defined the balance recently for the journal *Investigación en Educación Médica*:

> Technical skill is insufficient on its own just as behavioural attributes without the necessary technical competence are insufficient; both characteristics need to be present (and capable of being assessed) in order for a doctor to *earn* status that comes from being a medical professional.[37]

It seems strange to note the relative lack of ethics training when it comes to educating writers. While poets may have been asked to fill in a perfunctory form for university ethics approval or a 'research ethics' section of a grant application at some point in their lives, these are often limited in their use within the humanities to projects involving 'human subjects'. Most students completing a degree, master's, or even PhD in Creative Writing can do so with little more than a copy-and-pasted 'declaration' regarding their work's originality. It is hard to imagine, by way of contrast, a business or management degree that didn't include at least one module on 'business ethics'. Clearly, the mere existence of ethical oaths and pedagogy is no guarantee of ethical practice in medicine, law, teaching, business, or any other traditionally recognised profession. But it does underscore the degree to which these occupations conceive of their labour in relation to its social impact. This might be a way for poets or writers more generally to re-think the professionalisation of their field.

That's not to suggest poets are any less conscious of their social commitments and responsibilities. A running theme of this book has been the way communal values are constantly being expressed and re-evaluated through discussions arising from prize culture, publishing trends, or perceived wrongdoings. Its running argument has been that the semi-public discourse among poets and publishers on social media or in mainstream media coverage provides a self-regulatory function for maintaining what we might think of as community standards, in lieu of official administrative bodies. But if anything, the growing scope of debates regarding ethical issues – diversity and cultural representation, for example, or issues around plagiarism and appropriation – suggests more poets would relish and benefit not only from more career support and advice, but also from a more direct engagement with the ethics of poetic practice as an essential part of their creative development.

Some writers are already thinking about the teaching of creative ethics. The theme for the 2011 Australasian Association of Writing Programs (AAWP) conference was 'Ethical Imaginations', with a focus on 'the ethical considerations writers enter into when representing worlds via the written word'.[38] Noting the gap in ethics requirements for the study of creative writing versus medicine, journalism, or law, the Australia-based writer Shady Cosgrove makes a case for the natural link between these considerations and the teaching of writing. 'The relevance of research and representation as issues that affect creative writing is not an external imposition from university structures,' she argues. 'They are central to the craft of writing.'[39] Within this, a discrepancy between written forms soon emerges, however, with most attention on prose writing as a site of ethical concerns, and within that, Cosgrove, writing in 2009, notes that 'courses in creative nonfiction tend to include more discussion on matters of ethics and representation than those in fiction'.[40] While these discussions occasionally cross over into 'nonfictional' modes of poetry – the AAWP proceedings include a paper on lyric autobiography and another on 'witness poetry' – public discourse regarding representation tends to focus on narrative prose.

It helps to broaden the conception of what 'ethical considerations' might include. Jen Webb, director of the Centre for Creative and Cultural Research at the University of Canberra, and a poet herself, defines 'ethical writing' as 'the writing we do when we have consciously reflected on the meanings we are making, or the world we are representing'.[41] While the link between meaning-making, representation, and the importance of research help to emphasise the overlap between writing ethics and writing craft, there is a further sense in which an even more expansive notion of writers' professional ethics might connect the writing skills and career skills discussed above. Mirroring the sort of courses required on other professional degrees, Charles Sturt University in New South Wales introduced a course on 'Ethics and Law for Creative Industries' in 2012, covering contract law, liability, intellectual property and copyright, and other matters of social or professional ethics. Emma Rush, reflecting on the course's design, which she conceived alongside a similar course for medical students, suggests a central question arising 'about whether the technical excellence that university curriculums aim to develop is properly matched by an adequate grounding for practitioners-to-be (i.e. students) to meet the ethical aspirations of their profession'.[42]

As I argue in the chapter above, providing opportunities to engage with these practical issues is a matter of access and support. Shifting the understanding of professionalism away from a focus on qualifications or other means of occupational exclusion, towards a broader understanding that connects technical ability with essential career skills, but also with the values and ethics inherent to both skill sets, is a means of widening access to poetry by making 'the behaviours and markers of professionalism' (in my phrase above) a core consideration within writers' training, whatever form it takes. In this conception, professionalism is clearly distinguished from and made to respond to the pressures of entrepreneurial culture, highlighting poets' own 'contract with society'. In common usage, the word 'unprofessional' refers to behaviours and values that are often quite separate from the financial- or credential-oriented assumptions around a process of professionalisation. Being 'unprofessional' usually means having betrayed the social contract, acted irresponsibly, or put one's own interests before the group. In this, the idea of professionalism is primarily ethical. By re-asserting the ethical and social considerations expected of other professions, poetry's ideas of professionalism might also be turned inside-out, away from individualistic career development, towards a commitment of communal values.

Notes

1. Reprinted in A. Clutton-Brock, *Essays on Art* (London: Metheun, 1919), 120.
2. Anthony Anaxagorou (@Anthony1983), Twitter (2:32 p.m., 9 March 2018).
3. Jarrell, *Randall Jarrell's Letters: An Autobiographical and Literary Selection*, ed. Mary Jarrell (Charlottesville: University of Virginia Press, 2002), 413.
4. Gerber, *The Work of Art: Value in Creative Careers* (Stanford, CA: Stanford University Press, 2017), 11.
5. Auden, *The Dyer's Hand and Other Essays* (London: Faber, 1963), 14.
6. Daniel S. Palmer, 'Go Pro: The Hyper-Professionalization of the Emerging Artist', *ArtNews* (9 March 2016).
7. 'The Problem of Professionalization', *Chronicle of Higher Education* (23 March 2015).
8. Fox, 'Where There's Poems There's Brass?', personal website (23 February 2015).
9. *Poetry* magazine (October 1941), 26.
10. Jo Bell, 'On Your Marks...', in *How to Be a Poet: A Twenty-First Century Guide to Writing Well* (Rugby: Nine Arches, 2017), 13.
11. Jane Commane, 'How to Explore the World of Poetry Magazines and Journals', in *How to Be a Poet*, 99.
12. Bell and Commane, 'Welcome', in *How to Be a Poet*, 11–12.
13. Hamilton-Emery, *101 Ways to Make Poems Sell* (Cambridge: Salt Publishing, 2006), xiii.
14. Ibid., 20.
15. Bell, 'On Success', in *How to Be a Poet*, 156–57.
16. Kate Fox and Tamar Yoseloff, 'Poets and Spoken Word Artists Network Fees and Needs Survey, March 2015 Short Report', posted to Kate Fox's personal webpage (27 March 2015).

17 Qtd in Danuta Kean, 'Publishers are paying writers a pittance, say bestselling authors', *Guardian* (27 June 2018).
18 Ed Vaizey, '"The Creative Ecology": Speech at State of the Arts', available at Gov.uk (10 February 2011).
19 John Holden, *The Ecology of Culture* (Arts and Humanities Research Council, January 2015,), 2.
20 Hamilton-Emery, *101 Ways*, 12.
21 Meredith, *Modern Love and Poems of the English Roadside* (London: Chapman & Hall, 1862), 87.
22 Gerber, *The Work of Art*, 27.
23 Call posted to NAWE website (14 February 2016), for example.
24 Call posted to London Playwrights website (2016), for example.
25 Call posted to the Poetry School website (15 December 2016), for example.
26 Sylvia Plath interview with Peter Orr (BBC, 1962), reprinted in Peter Orr, *The Poet Speaks: Interviews with Contemporary Poets* (London: Routledge & Keegan Paul, 1966).
27 Bell, 'On Money', *How to Be a Poet*, 177.
28 Gerber, *The Work of Art*, 27.
29 Woolf, 'Professions for Women', in *The Collected Essays*, ed. Leonard Woolf, vol. 2 (London: Hogarth Press, 1966), 284.
30 'Jerwood Compton Poetry Fellowships selectors announced', Jerwood Arts website (10 April 2017).
31 Qtd in Natasha Onwuemezi, 'Nine Arches Press to mentor poets from under-represented backgrounds', *The Bookseller* (30 September 2016).
32 Banks, *Creative Justice: Cultural Industries, Work and Inequality* (London: Rowman & Littlefield, 2017), 86.
33 Rob MacKenzie, 'Should We Restrict the Title of "Poet"?', *Magma* blog (December 2010).
34 Gerber, *The Work of Art*, 28.
35 McRobbie, *Be Creative: Making a Living in the New Cultural Industries* (Cambridge: Polity Press, 2016), 40.
36 The charter is available in various places online, including the AMBI Foundation webpages, the ACP's *Annals of Internal Medicine*, and the *European Journal of Internal Medicine*, where it was published simultaneously in 2002.
37 Roger P. Worthington, 'Ethics and Professionalism in a Changing World', *Investigación en Educación Médica* vol. 4, no, 15 (July–September 2015), 175–178 (177).
38 Janie Conway, Herron, Moya Costello, and Lynda Hawryluk, 'Editorial Introduction', in *The Ethical Imaginations: Writing Worlds Papers: The Refereed Proceedings of the 16th Conference of the Australasian Association of Writing Programs, 2011* (AAWP, 2011).
39 Shady E. Cosgrove, 'WRIT101: Ethics of Representation for Creative Writers', Pedagogy vol. 9, no. 1 (Winter 2009), 134–41 (136).
40 Ibid., 135.
41 Jen Webb, 'Ethics and Writing', *The Conversation* (4 August 2016).
42 Emma Rush, 'Ethics in Creative Industries and Complementary Medicine', *AAPAE (Australian Association of Professional and Applied Ethics) 2019 Symposium: Educating Practitioners and Aspiring Practitioners – The Art of (Ethical) Survival* (published online, 1 December 2011). A similar course on 'Legal and Ethical Issues in the Creative Writing Profession' has also been introduced at Simon Fraser University in Vancouver.

Afterword

THE POETRY GAME

> I've sung what I was given –
> some was bad and some was good.
> I never did know from where it came
> and if I had it all to do again
> I am not sure I would
> play the poet game.
>
> – Greg Brown, 'The Poet Game'

This book has often foregrounded poetry's competitive side. The 'business' of poetry appears to pit poets and publishers against one another in unavoidable ways. The nature of publishing contracts, prizes, funding, jobs, academic institutions, and residencies all seems to necessitate an unequal distribution of resources and opportunities, whose value is determined through competition. For many, this is rationalised by a split-logic discussed in the final section of this book. On the one hand, these structures are regarded as separate from the writing itself, which therefore retains its independence. On the other hand, they're also said to have a positive influence on the work. Announcing the results of the 2017 Mick Imlah Poetry Prize, Alan Jenkins neatly expresses this incongruity in his assertion: 'Art is not a competition; but a competition may encourage art, and reward it.'[1] By such logic, neither the prospect nor the consequences of receiving (in this case) £3,000 for a single poem can ever pierce the creative bubble of its making. This doublethink serves the writer too, who can claim, like the novelist Nadine Gordimer, upon winning the Nobel Prize for Literature in 1991: 'I never thought about the prize when I wrote. Writing is not a horse race.'[2] In the context of publishing, these distinctions are analogous to the one in Marx's image of Milton, which I've discussed a few times. Milton's pure 'expression of his own nature' while writing *Paradise Lost* is split from his later position as a 'dealer in a commodity' when selling the manuscript.[3] In either case, writing's autonomy is rationalised by separating the moment of writing from the moment in which its value is inscribed.

While these contests might seem historically inextricable – poetry competitions and prizes were a key feature of ancient Greek culture, after all – this book is my attempt to understand poetry's changing dynamics in a period when competition has become a more general condition of life under neoliberalism. Wide-ranging attention economies, omnipresent technologies of self-assessment, and the creep of entrepreneurial thinking into everyday life have all contributed to a much more embedded and embodied sense of a competitive stake behind our ideas, words, and actions. The preceding chapters have attended to the pressures and anxieties resulting from this historical-economic environment, with the hope that acknowledging structures which are designed and determined to hide themselves will aid the search for modes of resistance. The more fluid effects of poetry's *generationalism*, its consumption as online *content*, its packaging as *full collections* or *debuts*, its attachment to *cities*, its communal response to *fakes*, or its status as *work* or *profession* might not be as visible as competitions, but they have become core mechanics in the more general game of poetry. The game metaphor proves weirdly persistent, in fact. Bourdieu's notion of poetry as a game of 'loser wins' in the introduction prefigured the *illusio* or collective belief in Chapter 2 in 'taking the game seriously' when it comes to prizes.[4] The influence of video games on the status of contemporary cities in Chapter 7 was followed by Cathy Park Hong's critique of 'post-identity' conceptualists slipping 'in and out of identities like a video game avatar' in Chapter 8.[5] Chapter 11 also concluded with Felix Dennis's sense of entrepreneurialism as 'all just a silly game'.[6] In these final pages, I want to revisit poetry's status as a 'game', suggesting some ways in which the experience of its competitive aspects might be balanced with a sense of play.

A World of Games

Any metaphorical sense of poetry's gameness needs reconsidering in relation to actual games' popularity in recent years. Eric Zimmerman's 'Manifesto for a Ludic Century' (2013) highlights the role of digital technologies in giving games a 'new relevance', driving participatory and non-linear media more generally. He also acknowledges the economic-political context:

> The ways that we work and communicate, research and learn, socialize and romance, conduct our finances and communicate with our governments, are all intimately intertwined with complex systems of information – in a way that could not have existed a few decades ago.[7]

'For such a systemic society,' he declares, 'games make a natural fit.' Zimmerman's emphasis on digital contexts can be extended to other forms of gaming as well. Console, computer, and mobile video games might be the most celebrated sector of our 'ludic century' in press coverage and economic terms, bolstered by streaming platforms, e-sports, Let's Play videos, and the fan culture and cinematic releases around games like Minecraft (2006), Angry Birds (2009), or Pokémon Go (2016). But the growing audience for digital games has coincided with a similar boom in tabletop gaming, as evidenced by the appearance of board game cafes, and in live-action games, with Quidditch or Humans vs Zombies matches played regularly on university campuses, inspired by franchises like *Harry Potter* or the *Hunger Games*. Beyond these, a great deal of online culture is also dedicated to documenting real-world games or challenges. All of this has contributed to what Sebastian Deterding describes as an increasingly 'gameful world', in which more and more people play games as a regular part of their day.[8]

As Zimmerman suggests, our now habitual gameplay has a natural affinity with the emergence of a 'systemic' information economy. Although he puts it in fairly neutral terms, it's clear that the abstraction of labour, the shift from tangible commodities towards symbolic goods and capital, technologies like 'contactless payment', and the value derived from so-called futures, quantitative easing, and cryptocurrencies in an era of extreme financialisation have rendered economic activity increasingly game-like. Of course, games are also a 'natural fit' with the competition infused into social activities, work, and personal lives by the same ideology. In this way, images of life as a kind of game obscure its economic bearings. Zimmerman's manifesto concludes with an aestheticizing turn, insisting that 'games are not valuable because they teach someone a skill or make the world a better place. Like other forms of cultural expression, games and play are important are beautiful.'[9] And yet, the fetishisation of playfulness on Silicon Valley 'campuses' decorated with ping-pong and foosball tables is merely emblematic of a more insidious impulse to 'gamify' work in general, using the design principles and technology behind digital games to incentivise employees. Contrary to Zimmerman's anti-instrumental take, 'play' (much like 'creativity' as discussed as discussed in several chapters here) becomes a perverse driver of productivity. A game-like atmosphere and game-like structures become a ruse for the self-exploitation they encourage; and the perceived autonomy of games-for-games'-sake serves a familiar enabling function.

Poetry and Games

The wider interest in games parallels a growing critical interest in the poetry's game-like qualities. Some of these arguments have a deep historical scope, as in Derek Collins' *Master of the Game: Competition and Performance in Greek Poetry*

(2004) or Anne Birrell's *Games Poets Play: Readings in Medieval Chinese Poetry* (2004). Classical texts also offer their own, often unfavourable comparisons between literature and games. Plato argues in the *Republic*, for instance, that 'mimetic' writing or art is 'a sort of game (*paidia*) and not a serious thing' and in the *Phaedrus* that compared to dialogical discourse most writing is mere 'amusement' (also *paidia*, in the original).[10] The Greek word *paidia*, Stephen E. Kidd suggests, could be translated as 'game' or 'trifle', with the same emphasis on 'delight', 'joy', or 'amusement' here.[11] Modern comparisons of poetry to games tend to be more positive, especially under the influence of Ludwig Wittgenstein's conception of 'language-games', through which the use of language is reframed as a game-like activity, epitomised by children's play within its rules.[12] Peter Lamarque, in this vein, examines 'the fundamental rules of the poetry game [...] in the Wittgensteinian sense, its rules and norms', such as 'the finegrainedness of language' or 'opacity', which in poetry take 'precedence over the more humdrum norms of communications'.[13] The range of poetry's game-like functions is also captured in Jonathan P. Eburne and Andrew Epstein's 2014 special journal issue on 'Poetry Games'. In the introduction, they claim: 'The notion of poetry as a game or project – in which the writer devises an idea, concept, or set of procedures or practices that help generate the work – has become central to contemporary poetry.'[14] Their insistence, contra Plato, that 'contemporary poetry games are far more than simply frivolous or playful for the sake of merriment alone', is born out in *Coin Opera*, an anthology of video game poems published by London-based Sidekick Books in 2009, with a second volume in 2014.[15] Jon Stone's introduction to the latter notes various features shared by poetry and games, including 'Resistance' – which might be read as a loose corollary to Lamarque's 'opacity' or John Crowe Ransom's earlier emphasis on playing 'hard to get' with the reader, making poetry 'a psychological game like poker rather than a logical game like chess'.[16] Much more important, Stone suggests, is poetry and games' shared sense of 'Play' within 'Formal restriction'. 'Play,' he writes, 'is one way of continually testing and adjusting the boundaries of culture, or conversely, through the apparatus of rules and goals, reinforcing certain ideals and models of behaviour.'[17] In this regard, poetic play has the potential to become 'a serious thing', without sacrificing 'joy' or 'amusement'.

These approaches celebrate the inherent gameness of writing or reading poems, whether through the interactions of rhyme, rhythm, or restrictive forms, or through more conceptual, procedural, or other constraint-based approaches. The relationship between the game-like nature of poems and the game-like nature of poetry as a field has received far less attention, however. As a means of reopening questions raised throughout this book towards other possible trajectories, I'll conclude by comparing three conceptions of gaming that might be applied to poetry as an industry.

The Playing Field

In my Introduction, I referenced the game metaphors employed in economic policy, citing NESTA's sense that 'a growing market is out there to be won by creative businesses that are willing and able to innovate, and that do not see any inherent conflict between creative and commercial excellence'.[18] Elsewhere, that report refers to 'key industry players' or 'players in the global market' in corporate language that focuses on 'winning' or 'levelling the playing field'.[19] Such rhetoric extends IBM founder Thomas J. Watson's sense that 'Business is a game, the greatest game in the world if you know how to play it.'[20] But as suggested above, game metaphors can be spun in different directions, depending on their positive or negative connotations (e.g. Plato vs Wittgenstein, for instance) and depending on the type of game we might be thinking of (e.g. Ransom's distinction between 'psychological' and 'logical' games). In his critique of business-game metaphors, Maurice Hamington argues against treating 'business as if it *were* truly a game, rather than merely *like* a game'.[21] Overly literal comparisons, he writes, encourage 'compartmentalized morality, truncated ethics, trivialized stakes, and the privileging of adversarial relationships'.[22] More generally, as noted above, game metaphors also mask the reality of labour relations.

But at various points, we've seen Bourdieu's love of game analogies as well, and his consistent emphasis on 'the rules of the game', 'moves', and 'play' within a 'field' of production. Rather than masking labour or social conditions, however, Bourdieu's game-speak is a means for emphasising the abstraction of work and class positions, subject to the game-like circulation symbolic capital in a field. The difference lies in motivations. Where business rhetoric rationalises competition by focusing on 'winning' a particular job or market or the 'greatest game' in general, Bourdieu's game analysis aims to understand the dynamics of a field. His study of 'the rules of the game', or, in a later text, *The Rules of Art*, is not offered as a strategy guide, but a means for better comprehending the ways in which

> the field as a structure of objective relations between positions of force undergirds and guides the strategies whereby the occupants of these positions seek, individually or collectively, to safeguard or improve their positions and to impose the principle of hierarchization most favourable to their own products.[23]

In other words, his concern is the *relational* forces which determine positions within a field and drive individuals or institutions to protect them. What these metaphors share – for business contexts or critical analysis of a field like poetry – is a sense of the 'rules' specific to that field and a related sense of the 'game' as an exceptional space, distinct from the rules or conditions of everyday life.

Game Theory

Game theory, on the other hand – with its grounding in mathematical, rather than sociological principles – presumes a universality for seemingly game-like human interactions. Game theory's founding text, 'On the Theory of Games of Strategy' (1928), opens with mathematician John von Neumann's assertion that 'any event – given the external conditions and the participants in the situation (provided the latter are acting of their own free will) – may be regarded as a game of strategy if one looks at the effect it has on the participants.'[24] Throughout the Cold War, von Neumann's thinking informed both nuclear strategy and economic policy in the United States, guided by his and the economist Oskar Morgenstern's influential *Theory of Games and Economic Behaviour* (1944). But as von Neumann stresses, game theory's applications, from war and economics to moral philosophy, social behaviour, population modelling, and voting habits, are predicated on rational participants 'acting of their own free will'. Ninety years later, the presumption of rational agents adopting deliberate strategies for success in a given situation explains the extent to which 'game theory has come to shape the unique practices of contemporary late-modern capitalism', according to S. M. Amadae.[25] With choices understood as a matter of individual agency in an open marketplace, Amadae shows von Neumann's ideas still in action: 'The exemplary neoliberal citizen and consumer *is* the strategic rational actor modelled by orthodox game theory.'[26]

Game theory's focus on rational choice marks a crucial distinction from the idea of games in Bourdieu's theory. At various points in this book, I have underscored the unconscious or structural nature of forces which, in Bourdieu's words above, 'undergird and guide' the occupants of a field. As John Guillory contrasts these approaches, Bourdieu's sociology elaborates 'a form of play whose inner truth is labor against an economism that would either reduce all practice to the explicit labor of accumulation or conceal the fact of labor altogether by representing all social action as play, as in game theory.'[27] Again, the 'inner truth' that a critic like Bourdieu seeks to reveal about the various kinds of labour supporting 'play' within a field are precisely the material conditions that game theory's economic applications seek to conceal. With a playful reframing of its 'joy' or 'art', game theory's deflections from labour are clear in the titles of popular books promoting *The Art of Strategy: A Game Theorist's Guide to Success in Business and Life* (2010) or *The Joy of Game Theory: An Introduction to Strategic Thinking* (2014). Under neoliberalism, the assumption of rational choices in game theory's mathematical models re-emerges in the imperative for entrepreneurial, self-branding, and self-regulating agents, whose supposed autonomy obscures the influence of other forces. Where Bourdieu's game accentuates relationality, game theory posits individuals for whom everything is a competition to be won by superior strategy.

Notwithstanding Steven Brams's claim that 'game theory provides a parsimonious framework and an important set of tools for the literary theory', its applications to literature have mostly been confined to analysis of characters' choices in narrative fiction.[28] A typical example is Michael Suk-Young Chwe's *Jane Austen, Game Theorist* (2013), which looks at Austen's 'systematic' and 'relentlessly theoretical' approach to understanding human choices and strategic thinking.[29] Barry O'Neill's analogous discussion of strategy and challenges in *Sir Gawain and the Green Knight* is one of few direct applications to poetry, although Eburne and Epstein suggest that

> game theory's combinatory mathematics for calculating rational strategy choice extends, in poetry games, to the virtual quantification of the 'author function', where the 'rational' choices of the creative subject become quantifiable, programmable, even digital.[30]

Still, in this regard, game theory's limited relevance to character and author decisions throws into relief the unquantifiable complexity of actual literary production.

Gamification

Finally, in recent decades, 'gamification' has put a strange twist on game theory's rationalist ideology. In its broadest conception, the term (coined by Nick Pelling in 2002) describes a process of rendering non-game activities game-like by introducing challenges and incentives. In its most prominent form, the trend has been fed in the past decade by the ubiquity of mobile devices, with smartphones and smartwatches providing the interface and feedback loops necessary for the gamification of consumption, work, and almost any other activity. Companies have expanded customer loyalty programmes to include personalised rewards and purchasing options. The so-called gig economy is characterised by the gamified models of transportation and delivery companies, or house-sharing and freelance platforms. On the same principles, the reach of gamification also extends into daily lives in the form of 'productivity' apps, philanthropic crowdfunding, educational software, and all areas of mental and physical well-being, through wearable wristbands and apps measuring exercise, mindfulness, or fertility.[31]

Gamification overshoots business game metaphors by making literal the game possibilities of life, work, and economic transactions. But it also inverts game theory's fixation on rational choice, drawing on behavioural psychology and a long history of marketing techniques to exploit irrational or unconscious human impulses. For this reason, danah boyd, a researcher at Microsoft and founder of the Data and Society Research Institute at NYU, describes gamification as 'a modern-day form of manipulation. And like all cognitive manipulation, it can help people and hurt people. And we will see both.'[32] For positive perspectives, gamification has an army of champions, like Yu-Kai Chou (several-times winner of 'Gamification Guru of the Year'), who has worked with Lego, Google, Huawei, and others, and who writes: 'There's a game that we're all playing right not whether we know it or not – the game of life.'[33] For Chou, the Matrix-like game being played 'whether we know it or not' is not manipulative, but offers opportunities for improved well-being: 'My vision for Gamification is a future where no one really works, but everyone plays and contributes to a happier and more productive society.'[34] Interpreting this vision from the opposite perspective, P.J. Patella-Rey describes gamification as an essential tool of a 'post-Fordist' knowledge economy, arguing: 'If and when it achieves what it promises, workers will be lured into exploitative conditions by genuine interest and motivation instead of economic coercion.'[35]

In keeping with this book's running theme, gamification is obviously bound up in self-regulation. Whether we imagine a happy delivery cyclist, who sees their work as a form of productive play or imagine that the same cyclist is 'lured into exploitative conditions' by a system of rewards, gamification works by turning the worker into their own manager. This is also clear in education, where gamification is increasingly employed as a mode of 'self-regulated learning'. 'Education is one of the fields where gamification will become a disruptive innovation,' leading to a 'revolution' in what Llorens-Largo et al. call 'gamified learning'.[36] For work, learning, or daily exercise, the promise of gamification is the degree to which it channels addictive and affective impulses into productivity.

Yu-Kai Chou's trademarked system 'Octalysis' (with courses for sale on his website or explained in his book, *Actionable Gamification*) promises to optimise your business or life by identifying 'eight core drives'. These map quite uncannily onto many of the issues discussed in this book as motivations within the field of poetry. The first drive, 'Epic meaning & calling' chimes absolutely with questions around vocationalism and the status of poetic labour or professionalism. The sense of personal 'Accomplishment' links with the rhetorical emphasis on 'craft', while 'Empowerment' aligns with the language of creative agency. 'Ownership' is an obvious factor in authorial identity, especially in the value of originality in debates around plagiarism or copyright. Chou's fifth drive 'Social influence' connects to many topics, as a measure of social capital within semi-public networks. 'Scarcity' speaks to the prestige associated with small rewards in poetry's restricted field. 'Unpredictability' or, as Chou puts it, 'wanting to find out what will happen next', connects with the uncertainty and anxiety often re-claimed as a creative source, while the eighth and final drive, 'Avoidance of something negative', captures the growing sense of economic and creative precarity faced by poets, publishers, and anyone involved with the form.

Conclusion

A final question might be asked, with implications for the many creative, ethical, political, economic, and personal questions raised in the course of this book: If the poetry industry is like a game, what sort of game is it like? Is it a zero-sum battle for resources and attention, to be 'won' by finding the best strategy, applying your own bit of game theory? Or is it a space for pure autonomous play, under threat from 'gamifying' forces working to impose exploitative competition? My own approach, often implicit, has been to treat the poetry industry as a game in Bourdieu's sense of a knowingly abstracted field, in which the positions of individuals, organisations, and institutions are constantly being renegotiated, consciously or not, through discursive exchanges of symbolic goods and capital. Making no assumptions about personal motivations, beyond those expressed in the flow of poetry-adjacent discourse, this approach has partly been a way to keep the bigger picture in view and partly a way to keep in mind the structures and pressures underlying my analysis as well. I've often thought about Joshua Clover's 2016 essay 'Unfree Verse' while writing this book, recalling its opening sentences: 'I am being paid for poetry right now. I can't feel it but I am. It's complicated. Or maybe it's not.'[37] Like Clover, I am writing while being paid a regular salary on a permanent academic contract which requires me to write and publish such things. Given those expectations and the increasingly game-like mechanisms for assessing my productivity, I have very little sense of this labour's autonomy. I cannot claim to have an objective view of the game I'm trying to understand. Every turn of my argument is bound by my complicity in it and those same uncritical drives, however much I've tried not to let them determine my critical positions.

Maybe it isn't so complicated, as Clover says. One's experience of the poetry game depends on one's own conception of it. How you see it affects how you play it. As a figure of speech, plenty see the 'game' as something best avoided, like Katherine Towler, whose memoir of the poet Robert Dunn admires him as someone who 'was not going to play the poetry game as it was defined by the elites of the world'.[38] In other cases, the game is unavoidable, or there to contend with. Ralph Story's description of Paul Laurence Dunbar as a 'master player in a fixed game' might chime with a continuing sense 'that as far as black writers are concerned, the game was (and is) fixed'.[39] I suspect most poets' feelings about the poetry game are as mixed as my own. Or as mixed as those of London-based poet Luke Wright, turning the figure of speech both ways in an interview where he admires Martin Newell as a poet who 'doesn't really (and I think he'd be the first to admit this) play the poetry game (i.e. flock to London, crave prizes or get big reviews)', then a moment later admires Salena Godden as a poet who has 'been in the game longer than me'.[40] It's just one example, but it captures a typical, likely unconscious ambivalence, and the tendency to treat the poetry game as something both external and perhaps eternal. It is a game that others seem to play or else avoid or maybe rope us into, and one that seems to have existed far longer than anyone now playing, which we can only do our best to survive and sustain.

I hope it has been useful to examine the language and structures by which the game of poetry becomes internalised. More than that, I have aimed to capture our historical moment from some practical perspectives, and the specific conditions under which poetry is now made and read. I don't believe the game is eternal in any inevitable sense. Rather, this book has tried to take up Sarah Brouillette's call 'to challenge the model of the asocial or antisocial flexible individualist by stressing that, though it is disseminated as a natural given, it is in fact historically produced, highly contested, and contingent'.[41] For all the rules and pressures, I would like to think we have options. The game now being played will continue to evolve, with new rules demanded by evolving conditions, experienced differently by every individual or organisation involved. Understanding the current state of play will be essential if more communal models of poetry are to emerge.

Notes

1. Alan Jenkins, 'The Mick Imlah Poetry Prize – Winners', *Times Literary Supplement* (21 December 2017).
2. Qtd in Robyn Dixon, 'Nadine Gordimer Dies at 90; Nobel Laureate Chronicled Apartheid', *Los Angeles Times* (14 July 2014).
3. Marx and Frederick Engels, *Collected Works: 1861–1864*, vol. 34, trans. Ben Fowkes (New York: International Publishers, 1994), 448. See Introduction and Chapter 11.
4. Bourdieu, *Practical Reason* (Stanford, CA: Stanford University Press, 1998), 76.
5. Cathy Park Hong, 'Delusions of Whiteness in the Avant-Garde', *Lana Turner* (3 November 2014).

6   Dennis, *How to Make Money: The 88 Steps to Get Rich and Find Success* (London: Ebury, 2011), 250.
7   Eric Zimmerman, 'Manifesto for a Ludic Century', first published online at Kotaku (9 September 2013), and reprinted in *The Gameful World: Approaches, Issues, Applications*, ed. Steffen P. Walz and Sebastian Deterding (Cambridge, MA: MIT Press, 2014).
8   See Deterding's chapter, 'The Ambiguity of Games: Histories and Discourses of a Gameful World', in *The Gameful World* (Cambridge: MIT Press, 2014), 23–64.
9   Zimmerman, 'Manifesto for a Ludic Century'.
10 Plato, *Republic*, trans. in Stephen E. Kidd, *Play and Aesthetics in Ancient Greece* (Cambridge: Cambridge University Press, 2019), 53. For the *Phaedrus*, see section 276e, trans. Harold North Fowler, in Plato, *Plato in Twelve Volumes*, vol. 9 (Cambridge, MA: Harvard University Press, 1925), available online at Tufts University's Perseus Digital Library.
11 Kidd, *Play and Aesthetics in Ancient Greece*, 53.
12 See Ludwig Wittgenstein's *Philosophical Investigations*, trans. G. E. M. Anscombe, P. M. S. Hacker, and Jonathan Schulte (London: Wiley-Blackwell, [1953] 2009).
13 Peter Lamarque, 'Semantic Finegrainedness and Poetic Value', in *The Philosophy of Poetry*, ed. John Gibson (Oxford: Oxford University Press, 2015), 35–36.
14 Jonathan P. Eburne and Andrew Epstein, 'Introduction: Poetry Games', *Comparative Literature Studies*, Special Issue: Poetry Games, vol. 51, no. 1 (2014), 1.
15 Ibid., 11.
16 Jon Stone, 'Introduction', in *Coin Opera 2: Fulminare's Revenge*, ed. Jon Stone and Kirsten Irving (London: Sidekick Books, 2014), 12; John Crowe Ransom, 'The Bases of Criticism', *Sewanee Review*, vol. 52, no. 4 (October–December 1944), 556–71 (564).
17 Ibid., 13.
18 NESTA (2006), 49, after several earlier repetitions.
19 Ibid., 35 and 47.
20 Qtd in various places, including Maurice Hamington, 'Business Is Not a Game: The Metaphoric Fallacy', *Journal of Business Ethics*, vol. 86, no. 4 (June 2009), 473–84 (473).
21 Ibid., 474.
22 Ibid., 477.
23 Bourdieu and Loïc J. D. Wacquant, *An Invitation to Reflexive Sociology* (Chicago, IL: University of Chicago Press, 1992), 101.
24 Von Neumann, 'On the Theory of Games of Strategy', in *Contributions to the Theory of Games*, vol. 24, trans. S. Bargmann, ed. A. W. Tucker and R. D. Luce (Princeton, NJ: Princeton University Press, [1928] 1959), 13–42 (13).
25 Amadae, *Prisoners of Reason: Game Theory and Neoliberal Political Economy* (Cambridge: Cambridge University Press, 2015), xvi.
26 Ibid., xvi. Emphasis added.
27 Guillory, 'Bourdieu's Refusal', *Modern Language Quarterly*, vol. 58, no. 4 (1997), 367–98 (385).
28 Steven Brams, *Game Theory and the Humanities: Bridging Two Worlds* (Cambridge: MIT Press, 2011), 1.
29 Suk-Young Chwe, *Jane Austen, Game Theorist* (Princeton, NJ: Princeton University Press, 2013), 1.
30 See Barry O'Neill, 'The Strategy of Challenges: Two Beheading Games in Medieval Literature', in *Game Equilibrium Models*, vol. 4, ed. R. Selten (Berlin: Springer, 1991); Eburne and Epstein, 'Introduction: Poetry Games', 4.
31 It's worth saying that gamification is not entirely contingent on digital technology. Perhaps the clearest example is McDonald's Monopoly promotion, running annual

since 1987 – a particularly layered instance of gamification as well, given that the original board game was intended to educate people about the hazards of private monopolies.

32 Response to 'The Future of Gamification' survey, conducted by Janna Anderson and Lee Raine, Pew Research Center (18 May 2012).
33 Yu-Kai Chou, personal website, no date.
34 Chou, 'The 10 Best Social Products That Use Gamification to Literally Save the World', personal website.
35 P. J. Patella-Rey, 'Gamification and Post-Fordist Capitalism', in *The Gameful World*, 289.
36 F. Llorens-Largo et al., 'LudifyMe: An Adaptive Learning Model', in *Formative Assessment, Learning Data Analytics and Gamification in ICT Education*, ed. Santi Caballé and Robert Clarisó (London: Elsevier, 2016), 250.
37 Joshua Clover, 'Unfree Verse', Poetry Foundation blog (15 April 2016).
38 Katherine Towler, *The Penny Poet of Portsmouth: A Memoir of Place, Solitude, and Friendship* (Berkeley, CA: Counterpoint, 2017), 47.
39 Ralph Story, 'Paul Laurence Dunbar: Master Player in a Fixed Game' (1983), *African-American Poets: Phillis Wheatley through Melvin B. Tolson*, ed. Harold Bloom (New York: Chelsea House, 2003), 149n1.
40 Luke Wright, interview with Michael Pedersen, 'Luke(y)-likely: An interview with Luke Wright of Nasty Little Press', *The Skinny* (3 July 2014).
41 Brouillette, *Literature and the Creative Economy*, 4.

INDEX

Actionable Gamification (Chou) 222
Adonis, Andrew 178
Adorno, Theodor 8, 191
Against Creativity (Mould) 5, 13, 131, 184
Against Meritocracy (Littler) 180, 183, 187
Ahmad, Aisha 114
AHRC. *See* Arts and Humanities Research Council
Alizadeh, Ali 156
Allen, Kim 114
Amadae, S. M. 220
amateurism 177–78, 208–9
The Amateur (Merrifield) 177
Amazon 93, 96–98
Americans for Generational Equity (AGE) 27
Anaxagorou, Anthony 201
Anderson, Chris 172
Antigonick (Carson) 97
The Anxiety of Obsolescence (Fitzpatrick) 85
Apollinaire, Guillaume 124
Arcangel, Cory 193
Arendt, Hannah 171–74, 178
The Argonauts (Nelson) 157
Armitage, Simon 25, 34–35
Armour (Kinsella) 47
The Art of Falling (Moore) 107
The Art of Strategy: A Game Theorist's Guide to Success in Business and Life 221
Arts and Humanities Research Council (AHRC) 162–63, 205
Arts Council England (ACE) 2, 45, 47, 111, 113, 134n17
Arts Council of Northern Ireland 146
arts funding 1–3, 45, 47–49, 64
Assassin's Creed 128

Astley, Neil 91–92
Auden, W. H. 112, 202
Australasian Association of Writing Programs (AAWP) 211
authorship 137–39, 143–46
Autobiography (Williams) 175–77
autonomy 5–13, 61, 64, 69, 173–74, 179, 190–92, 207, 215, 217, 221, 223

Baby Boomers and Generational Conflict (Bristow) 28
Bajorek, Jennifer 9
Banks, Mark 13, 207–8
Banville, John 154
Barnes, Julian 46
Barnhisel, Gregory 97
Barry, Peter 32, 35–36
Barthes, Roland 138, 164
Baudelaire, Charles 124
Beard, Mary 178
Beasley, Sandra 144
Be Creative: Making a Living in the New Culture Industries (McRobbie) 13, 209
Behrle, Jim 193
Bell, Jo 203–4, 206
Benjamin, Walter 94–95, 129
Benson, Fiona 107
Berger, John 49
Bernard, Jay 130
Bernes, Jasper 10, 14
Bernstein, Charles 111
Berry, Liz 43, 107
Beyond the Lyric (Sampson) 30, 36
Bird, Hera Lindsay 67–68
Birrell, Anne 218
Bishop, Elizabeth 84

Black Cat Bone (Burnside) 158
Blair, Tony 1, 3, 186
Blake, William 81, 123–24, 130
Booker prize 46, 49
Book of Younger Poets (Salt) 25, 36, 38–39
bookworks 96
Borodale, Sean 50
Bourdieu, Pierre 9–11, 29, 38, 46, 54, 64, 216, 219–21, 223
Bowling Alone: The Collapse and Revival of American Community (Putnam) 127
Bradbury, Malcolm 154
Brams, Steven 221
branded self 192–93
Breakfast at Tiffany's 169
Bristow, Jennie 28
British Poetry Since 1945 (Lucie-Smith) 23, 25
The Broken Word (Foulds) 107
Brouillette, Sarah 3–4, 13–14, 130, 224
Brouwer, Joel 76, 79, 80
Brown, Jericho 84
Brown, Mark 50
Brown, Nicholas 7–8, 191
Brownjohn, Alan 32, 35–36, 175
Bunting, Basil 174
Burgin, Christine 95
Burnshaw, Stanley 77
Burnside, John 158
Burt, Stephanie 68, 126
Byatt, A. S. 154
Byrne, James 25, 26

Cain, Sian 93
Caines, Michael 49–50
Cairncross, Frances 121
Cake Wrecks 101
Callan, Ainé 147–48
Cambridge Companion to American Poetry Since 1945 91
Canfield, Jack 201
Cantillon, Richard 183
Capildeo, Vahni 158
Capital (Marx) 173–74, 192
Capote, Truman 155
Carr, Nicholas 63
Carson, Anne 84, 86, 96
Carson, Rachel 178

Carter, Angela 154
The Case for Working with Your Hands (Crawford) 172
Cassuto, Leonard 202
Castells, Manuel 121
'Cat Person' (Roupenian) 68–69, 71n21
Celebrity, Aspiration & Contemporary Youth 114
Chaffee, Michelle 185, 188
Chou, Yu-Kai 222–23
Chwe, Michael Suk-Young 221
Citizen (Rankine) 86, 158–59
Clarke, John Cooper 188, 194
Clegg, John 78
Clutton-Brock, Arthur 202
Coates, Dave 50
Cobbing, Bob 99
Coetzee, J. M. 154
Cohen, Leonard 194–95
Coin Opera 218
Cole, Teju 130
Coleridge, Samuel Taylor 81, 139–43
Coleridge, the Damaged Archangel (Fruman) 143
Collins, Derek 217
Commane, Jane 203
community 30–31, 36, 63, 110, 115, 127–28, 142–43, 204–5, 211–12
Complete Works project 206
conceptual writing 143–46
'Conjectures on Original Composition' (Young) 143
Contemporary British Poetry and the City (Barry) 33
Convergence Culture: Where Old and New Media Collide (Jenkins) 53, 61
copyright 63, 137–39, 143, 149, 211, 223
Corcoran, Josephine 193
Cosgrove, Shady 211
Costa Award for Poetry 79, 107, 109, 115, 116, 125
Coutard, Oliver 125
Cox, George 3–4
The Crack Up (Fitzgerald) 95
craft 94, 171–76, 190, 223
The Craftsman (Sennett) 171–72
Crawford, Matthew 172
Crawford, Robert 25
creative class 12, 130, 184, 186

creative economy 3–5, 9, 12, 14, 173, 186, 204–5, 207
creative industries 3–5, 7–8, 10, 13, 130, 173, 183, 186, 204
Creative Justice: Cultural Industries, Work and Inequality (Banks) 13, 207–8
creative writing 3–6, 153–65, 211
   QAA benchmark 163
creativity 4–5, 12, 131, 143–44, 164, 171, 184, 186, 195, 217
credentialism 29, 38, 115, 208–9, 212
Critical History of Pamphlets (Davies) 78
'The Cult of the Noble Amateur' (Watts) 84–85, 102
Cultural Capital: The Rise and Fall of Creative Britain (Hewison) 12–13, 186–87
The Cultural Industries (Hesmondhalgh) 13
Curren, Malachy 148

Dardot, Pierre 184
Dauncey, Hugh 114
Davies, Myles 78
Davies, Terence 170
Dawe, Gerald 23
Dawson, Delilah 193
Day (Goldsmith) 143
Deahl, Rachel 157
Dear World & Everyone in It 25, 28, 36–37
The Death of Distance: How the Communications Revolution Will Change Our Lives (Cairncross) 121
'Death of the Author' (Barthes) 138
Debord, Guy 129
de Certeau, Michel 129
de Cervantes, Miguel 80
'The Deer at Exmoor' (Ward) 139
'The Deer' (Mort) 139
The Defence of Poetry (Shelley) 122
Defoe, Daniel 80
de las Rivas, Toby Martinez 111
Delillo, Don 154
Dennis, Felix 195–97
Department of Culture, Media and Sport (DCMS) 3
De Quincey, Thomas 139–41, 143
Deresiewicz, William 190–91
Derrida, Jacques 154, 160, 164
Descartes, René 138, 153

Deutsch, Babette 77
Dickinson, Emily 95, 170, 175
Didion, Joan 155
Divan (Hafez) 82–83
Donaghy, Michael 31, 35
Don't Call Us Dead (Smith) 158
Don't Let Me Be Lonely (Rankine) 158–59
Doren, Mark Van 77
Dowden, Edward 84
Drake, Robert M. 100
Driver 128
Drysalter (Roberts) 79
Duchamp, Marcel 144
Dunlap, Amy M. 97
Dworkin, Craig 144
The Dyer's Hand (Auden) 202

e-books 93–94
Eburne, Jonathan P. 218
Eco, Umberto 154
'ecology' 204–5
The Economy of Prestige (English) 43
Edwards, Jonathan 107
Ehrenfield, Tom 188–89
81 Austerities (Riviere) 194–95
Eliot, T. S. 22, 124, 153, 165, 170
Elkin, Lauren 130
Ellams, Inua 201
Emerson, Lori 81
Emerson, Ralph Waldo 83–84
English, James F. 43–44, 52
entrepreneurship
   creative 5, 183–86, 190–91, 198n42
   modern usage 189
   poet as 183–205
Epler, Barbara 98
Epstein, Andrew 218
Eric Gregory awards 112
An Essay on Criticism (Pope) 156
Essay on the Nature of Trade in General (Cantillon) 183
Estrada, Mary Michaels O. 110
Evans-Bush, Katy 48, 52, 140, 142
Everett, Edward 84

Facebook 6, 63, 69, 128, 139, 142
Farley, Paul 130
Fennelly, Beth Ann 80

ficto-criticism 164
The Firebox: Poetry from Britain and Ireland after1945 (Picador) 25
Fire Songs (Harsent) 49–50
The First Book: Twentieth-Century Poetic Careers in America (Zuba) 10, 14, 106, 110–11, 115
First Pressings 25
Fisher, Allen 129
Fitzgerald, F. Scott 95
Fitzpatrick, Kathleen 85
Flood, Alison 43, 55, 102, 149–50, 166, 198
Florida, Richard 4, 130–31, 184
Folsom, Ed 81
Forbes, Peter 23, 31, 33–34, 36–37
Formsby, Rank 49, 50, 146–48
Forward prizes 43–4, 50, 53, 60, 79, 116, 125, 159, 195–96
Foster, Jodie 141
Foucault, Michel 12–13, 137–38, 149, 154
Foulds, Adam 107
Fox, Kate 174, 202, 204
Fraistat, Neil 76
France, Linda 24, 33
Friedman, Thomas 121
Frolic Architecture (Howe) 99
Frost, Robert 80
Fruman, Norman 143

Gaiman, Neil 155
Galvin, Rachel 122
games 216–17
  analogies 219
  playing field 219–20
  and poetry 217–19
Games Poets Play: Readings in Medieval Chinese Poetry (Birrell) 218
game theory 220–21
gamification 221–23, 225n31
Garber, Megan 68–9, 71n21
generationalism 26–30
The Generation of 1914 (Wohl) 26
Geocities 127–28
Geoffrey Faber Prize 107
Geography III (Bishop) 84
Gerber, Alison 13, 202, 205, 209
Getaway 128

Gifford, Terry 123
Gill, Nikita 101
Global Creativity Index 184
Global Entrepreneurship Index 184, 197n6
Golden Treasury (Palgrave) 22
Goldin, Nan 132
Goldsmith, Kenneth 143, 144–46, 148
Gone with the Wind 145
Gordimer, Nadine 215
governmentality 12
Graham, Jorie 158
Grand Theft Auto 128
Graves, Robert 22
Great British Bake Off 172
Great British Sewing Bee 172
Gregson, Tyler Knott 100
Griffin Prize 50, 107, 115
Griffiths, Bill 130
Guern, Philippe Le 114
Guillory, John 220
Gutenberg, Johannes 94
Gutkind, Lee 155

Halberstam, Jack 124
Hamilton, Ian 24
Hamilton, Nathan 25, 36–37
Hamilton-Emery, Chris 91–92, 204, 205, 209
The Handbook of Creative Writing (Twitchell) 113
Hanson, Michael 132
Harsent, David 49–50
Harvey, Laura 114
Hatch, Mark 172
Haussmann, Baron Georges-Eugène 125, 129
Heaney, Seamus 23, 151, 156, 158
Hearn, Alison 192
Heidegger, Martin 94
Hentea, Marius 106
Hepburn, Audrey 169
Herbert, Susannah 44
Herd, David 31–32
Her Heart Poetry 101
Hesiod 169–70
Hesmondhalgh, David 13
Hewison, Robert 12, 13, 186
Higgins, Kevin 148

Hilborn, Neil 65
H is for Hawk (MacDonald) 157
Hollis, Matthew 108
Honest Ulsterman magazine 146–48
Hong, Cathy Park 144
Hong, Judy 172
Horkheimer, Max 191
Howard, Liz 107
Howe, Neil 27
Howe, Sarah 50–52, 107, 157
Howe, Susan 99
How to Be a Poet: A Twenty-First Century Guide to Writing Well (Bell and Commane) 203–7
How to Get Rich (Dennis) 196
'How to Make a Killing from Poetry' (Lewis) 193
How to Make Money (Dennis) 196
Huehls, Mitchum 14
Hughes, Ted 156
Hulse, Michael 24, 31
Human Chain (Heaney) 158
The Human Condition (Arendt) 171
Hunt, Jeremy 48

Identity Parade: New British and Irish Poets (Lumsden) 22, 25, 32, 36
In Cold Blood (Capote) 155
Indecency (Reed) 107
Infinite Citizen of the Shaking Tent (Howard) 107
iPhone 6
#IrishPoets2015 campaign 146–48
Ivory, Helen 142

Jacobs, Jane 133, 178
Jameson, Frederic 8, 191
Jane Austen, Game Theorist (Chwe) 221
Jarmusch, Jim 170–73, 175–76, 178
Jayne, Samantha 187, 188
Jenkins, Alan 215
Jenkins, Henry 53, 61
Jennifer, G. 62, 66
Jess, Tyejimba 86
Jobs, Steve 6
Jones, Saeed 64
Joyce, James 177
The Joy of Game Theory: An Introduction to Strategic Thinking 221

Kafka, Franz 178
Kallinikos, Jannis 100
Kant, Immanuel 138
Karmel, Annabel 187–88
Kaur, Rupi 60, 84, 100, 188
Kay, Jackie 59
Kennedy, David 24, 31
Kestenbaum, Jonathan 3
Key, Amy 51–52
Kid A 191
Kidd, Stephen E. 218
Kindle 93, 97
Kinsella, John 47
Korn, Peter 172
Kristeva, Julia 154
Kuhl, Nancy 113
Kuskin, William 76–77

labour 169–79
Lamarque, Peter 218
Lasky, Dorothea 80
Lasky, Kim 153, 163
Latour, Bruno 94
Laughlin, James 97–98
Laval, Christian 184
Lawson, Mark 46
Lazer, Hank 91
Leadbeater, Charles 4
Lear, Edward 156
Leav, Lang 101
Leaves of Grass (Whitman) 81–82
Lefebvre, Henri 129
Leong, Michael 145
Les Fleurs du Mal (Baudelaire) 124
Levine, David 189
Levine, Philip 169–70
Levitt, Marcus C. 77
Lewis, Michael 193–94
Lewis, Robin Coste 107
Lightman, Ira 139–44
Literature and the Creative Economy (Brouillette) 14
Littler, Jo 183–84, 187
The Lives of Poets (Schmidt) 44
Lockwood, Patricia 66–67, 157
Lodge, David 154
London's National Portrait Gallery 132
Loop of Jade (Howe) 50–52, 107, 157

Lost Lunar Baedeker (Loy) 84
Lotinga, Stephen 93, 157
Lovelace, Amanda 101
Love & Misadventure (Leav) 101
Loy, Mina 84
Lucie-Smith, Edward 23, 25
Lumsden, Roddy 22–25, 32, 34
Lung Jazz: Young British Poets for Oxfam (Swift) 25, 36
Lyrical Ballads (Wordsworth and Coleridge) 81–82

MacDonald, Helen 157
Mack, Ian 192
Madsen, Spencer 65
Maguire, Sarah 33, 36
Mailer, Norman 155
The Maker Movement Manifesto (Hatch) 172
Makers: The New Industrial Revolution (Anderson) 172
Mannheim, Karl 28
Maris, Kathryn 48
Marketing Literature: The Making of Contemporary Writing in Britain (Squires) 14
Marx, Karl 7–8, 173, 176, 192, 215
Marx, Leo 133
Master of the Game: Competition and Performance in Greek Poetry (Collins) 217–18
Masters of Craft: Old Jobs in the New Urban Economy (Ocejo) 172
Maxim 196
McCrum, Robert 156
McDaniel, Hattie 145
McGurl, Mark 14, 78, 193, 208
McKeon, Michael 80
McLuhan, Marshall 61, 121
McMeel, Andrews 101
McMillan, Andrew 49, 107
McMillan, Ian 35
McRobbie, Angela 13, 209
Memorial (Oswald) 46–47
Mendick, Heather 114
Merrifield, Andy 177–78
Mick Imlah Poetry Prize 215
Miles, Jack 156
Miller, Kei 43

Milliot, Jim 157
Mirrlees, Hope 124
Mitchell, W. J. T. 100
Mitchell, William J. 100
A Moon Shaped Pool 191
Moore, Kim 107
Moretti, Franco 75
Morgan, David R. 139–42
Morgenstern, Oskar 220
Morley, David 24, 31, 80
Morozov, Evgeny 114
Morris, William 81, 94, 133, 176
Morrison, Blake 23
Morrissey, Sinéad 49, 105, 107–8, 157
Mort, Helen 139
Motion, Andrew 23, 45
Mould, Oli 5, 13, 131, 184–85, 189–90
MTV 27, 70n9
Mumpreneur (Karmel) 187–88
My Family and Other Superheroes (Edwards) 107

Nagra, Daljit 109
National Endowment for Science, Technology and the Arts (NESTA) 3–4, 7, 10, 219
Nelson, Maggie 156
neocracy 114
neoliberalism 5, 11, 184, 187, 216
Neoliberalism and Contemporary Literary Culture (Huehls and Smith) 14
Netflix 6, 157
New British Poetry (Graywolf) 25
New Directions 95–99
New/Next Generation poets 21–25, 28–29, 31–38
The New Poetry 22, 24, 25, 31
News from Nowhere (Morris) 133
The New Testament (Brown) 84
New Younger Irish Poets (Dawe) 23–24
Night Sky with Exit Wounds (Vuong) 107
The Novel After Theory (Ryan) 154
A Novelette (Williams) 176
The Novel (Moretti) 75–76
Nox (Carson) 86, 96–97

O'Brien, Sean 34
Ocejo, Richard 172

O'Donoghue, John 92
O'Hara, Frank 175
Olds, Sharon 49
Olio (Jess) 86
On Borrowed Time: How the Growth in Entitlement Spending Threatens America's Future (Howe and Peterson) 27
O'Neill, Barry 221
101 Ways to Make Poems Sell 204
online poetry 59–70
The Origins of the English Novel (McKeon) 80
O'Sullivan, Feargus 132
Oswald, Alice 46–49
Oxford Companion to Twentieth-Century Poetry in English (Hamilton) 24, 36
Oxford Handbook of Contemporary British and Irish Poetry 91
The Oxford Handbook of Creative Industries 13

Padgett, Ron 175
Palmer, Daniel 202
pamphlets, poetry 78–79, 87–88
Paradise Lost 192
Parallax (Morrissey) 157–58
Paris: A Poem (Mirrlees) 124, 125
Parmar, Sandeep 108
Parsons, Deborah 130
participatory culture 52–55
Patella-Rey, P. J. 222
Paterson (Jarmusch) 170–79
Paterson, Don 31, 158
Paxman, Jeremy 43–44
Penguin Book of Contemporary British Poetry (Morrison and Motion) 23
Peppard, George 169
Perloff, Marjorie 144
Perry, Rebecca 107
Peterson, Peter G. 27
Phillips, Emilia 156
Pickard, Tom 174
The Pinch: How the Baby Boomers Stole Their Children's Future – and Why They Should Give It Back (Willetts) 27
Place, Vanessa 143, 145–46, 148
Place (Graham) 158
plagiarism 139–43
Plath, Sylvia 156
Plunkett, Adam 66

Poehler, Aaron 142–43
Poems in Their Place: The Intertextuality and Order of Poetic Collections (Fraistat) 76
poetry
 as digital content 59–70
 creative/critical modes 153–65
 genre problem 155–57
 debut culture 105–17
 games 215–24
 gamification 221–23
 modern collection 75–86
 participatory culture, theory of 52–55
 plagiarism in 139–43
 prize scandals 43–55
 promotion 21, 63, 76, 92, 109–10, 132, 193
 self-regulation 9–13
 as work 169–79
'Poetry and Spoken Word Artists Network Fees and Needs Survey' (Fox and Yoseloff) 204
'Poetry as Nonfiction' (Miles) 156
Poetry Book Society (PBS) 45–47, 49
The Poetry Business Book of New Contemporary Poets 36
Poetry Is Not a Project (Lasky) 80
Poetry Revival movement 32
Poetry Today (Thwaite) 24
Poetry Wars (Barry) 32, 35
Poets House 132–33
Poindexter, Christopher 100
Pollard, Clare 25, 26, 35, 92, 113
Pool, Ithiel de Sola 61
Pope, Alexander 156
Potts, Robert 31–32
Pound, Ezra 125, 129
Practice of Everyday Life (de Certeau) 129
Priestdaddy (Lockwood) 157
Princeton Encyclopedia of Poetry & Poetics (Kuskin) 76–77
print-on-demand technology 91–92
Private Eye magazine 51
'The Problem of Professionalization' (Cassuto) 202
professionalism 201–12
 ethical dimensions 211–12
The Program Era (McGurl) 14, 193, 208

The Progress of Romance (Reeve)
  75–77, 87n11
Prynne, J. H. 130
Pulitzer Prize for Poetry 79
Pullman, Philip 204
Purdy, Daniel 83
Putnam, Robert 127
Pynchon, Thomas 154

Quality Assurance Agency (QAA) 163
Quarter Life Poetry: Poems for the Young, Broke and Hangry (Jayne) 187
A Quiet Passion (Davies) 170

Rankine, Claudia 86, 158–60, 165
Ransom, John Crowe 218
Reactions 25
'The Red Wheelbarrow' (Williams) 176
Reed, Justin Phillip 107
Rees-Jones, Deryn 130
Reeve, Clara 75
Reid, Christopher 23
Research Excellence Framework (REF) 161–64
Rich, Adrienne 178
Riding, Laura 22
Riley, Peter 28, 112
Rimbaud, Arthur 189
Riordan, Maurice 108
The Rise of the Creative Class (Florida) 4, 130
The Rise of the Network Society (Castells) 121
Riviere, Sam 194
Roberts, Michael Symmons 43, 79, 130, 158
Robertson, Robin 23
Roupenian, Kristen 68–69
Royle, Nicholas 164
Rush, Emma 211
Rushkoff, Douglas 65
Ruskin, John 94
Rutherford, Jonathan 125
Ryan, Judith 154–55

Saboteur Awards 54
Salt Publishing 91–92
Sampson, Fiona 30, 49–50
Say, Jean-Baptiste 183
Schmidt, Michael 24, 44
Scholes, Lucy 170–71
self-employment 187
self-promotion 192–93
Sellers, Jefferey M. 126
Sennett, Richard 94, 171–72
Shelley, Percy Bysshe 122
'Shepherdess O Eiffel Tower' (Apollinaire) 124
Shop Class as Soulcraft (Crawford) 172, 175
SimCity 128
Sir Gawain and the Green Knight 221
Sixty Women Poets (France) 24, 33
Skoulding, Zoë 130
Smith, Danez 59, 158
Smith, Maggie 66–67
Smith, Neil 132
Smith, Rachel Greenwald 14
Smith, Robert 189
Smith, Stan 35
soft capitalism 132
Solnit, Rebecca 130
Song of Myself (Whitman) 82
Songs of Innocence and Experience (Blake) 81, 123
Soul Says (Vendler) 122
Spaulding, Daniel 10
Sperling, Matthew 91
Spicer, André 114
Spontaneous Particulars: The Telepathy of Archives (Howe) 99
Spring and All (Williams) 170, 176–78
Squires, Claire 14, 45, 116
The Startup Garden: Ideas and Resources for Entrepreneurs (Ehrenfield) 188
Statement of Facts (Place) 143
Stevens, Wallace 84, 175
Stevenson, Debris 202
Stewart, Garrett 96
Stone, Jon 218
Strauss, William 27
Stuff 196
The Success Principles: How to Get from Where You Are to Where You Want to Be (Canfield) 201, 204
Sullivan, Hannah 105–8, 115, 157
Sutherland, Keston 31
Swainson, Bill 23

Swift, Todd 25, 49
Szirtes, George 43

Tate group of British art galleries 132
technologies, poetic 91–102
  e-books 93–94
  print-on-demand 91–92
Tedeschi, Stephen 128–29
Ted Hughes Award 54
Tempest, Kate 130
Terror (de las Rivas) 111
That This (Howe) 99
Theory of Games and Economic Behaviour
  (Morgenstern) 220
'Theory of the *Dérive*' (Debord) 129
Thibaudet, Albert 76
Thompson, E. P. 124
Thoreau, Henry David 83
Three Poems (Sullivan) 105, 107, 115, 157
Thwaite, Anthony 24
'Time, Work-Discipline, and Industrial
  Capitalism' (Thompson) 124
Times Literary Supplement(TLS) 30
Tivnan, Tom 156
'Tradition and the Individual Talent'
  (Eliot) 170
Treatise on Political Economy (Say) 183
Trump, Donald 59–60, 64–65, 68, 146, 149, 157
T. S. Eliot prize 45–54, 79, 105–9, 112, 115–16, 125
Tuma, Keith 36
Twichell, Chase 113
Twitter 6, 48–50, 52, 54, 63, 66, 97, 114, 141, 145, 147–48, 178

Ulysses (Joyce) 177
unprofessional 212
Untermeyer, Louis 77
Urbanization and English Romantic Poetry
  (Tedeschi) 128
Usher, Nikki 54
US National Book Award 107
Utopia is Creepy (Carr) 63

Vaizey, Ed 204
Vendler, Helen 122
Verbal Arts Centre 146–47

viral poems 65–68
Voice Recognition:21 Poets for the21st Century
  (Pollard and Byrne) 25, 26, 36
von Goethe, Johann Wolfgang 82–83
von Hammer-Purgstall, Joseph 82
Voyage of the Sable Venus and Other Poems
  (Lewis) 107
Vuong, Ocean 107

Wallace, David Foster 154
Whalley, Charles 51
Walser, Robert 95, 98
Wandor, Michelene 162–63
Ward, Christian 139, 144
The Waste Land (Eliot) 124, 156, 177
Watson, Thomas J. 219
Watts, Rebecca 84–85, 102
Webb, Jen 211
Weinberger, Eliot 96
What Work Is (Levine) 169
Wheatley, David 30, 36, 49, 109, 113
White, Jonathan 26–27
White Mule (Williams) 97
Whitman, Walt 81–82, 189
The Whole Harmonium (Stevens) 84
Why We Make Things & Why It Matters
  (Korn) 172
Wilkinson, Jessica L. 156
Willetts, David 27
Williams, David A. 50
Williams, William Carlos 97, 170, 175–76
Wilson, Elizabeth 130
Winterson, Jeannette 154
Wittgenstein, Ludwig 218
Wohl, Robert 26–27
Wolfe, Tom 155
Wolff, Janet 130
Wooten, William 30
Wordsworth, William 81, 121, 123–24
work
  economic definition of 174
  poetry as 169–79
Working on My Novel (Arcangel) 193
The Work of Art: Value in Creative Careers
  (Gerber) 13, 202, 205, 207
The Work of Art in the Age of Deindustrialisation
  (Bernes) 14

'Work of Art in the Age of Real
    Subsumption, The' (Brown) 7–8, 191
Works and Days (Hesiod) 169
*The World Is Flat: A Brief History of the
    Twenty-First Century* (Friedman) 121
Wyatt, Thomas 48

Yeats, William Butler 84
York, Jake Adam 80

Yoseloff, Tamar 204
Young, Edward 143
Younger Irish Poets (Dawe) 23
'You're Dead, America' (Smith) 59
Yousef, Nancy 10

Zimmerman, Eric 216–17
Zuba, Jesse 10, 14, 106–8, 110–11, 115
Zukofsky, Louis 170

www.ingramcontent.com/pod-product-compliance
Lightning Source LLC
Chambersburg PA
CBHW021824300426
44114CB00009BA/319